Attitudes toward English Usage

THE HISTORY OF A WAR OF WORDS

Edward Finegan
University of Southern California

TEACHERS COLLEGE PRESS
Teachers College, Columbia University
New York/London   *1980*

Copyright © 1980 by Teachers College, Columbia University

All rights reserved

Published by Teachers College Press, 1234 Amsterdam Avenue, New York, N.Y. 10027

Library of Congress Cataloging in Publication Data

Finegan, Edward, 1940–
    Attitudes toward English usage.

    Bibliography: p.
    Includes index.
    1. English language—Usage. 2. English language
in the United States. 3. Linguistics—History.
4. Lexicography—History. I. Title.
PE1098.F5   420'.973   79-28462
ISBN 0-8077-2581-1

Manufactured in the United States of America

86 85 84 83 82 81 80 1 2 3 4 5 6

Grateful acknowledgment is made for permission to use quotations from the following copyrighted works:

The American Heritage Dictionary of the English Language (1969): usage note for *enthuse.* Used by permission of Houghton Mifflin Company.
The Authority of Law in Language, by George P. Krapp (1908). Used by permission of the University of Cincinnati.
"The Dictionary as a Battlefront: English Teachers' Dilemma," by Mario Pei, in *Saturday Review,* June 21, 1962. Used by permission.
"Dr. Kinsey and Professor Fries," by John C. Sherwood, in *College English,* vol. 21 (1960). Copyright © 1960 by the National Council of Teachers of English. Used with permission.
The House of Intellect, by Jacques Barzun: excerpts from pp. 240, 241, 244–245. Copyright ©1959 by Jacques Barzun. Reprinted by permission of Harper & Row, Publishers, Inc., and Martin Secker & Warburg Ltd, London.

FOR MY FATHER AND MOTHER

Acknowledgments

THIS STUDY HAS been a long time in process, and I am indebted to scholars and friends alike for aid and encouragement. Robert T. Roe suggested the topic and guided me through the early research on several chapters. Allan Casson, Thomas M. Cofer, J. J. Lamberts, the late Albert H. Marckwardt, and several anonymous reviewers provided thoughtful suggestions to aid readability and accuracy. Robert J. Baumgardner, Richard H. Brown, James T. Heringer, and Carol Lord commented usefully on sections of chapters seven or eight. Laura Whitehall has been an invaluable editor of the whole.

Others at USC have contributed in less tangible ways. Besides gratitude for the generally warm and supportive atmosphere provided my linguistics colleagues, I thank Steve Krashen, who may recognize echoes of our conversations here and there in the book, and Elinor Ochs, whose thinking about the social character of language has deeply influenced my views. Larry Hyman also deserves thanks for chairing us all so energetically, and Dean David Malone for his support of our work.

For their friendship and support I am also grateful to Jim Walker, Michael Weber, Marianne Boretz, and Mike Craig.

It is customary to absolve from the failures due to one's own limitations those generous people who have helped one write a book; certainly in this work what faults remain are mine.

Contents

Foreword

by Charlton Laird

AMONG THE ENDURING SATISFACTIONS are those that grow from the opportunity to say publicly that a good book is a good book. This one is, and it will long endure for the audiences to whom it is addressed. I envisage for it at least three sorts of readers: linguistic scholars, especially the analysts of American English; teachers of English and related subjects; and the literate public, many of whom love language and some of whom hate what they conceive to be "bad grammar."

The first group, the professional students of language, will not need me to tell them that *Attitudes toward English Usage* is required reading. They know that until now we have had no scholarly, detailed history of English usage; and whereas they may be less intrigued by usage than they are by syntax, phonology, semiology, or some other linguistic manifestation, they do know that it is important and that it is their business.

Many linguists double as teachers, for two-hattedness is not uncommon among scholars, who may wish to pursue language as a true love but find they must teach it if they are to live by it. Likewise, many teachers who do not profess linguistics are professionally involved with language. To these latter—as to the interested reader at large—one might make two observations: first, the history of learning is to a considerable degree the evolution of plausible error, and thus no book on a learned subject can be trusted implicitly and forever. Second, this particular volume is probably as trustworthy as such a study can be. Finegan knows his subject, and he has been faithful in his undertaking. Much remains to be learned about the history of usage, but our author has used the available literature with diligence and due caution—and also with an eye to cogent and curious exemplars.

The third group is the largest. The literate public that will read this book includes (one hopes) a host of people who are interested in language and in learning something new that will enhance their understanding and enjoyment and use of the English language in particular. Many of these people have no particular axe to grind. But some of them represent one side of the "war" chronicled by Finegan.

The antagonist group numbers among its adherents a relatively silent majority who assume that "English" is *mainly* usage, a set of rules that govern oral and especially written conduct, that is, how to use the native

ix

tongue and not be "wrong." But the group comprises also various commentators who are anything but silent! Some of them may not know
much about language, but they trust they know what is right and believe
that in usage the "right" should triumph. They include a few writers,
many journalists and editors, some administrators and executives, and
numerous other conscientious and highly placed persons—some ad-
mirably learned and accomplished. They incline to believe that their own
usage is the only possible correct one, because it is presumed to be
universal, grammatical, traditional, or logical, or to possess some other
immutable virtue; whereas they accuse the usagists of having *no* standards, of believing that in usage "anything goes." They may fear quite
genuinely that without the triumph of their convictions the native tongue
will decline and become extinct; and they are baffled to know why
linguistic scholars, who are surely a learned lot and should be well-
meaning, do not aid and abet them.

Usagists generally do not support purist positions. They believe that all
language has its uses, and hence all of it is precious. They doubt that
puristic animadversions will much alter usage: no number of singers in-
toning "Rain, rain, go away" has ever brought on a drought; and speech,
like precipitation, has its own laws of conduct. They deny that if one
locution is undeniably right, in the sense that many native speakers
prefer it, all alternative locutions must *per se* be wrong. They generally
do agree with purists that even the native language needs to be taught and
that standards should be upheld; but they tend to recognize language
levels and to use terms like *appropriate* and *inappropriate* and to restrict
the concepts of *correct* and *incorrect*. They doubt that "bad grammar" is
killing the language; all bodies of speech have been used crudely by
stupid or careless people, but among the thousands of tongues that have
died none has been exterminated by the blunders of its users. As for
American English, they find it thriving, at home and abroad, and they
surmise that Mother Tongue is more self-reliant than some of her
defenders understand.

Here, then, is the central issue of the book—a schism between usagists
and purists, between "liberals" and traditionalists. Finegan, like most
linguists, is a usagist—I am of course distinguishing here between
"linguists" who study language *per se* and other persons, also called
"linguists," who may be fluent in several languages but do not much
study language as a phenomenon. Most linguists of the first sort are
usagists because they feel that the facts of language force them to be, and
anyhow they are delighted by variety in language. They believe that
uniformity in speech would be dull—and is fortunately impossible. As a
scholar, Finegan has his preferences, but he has striven hard to be objec-

tive and impartial—to see merit in both liberal and traditionalist views. I should say that he has succeeded as no one else has—that he has traced the growth of this schism through the centuries and has described it revealingly as it survives today.

Prologue: Babel and Ivory— A Tale of Two Towers

SCIENTISTS PURSUE UNDERSTANDING of the physical world knowing that where contrariety is found, a higher generalization will bring harmony. No such assurance accompanies the social and cultural investigator. Human society is not only multifaceted but often contradictory. Wars flare up in the pursuit of peace. Voters turn politicians out of office whom pollsters predicted to be shoo-ins. Population figures soar as family planning units prosper.

If the physical world is opaque, the human world stubbornly resists categorization. If the facts of chemistry are complex, the phenomena of anthropology are recalcitrant. And, as if to make the road to insight more treacherous, cultural values are so near to us, so integral a part of our vision, that we easily overlook their pervasive influence on our general perceptive mechanisms. Only the most sophisticated grasp the relativity of world views. To one people, their religion is their truth, indeed God's truth, and other views seem aberrant if not perverse. Few adults choose their religious convictions after systematic weighing of alternative creeds. If we don't derive religion with the color of our eyes, we seem to absorb it at our mothers' breasts. Politics we ingest at every family meal. Moral and cultural values seem to reside in our marrow, and it requires Herculean strength of mind to see the relativity of these values, to recognize that not all those outside the shelter of our beliefs are perverse, while some allies within regrettably are. The more insulated we keep ourselves from other perspectives, the more confident we become of the accuracy of our perceptions. Once during a political contest I was persuaded that the pollsters must be fishing in the unstocked pond, for my views and those of my friends, bolstered by campaign acquaintances, predicted a whale of a victory for the candidate who ultimately lost.

Language, too, is a phenomenon intimately tied to our thoughts, feelings, and perceptions—to our inmost selves. We take for granted its nature and adequate functioning. But language is a cultural transaction, not a chemical process like breathing, and it is laden with social and cultural values. However complex the chemistry of breathing, understanding of it is shared by scientists around the world and taught to

1

pupils in essentially like ways. The same is not true of religion or politics or philosophy. Nor is it true of language. These are cultural enterprises; they vary from society to society and evolve over time. They are created by people as adaptations to a common biological heritage, but they are realized differently in different societies. Cultural enterprises are created rather than "natural," and they sort people into clusters that are separated one from another. Each culture represents achievement—successful accommodation to an environment; therefore each group has an obvious stake in ranking its own achievements high and perceiving its culture as being more in harmony with nature than others. Moreover, the human origins of cultural adaptation are frequently lost to history, and mythological or supernatural explanations for otherwise inexplicable states of affairs are evolved.

Language is special among cultural ventures. It is at once natural and created. Children must learn the peculiar linguistic system created by their culture; yet its acquisition seems natural to them. From our earliest utterances, language distinguishes us from the children of other nations in ways that skin color and eye slant fail to do.

In the realm of knowledge language is unique. No other human enterprise has so long a tradition of analysis. Like the universe itself, language has intrigued philosophers from the time of our earliest recorded speculations. We have Panini's analysis of Sanskrit from the fourth century B.C. and Aristotle's and Plato's reflections on Greek. Today, after these millennia of investigation, language has become the subject of a distinct discipline, whose practitioners acknowledge the limitations of their understanding despite contributions from logic, paleography, archaeology, sociology, anthropology, philosophy, biology, neurology, psychology, and acoustics.

Alongside this scholarly endeavor, and often at odds with it, is the wisdom of a still older folk tradition. "In the beginning was the Word," the Evangelist relates. "And the Word was with God. And the Word was God." In Genesis we read that God called the light Day and the darkness Night, that he called the firmament Heaven and the dry land Earth and the waters that were gathered together Seas.

Genesis also provides an explanation for the multitude of tongues in the world. There was at first, after the earth had been populated, one language and one vocabulary. But when the inhabitants of the plain in the land of Shinar started to build a ziggurat "with its top in the heavens," the Lord said, "The people have all one language, . . . and now nothing will be restrained from them. . . . Come, let us go down and there confuse their language, that they may not understand one another's speech." And the city with its tower came to be called Babel, and from there the Lord scattered the people abroad.

Plato's Cratylus believed that there exists a right name for every creature, and that, given a right name, others can only be wrong. That view, taken a step further in modern times, sees rightness or wrongness inhering in particular morphological forms and syntactic collocations. Thus, beside right words and sentences there are deviations that mimic real words or are "wrongly" used: *irregardless* is a sham word, and *like* is misused when it masquerades as a conjunction in "like a cigarette should." By further extension of this view there are misspellings like *accomodate* (with a single *m*) and mispronunciations like "*real*-a-tor" (for *re*-al-tor) and grammatical errors like *between you and I*.

If we examine the attitudes of Americans toward their language we find contradictions. We are thought to be purists in our judgments but inelegant in our practice. Americans readily confess to knowing no grammar and sometimes to not speaking English well. Still, we are linguistic chauvinists and fare poorly in the multilingualism that confronts us on the Continent. There is a robustness to our language that Mencken described and celebrated. But there is also a pattern of inhibition, especially in matters of "grammar" and spelling. Linguistically we are an insecure nation, and, like the English and the French, we tend to rely heavily on dictionaries for definitive pronouncements about what is correct. Oddly enough, however, we also have a group of language professionals who insist that the school tradition which has influenced most of us was wrong-headed and has set unrealistic standards of language correctness. The basis for that school grammar, they say, largely ignored the nature of language and linguistic change. Although the views of these linguists have had considerable impact on scholarly opinion in the last seventy-five years, they are often challenged or disregarded by many of the influential people who are responsible for writing and selecting handbooks, discussing language in the popular media, and evaluating the literary output of American culture.

If we ask where American attitudes toward linguistic correctness have come from, we confront contradictory traditions. One is essentially the tradition that infuses the work of modern linguists and lexicographers. It sees language as a convention of society, devoid of inherent rightness or wrongness and governed by the requirements of communication between people. The other is folklorish and classical and perpetuates a view of language that contradicts Locke's analysis of it as a social convention. It envisages language as having an inherent correctness, much as Cratylus did, and it regards language change as corruption.

Teachers have been torn between the two approaches—the one descriptive, the other prescriptive, but both normative. Teachers have an obligation to teach what is known of a subject and they also have an obligation to honor the beliefs and evaluations of the society they are representing. In the matter of language, teachers have been accused of failing to meet adequately the demands of either tradition. Linguists have faulted them for propagating the myths of prescriptivism, and guardians of tradition have criticized them for failing to teach the arts of clear writing and eloquent speaking.

In this book I tell the story of a conflict that has been waged in America for over two hundred years, having erupted in England before that. In such a history of attitudes toward "correct English" or "good grammar" I explore a subject of vital interest to English teachers and prospective teachers; and I hope the material will be useful to them. I also hope to persuade the disputants themselves that the claims of neither side are as perversely motivated as has been charged and that both sides have some validity. Thus far, efforts to teach the art and science of the English language have too often been undermined by the obstinate intractability of influential people on both sides of the issues.

Perhaps mere familiarity with the long-standing dispute cannot moderate the views of zealots either conservative or liberal. But it may not be too much to hope that teachers will be more critical of the claims on both sides as a result of such familiarity. And this same perspective may help persuade a wider audience of Americans that if English teachers focus more on literature, effective composition, and language analysis than on particular items of usage, students will derive greater benefit from their English classes than many of us derived from our own.

CHAPTER I

Introduction: Popular and Scholarly Views of "Good English"

"Winston tastes good, like a cigarette should."

"As, damn it!"—A FIRST-GRADE BOY

". . . anyone who complains that its use as a conjunction is a corruption introduced by Winston cigarettes ought, in all fairness, to explain how Shakespeare, Keats, and the translators of the Authorized Version of the Bible came to be in the employ of the R. J. Reynolds Tobacco Company."   —BERGEN EVANS, 1960

AT ITS PEAK of popularity in the mid-sixties, the advertising slogan "Winston tastes good, like a cigarette should" was denounced by *Saturday Review* magazine. *SR*'s communications editor claimed that, despite its frequent occurrence, *like* "still offends us" when used as a conjunction. The passing of a few weeks saw the editor's words pale beside the flushed enthusiasm in the applauding letters that swamped his desk. For months afterwards readers wrote in to condemn detested expressions like "Drive Slow" and "I'll try and go." Their sentiments ranged from plain gratitude to ecstatic "love" over *Saturday Review*'s "good grammar" campaign.[1]*

Readers called Winston's jingle "a cause of shame to its creator," "an abiding object of scorn," "a constant reproach," even a "sin." A woman from Florida wrote that "Our educable young people need not be demoralized at every turn." And abstainers found Winston's grammar "as irritating as tobacco smoke." It was reported with obvious approval that a posse of vigilantes had torn down and destroyed a *Drive Slow* sign in one American town, while grammatical guardians all across the country were boycotting both Winstons and Tareytons ("Us Tareyton smokers would rather fight than switch"). Some extremists even claimed to have quit smoking altogether—not because of the Surgeon General's

*Numbered reference notes are gathered at ends of chapters.

5

hazard warning on every pack, but to punish the R. J. Reynolds Tobacco
Company for flaunting bad grammar!

Some sixty years earlier a similar flood of letters had inundated the
American press with objections to Rudyard Kipling's "Recessional";
grammatical sensibilities were aroused by the poet's use of a singular verb
with a compound subject: "The tumult and the shouting dies!"[2] Across
the Atlantic, earlier still, the British government in certain treaty negotia-
tions with the United States made concessions on weighty matters like the
Alabama claims and the Canadian fisheries but "telegraphed that in the
wording of the treaty it would under no circumstances endure the inser-
tion of an adverb between the preposition *to*, the sign of the infinitive,
and the verb."[3] The faded might of the split infinitive has yielded to the
intemperate wrath aroused by *like* as a conjunction. When polled for his
opinion on this point of grammar, *New York Times* writer John Kieran
replied, "Such things . . . persuade me that the death penalty should be
retained."[4] And poet John Ciardi confessed that he'd rather hear his
first-grade son swearing "*As*, damn it!" than using *like* as a conjunction.[5]
More recently, *hopefully* (in the sense "I hope that . . . ") has drawn fire
from writers in *Newsweek* (February 13, 1978) and *Time* (January 1,
1979) and from Edwin Newman on NBC's "Today" show (November 17,
1978). And *Time* reported on March 26, 1979, that three grammatical
hot lines were available to Americans troubled about particular points of
usage. (Ironically, only the Arkansas dial-a-grammarian scored a perfect
3 on *Time*'s disguised quiz. The other two hot lines—one of which is provided toll free to Kansans—disappointed *Time*'s reporter with "wrong"
answers!) Thus the sometimes sanctimonious support that readers gave
to *SR*'s grammatical campaign reflects a common conviction among
English speakers on both sides of the Atlantic that of the several ways to
say a thing, there is only one right way—and that the wrong ways can be
sinfully bad.

Speakers of English have been preoccupied with correct linguistic
usage since before our earliest grammars and dictionaries were composed. Some of them call to mind Shakespeare's pedant Holofernes, who
railed against pronouncing *doubt* and *debt* as if they had no *b*: "I abhor
such fanatical phantasimes, such insociable and point-device compan-
ions; such rackers of orthography. . . . This is abhominable—which he
would call abbominable" (*Love's Labour's Lost*, V, i).

Holofernes first uttered his futile detestations a decade before America
had its earliest permanent English settlement. Four centuries later, on
this side of the Atlantic, a truly extraordinary reaction against "fanatical
phantasimes" burst forth, and it shook the literate world. In 1961, shortly after the G. & C. Merriam Company published *Webster's Third New*

International Dictionary, the editorial staff must have feared they had fired a fatal shot through the English-speaking world; for the frenzy of journalists, educators, and book reviewers conveyed the impression that the English language had been mortally wounded. I will discuss this development in detail in a later section; here I merely indicate how incendiary the dictionary's treatment of a small number of contested entries was.

Mario Pei, a professor of Italian and well-known author, accused *Webster's* editors of blurring "to the point of obliteration the older distinction between standard, substandard, colloquial, vulgar, and slang." As he interpreted the new dictionary, "Good and bad, right and wrong, correct and incorrect no longer exist."[6]

Across the nation editors and educators rallied in support of Pei's judgment. A few hinted that the good old red-white-and-blue American dictionary was now mostly pink. "Small wonder that our English-speaking world . . . is having trouble with creatures like beatniks—not to mention Nikita Khrushchev and his kind," lamented the Washington *Sunday Star* (September 10, 1961). The *Detroit News* (February 10, 1962) found the dictionary motivated by a "bolshevik spirit" and called it "a kind of Kinsey Report in linguistics."[7]

Through the pen of Wilson Follett, *The Atlantic* (January 1962) accused the dictionary of a "sort of theoretical improvement that in practice impairs. . . ." As Follett assessed it, "we have seen the gates propped wide open in enthusiastic hospitality to miscellaneous confusions and corruptions." And "Worse yet," he said, the *Third* "plumes itself on its faults and parades assiduously cultivated sins as virtues without precedent."

English professor A. M. Tibbetts called the three-and-a-half-million-dollar investment an "inelegant, five-and-dime store approach to language . . . as democratic and mechanical as a bean picker."[8]

Much of the criticism heaped on the new *Webster's* represented straightforward opposition to the impartial recording of language customs in a dictionary. Many reviewers maintained that in lieu of an official national academy to preserve the purity of the mother tongue, reputable American dictionaries, successors to the original "Webster's" (i.e., Noah Webster's, 1828), must assume the role of guardian of good grammar. They must carefully elect the words and meanings they list, rigorously weeding out every questionable usage. "The Custodians of Language," Pei told his fellow Americans, "hold that there is a right and a wrong way of expressing yourself, and that the right way should be prescribed by works of a certain description, chief among them the dictionaries of the language."[9] Most language custodians in America felt that in the new dictionary an already indiscriminate linguistic democracy had yielded to anarchy. Even *The New York Times*—the *Third's* most often cited source of usage examples—lamented that the Merriam editors had not lived up to their public responsibility in the new "say-as-you-go dictionary."

Opposed to the position of these reviewers, of course, were the compilers of the dictionary. The *Third*'s editor in chief believed that lexicography "should have no traffic with guesswork, prejudice, or bias, or with artificial notions of correctness and superiority. . . . If a dictionary should neglect the obligation to act as a faithful recorder and interpreter of usage, it cannot expect to be any longer appealed to as an authority."[10] *Webster's* lexicographers took the function of a dictionary to be the faithful and scrupulous recording of actual language usage, which they identified as whatever language forms appropriate groups of people use in speaking and writing. This is a view in which descriptive linguists concur. They claim that the setting of value on linguistic forms is a social, not a lexicographic, matter. They maintain that lexicographers should record what society *does* with language, not what society says *should* be done or what society *thinks* it does. Linguists and lexicographers espousing this view, often considered liberal or even leftist, regard the proper function of grammars and dictionaries as exclusively descriptive: their books describe actual language practice.

Descriptive linguists do not recommend that a grammar of nonstandard English be taught in schools and colleges, where a command of standard English is assumed as the accepted goal. But if it were desirable to have descriptions of particular varieties of *spoken* English—English spoken on the Bowery, for example, or by United States Senators, or eleven-year-old Hopi Indians, or atomic physicists—then such grammars should accurately reflect the customary usage and pronunciation of those speakers. A hypothetical illustration: If atomic physicists ordinarily speak of the "nuculus" of an atom and of "nucular" energy, then a grammar of their English has an obligation to say so. In recording such a usage linguists would not be making a value judgment; they would be saying not that "nucular" is as good as or better than "nuclear" but merely that it is the form physicists ordinarily use.[11] A factual illustration: Quite a few educated American house hunters of my acquaintance seek assistance these days from a "*real*-a-tor" rather than a "*re*-al-tor"; descriptivists think it would be misleading for a dictionary to ignore this usage or to label it restrictively—assuming, of course, that its citation files for a wider sample of educated speakers validated my own observations. (As a matter of interest, *Webster's Third*—on the basis of mammoth citation files—labeled the pronunciation "*real*-a-tor" *substandard* and the pronunciation "nu-cu-lar" *chiefly substandard*. Whether or not the intervening two decades have witnessed sufficient spread of these pronunciations to warrant different labels is difficult for an individual to tell.)

The linguists' concern has been that school grammar, in stressing and continually testing disputed usages, has given the impression that nonstandard *spoken* varieties of English (and sometimes merely informal standard ones) are "bad" or "ungrammatical" English and has failed to distinguish the functions of these varieties and those customary in more formal communication, especially in writing. They have also quarreled with too-narrow and too-rigid definitions of "standard English" itself, definitions that reject the usages of many educated and cultured speakers and writers.

Different linguists would doubtless have different answers to questions about particular disputed usages. (Is "nucular" standard spoken English? Should students be taught not to write "different than" and not to say "It's me"? Should they be taught to say or write "Whom did you see?" Are *through* and *thru* equally good?) But the linguists' answers would be alike in not being absolutely Yes or No; and in most cases they would probably begin with "It depends"—on the social and linguistic background of the speaker or writer *and* of the person or persons addressed; on the topic of discussion and its setting; on the nature and context of the usage in question; and so on. And they would insist that students should learn the *differences* between standard varieties of English and other varieties *without* being made to feel the other varieties are "inferior." Linguists think students should understand that all varieties of English—including standard written English—have evolved to meet communicative or social needs of the linguistic communities using them. (Additionally, linguists want teachers to be aware of the similarities among all the varieties of English, so that its underlying systematic nature will be better understood; and many of them would like to see students become familiar with the outlines of the historical growth and development of their language. But these features of a full-scale program of language study are beyond the scope of my concern with ideas about "good usage.") For my purposes here, the view of descriptive linguists may be summarized thus: the correctness of "grammar" or "English usage" is relative.

Obviously this relativist view is not universally shared. Wilson Follett, a distinguished editor and teacher, could hardly contain his rage when he heard usage so defined. "Let those who choose define usage as what a swarm of folk say or write by reason of laziness, shiftlessness, or ignorance; the tenable definition is still what the judicious do as a result of all that they can muster of conscious determination."[12] The absolutist view of correctness is also represented by Edwin Newman, who in *Strict-*

ly Speaking (1974) cites hundreds of "wrong" and "impossible" usages culled from *The New York Times, Esquire* magazine, and other periodicals. For example: "'Different than,' rather than different from, is wrong. So is 'augur for.' Augur does not take for after it. It cannot take for after it." That *augur* has in fact taken *for* after it in the pages he cites does not shake Newman's faith in his index of impossible usages. Unlike these rigid custodians of language, descriptive linguists do define what a swarm of folk say or write—by reason of laziness, shiftlessness, ignorance, or anything else—as *their* usage, and what the judicious speak and write, for whatever reasons, as *their* usage. They maintain that different usages are appropriate to the different uses and users of English.

Follett believed that linguistic scholarship, using such definitions, was "dedicating itself to the abolition of standards" and that "the new rhetoric evolved under its auspices is an organized assumption that language good enough for anybody is good enough for everybody." He called for a "philosophy of usage grounded in the steadfast conviction that the best, whether or not we have it in us to attain it, is not too good to be aspired to."[13] Language guardians like Follett prefer basing grammars and dictionaries on standards other than current custom. The rules they favor would delimit what they regard as the best possible English; and insofar as such rules portray a potential rather than an actual state of affairs, they are properly called linguistic exhortations or prescriptive rules.

The position taken by Follett, Pei, Newman, certain critics of *Webster's Third,* and *Saturday Review*'s letter writers, has often been referred to as a "doctrine of correctness," while the view of most modern linguists and the lexicographers who compiled the *Third* has been termed a "doctrine of usage."

Adherents of a doctrine of correctness strive to mold linguistic practice according to selected patterns of grammar; they attempt to retard the pace of language change or halt it altogether; they are idealistic and prescriptive; some are elitist; they make explicit value judgments about English locutions. As the editor of *The American Heritage Dictionary* acknowledged about its panel of prescriptive usage consultants, "They have eschewed the 'scientific' delusion that a dictionary should contain no value judgments."[14] Another prescriber, former *Fortune* magazine editor Dwight Macdonald, appearing on the "Today" show in 1975, told host Edwin Newman that he considered one of his editorial duties to be slowing down of the acceptance of new usages. On the same broadcast Theodore M. Bernstein of *The New York Times* agreed with Macdonald and with writer Jean Stafford that their position with respect to linguistic correctness is and should be "elitist." Stafford, winner of a Pulitzer

Prize, remarked that a usage must be accepted by the "educated," not merely "widely accepted," in order to be correct.

Supporters of a doctrine of usage, on the other hand, attempt to base rules of grammar and lexical entries in dictionaries on actual language practice. It is their goal to be realistic and descriptive. They make no explicit value judgments about the logic, utility, or esthetics—i.e., the "correctness"—of particular lexical or grammatical items, but report the known facts about the ways in which a given form, meaning, or pronunciation is actually used and in what circumstances.

The word *grammar* has a variety of meanings in America. Almost any book about a particular language can be called a "grammar." To most professional grammarians "grammar" means a relatively complete and systematic description of the language in a community, however large or small, rural or urban, technologically advanced or primitive. Among linguists of the transformational-generative school, a "grammar" describes the internalized, psychological system of elements and rules underlying the use of one's native language. And there are other related senses of the word. But to most Americans "grammar" suggests a code of good conduct regulating spoken and especially written English. For violation of its precepts we are said not to know grammar or to have bad grammar; and, as with other codes of etiquette, disregard of this one can elicit judgments of educational, social, and even personal inferiority. Like other etiquettes, this one too has intricate and subtle applications, though most of us are unaware of their complexity. A word or phrase that goes unnoticed in one set of circumstances may brand a speaker as boorish if used on another occasion.

Because we customarily think of preschoolers as knowing little or no grammar in this last sense, we can call this linguistic etiquette "school grammar." Great effort is expended teaching this protocol, and it is this kind of grammar that is talked about in schools and in newspaper discussions. The linguistic punctilios that constitute school grammar are often taught as absolutes: *ain't* is wrong; *as* is the right conjunction, *like* is wrong; *whom* is correct in this structure but not in that one; use *I*, not *me*, in this phrase; *infer* cannot mean "imply"; and so on. Embracing perhaps several hundred generally unrelated linguistic usages, such a code of fashion must be taught in the schools because it is not much observed in ordinary spoken communication and therefore cannot be acquired the way a child absorbs the vast bulk of his internalized linguistic system—without conscious effort or formal instruction. This grammatical *savoir faire* covers just a portion of our English language and draws attention to itself only when we venture outside our immediate familial and social milieu. Like other codes of convention school grammar is a social artifact, though not unimportant; indeed, in the United States (as in some other countries) its traditional importance is unmatched by any other academic subject, reading and perhaps arithmetic excepted.

Not everyone agrees that school grammar should play a major role in education; fewer still approve the influence wielded by its nice distinctions in socioeconomic advancement. Because many recent debunkers of this absolute code of conduct have in fact been professional students of language, I shall for convenience group supporters of a relativistic view of correct English under the label *linguist*. Of course, many linguists have expressed little or no interest in the correctness controversy or in the debate over the role that the mastery of particular items of English usage should play in the schools. Most linguists have directed their energies instead to historical or descriptive problems in the grammar and phonology of English or to analysis of other languages. They have taken their transcriptions of speech as given, much as historical linguists and philologists accept the language forms of extant texts. Linguists afford the spoken word primacy over the written; they regard writing as a sometimes pallid reflection of speech. For descriptive and historical linguists of all persuasions, a relativist view of correctness and the primacy of speech over writing are working assumptions.

But how shall I characterize Pei, Follett, Macdonald, Newman, the writers of *SR*'s letters, and their company? It is difficult to choose a fair and telling designation for the various antagonists of the relativistic approach. *Purist* and *absolutist* are harsh and too rigid to encompass many who ought to be included. *Conservative* is too broad, perhaps too political. *Rhetorician* is narrow and too professional. *Traditional grammarian*, sometimes shortened to *traditionalist*, fits more comfortably, and I shall use it, though it is perhaps not so well tailored as *linguist* is to its wearers. The truth is that many of those I shall call traditional grammarians have not been professional grammarians at all. Some are authors, editors, and teachers of composition; some are professors of history, rhetoric, and literature; some are social critics, journalists, television and radio commentators; in the past there were many clergymen and amateur philosophers among them. What they share is the belief that acceptance and practice of their principles and preferences would improve the English language and the lives of its users.

Because they understand and propagate the orthodox rules about *who* and *whom, shall* and *will, like* and *as*, various traditionalists are popularly considered grammarians, and it will serve my purpose to follow custom in this regard. And because traditional grammarians have been concerned with protecting the English language from what they take to be degeneration and debasement, it will be appropriate at times to refer to them as *language guardians.* And, taking a cue from the form of their guidance, I shall on occasion call them *prescriptivists* and *prescribers,* in contrast with the linguists, who are *descriptivists* and *describers.*

It must be admitted that none of these labels is ideal! Readers should bear in mind, as they come across generalizations about *linguists* or *traditional grammarians,* that the terms have been chosen to characterize two warring factions—the supporters and opponents of a relativistic view of language correctness. Often I will have need to refer to both groups and so I will sometimes use "grammarians" as an umbrella term for all writers about English.

The term *usage* also needs a word of explanation, though my employment of it is in keeping with customary interpretations over the past fifty years. "Usage" sometimes refers to the complete set of lexical, grammatical, and phonological or orthographical occurrences in speech and writing (that is, to everything that people say or write, with special reference to the way they do it). Often, however, the term's reference is limited to that subset of linguistic items whose social or functional status is debatable (that is, to locutions whose "correctness" is in question). For each debatable item or questionable "usage," there is another that language guardians consider better or worse and hence to be preferred or avoided (*whom/who*; "that thing"/"dat ting"; *different from/different than;* "nucular"/"nuclear"; and so forth).

There has been disagreement between the advocates of actual usage and the proponents of correctness since grammars and dictionaries were first compiled. Linguists and traditional grammarians have quarreled for generations about what is correct English, what the standards for correctness should be, and who should set them.

The appearance of *Webster's Third,* in 1961, crystallized the issues. More than that, it politicized them and gave diverse tractarians occasion to cloud the debate and lobby for their views in the ensuing storm. The depth and character of the convictions threatened by the *Third*'s treatment of usage can be highlighted by noting that *The New York Times* in its editions of November 30, 1961, dubbed the new dictionary "Webster's Third (or Bolshevik) International." Further, the president of a respectable publishing firm sought to buy out the Merriam Company and scuttle the *Third,* alleging that the world of scholarship was "horrified" at its permissive standards.[15] Finally, the hint of linguistic promiscuity latent in the already cited comparison between the *Third* and the somewhat notorious "Kinsey Report" is a reminder of the moral and puritanical overtones that often surround discussion of English usage. Clearly, the tug of war between description and prescription in English lexicography and grammar, though four hundred years in the waging, remained taut and unresolved in 1961.

And so it continues. While the doctrine of usage is gaining support in some school books and already dominates lexicography, many teachers of English still favor a form of the centuries-old doctrine of correctness for dictionaries, handbooks, and school grammars; and in general both educated and uneducated opinion agrees with them. Indeed, traditionalists blame much that is wrong in our schools and public places on the rise of structural, descriptive linguistics and the alleged easing of language standards. Television commentator Edwin Newman has linked the decline of public confidence in government with the looser language standards of politicians; he has placed two such indictments on the best-seller lists since 1974. In the last month of 1978 and the first month or so of 1979 I happened upon discussions of the poor state of the language in *Saturday Review, Newsweek,* and *Time* magazines, as well as on television—on the "Today" show, on a local Los Angeles news broadcast, and (for an entire week!) on the Dick Cavett show. "All Things Considered," a syndicated news program on National Public Radio, has reported that the most "irate" mail received from listeners deals with the "improper" use of English by the broadcasters. And a New Jersey professor of English has been receiving nationwide attention for his newsletter, *The Underground Grammarian,* which details the decline and fall of the English language with illustrations from memoranda issued on his campus. Finally, even *Esquire* magazine now publishes a monthly column on English usage. Ironically, as gracefully as it is written, its author learned English not as a native language from family and friends but from grammar books as a foreign language (his fifth in fact!); quite understandably he takes a consistently conservative and sometimes unnaturally rigid view of correctness. Uneasiness, then, over the state of the language is not limited to a few Americans in publishing houses or on university campuses nor even to teachers of English. It is a matter of deep and widespread and continuing concern.

It was late in the sixteenth century, after English had started to replace Latin as a medium of learned discussion in Britain, that Englishmen first complained about the absence in their use of the vernacular of the kind of regularity and certainty to which they were accustomed in the classical language. They began writing handbooks to supply this want, and since then Englishmen and Americans have continued publishing grammars and lexicons of their language. While some grammarians and dictionary makers lamented linguistic alteration and tended to regard the descriptions and strictures of their predecessors as nearly immutable, others strenuously objected to analyses based on anything but actual current usage. As usage changes, these latter argued, grammars and lexicons must also change; the rules are dependent, not primary, and cannot be considered sacrosanct. But the more conservative codifiers, noting the variety of English and American dialects and the natural tendency of tongues to change, were convinced that without powerful safeguards English speakers would find themselves unable to read the literature and written records of earlier periods and unable to communicate across countries (or possibly even counties). Dwight Macdonald expressed this fear in 1962, saying that without "brakes applied by those who know and care about the language, . . . the change will be so fast and so dominated by the great majority who have other things to do besides worrying about good English that the result will be a jargon as cut off from the race's culture and traditions as the Pidgin English of the South Seas."[16] To further complicate things, the relationship between speech and writing has confounded nearly all literate English speakers; and the linguists' focus on spoken systems has not helped. In 1975, *Newsweek* warned that, with speech taking priority over writing, a second tower of Babel was building![17]

Continued struggle over four centuries has dragged to the surface several underlying causes of disagreement and misunderstanding. Changing social and educational conditions have demanded clearer expositions of each viewpoint. In America, especially, dramatic increases in the numbers of students from lower socioeconomic levels and from foreign cultures have forced educators to reconsider the linguistic needs of students and the purposes and means of teaching them English grammar and spelling. Supporters of the idea that usage determines correctness in language began abandoning a right-or-wrong approach in favor of a relativistic one that distinguished varieties of English according to level and function. But as they groped their way toward objective analysis of what this might mean in terms of linguistic correctness, they met resistance from traditional grammarians who found their objective criteria irrelevant.

In this century, grammar has provided a battering ram both for supporters and for opponents of progressive education. Liberals claimed that objectives for language instruction have not remained consonant with the changing social situations of students, while conservatives, generally cool to universal education at all levels, deplored the diluting of traditional ideals. Language guardians feared that the permissiveness associated with progressive education was infecting the teaching of grammar and would ultimately contaminate the language itself if left unchecked.

Besides straightforward differences of opinion, we find that misunderstanding, hostility, and bigotry have contributed at times in this century—as before—to the confusion surrounding the composition of dictionaries and grammars and the teaching of English usage. Philosophical differences over the nature of language, the purposes of education, the function of science (especially its role in language studies), the value of democracy, and ultimately the character of human society have obscured discussions ostensibly about English usage.

Beginning with early British views, the chapters that follow examine the opinions that scholars and laymen from various walks of life have expressed about correct English in grammars, dictionaries, and handbooks. A look at the development of a doctrine of correctness and of opposition to it in the nineteenth and twentieth centuries reveals that the chasm separating these views goes far deeper than mere technical disagreement about the status of specific items of usage. A historical survey of American views of linguistic propriety helps uncover certain veiled assumptions embodied in the letters to *Saturday Review,* in the imbroglio surrounding *Webster's Third,* and in the attitudes of countless Americans toward the proper use of the national tongue. It also subjects to scrutiny the linguists' assumptions and the successive refinements of their position resulting from the vigorous opposition of traditional grammarians.

Since a good deal of the antagonism between descriptivists and language guardians stems from a bilateral misunderstanding of intentions and aspirations, a historical overview provides a perspective for evaluating the two opposing views of propriety in lexicography and grammar. The Danish linguist Otto Jespersen, perhaps the world's most distinguished student of the English language (and sometimes affectionately referred to as "the great Dane"), has identified seven kinds of standards commonly applied in classroom and newspaper discussions of linguistic correctness. Besides the standard of authority, he noted appeal to geographical, literary, aristocratic, democratic, logical, and esthetic standards.[18] We shall find these same criteria and others learnedly discussed throughout our historical search.

Notes

[1]Richard L. Tobin, "Like Your Cigarette Should" (1966), p. 59. Letters appeared in 1966 in the June 11, July 9, and August 13 issues of *Saturday Review.*

[2]Reported by Brander Matthews in *Parts of Speech* (1901), p. 217.

[3]Thomas R. Lounsbury, *The Standard of Usage in English* (1908), p. 242; cited also in W. H. Mittins et al., *Attitudes to English Usage* (1970), p. 70.

[4]Reported in *Time* (August 22, 1969), p. 50.

[5]"Manner of Speaking" (1961), p. 30.

[6]Mario Pei, "The Dictionary as a Battlefront: English Teachers' Dilemma" (1962), p. 45.

[7]Reviews of *Webster's Third* appearing originally before June 1962 are cited from James Sledd and Wilma R. Ebbitt, eds., *Dictionaries and THAT Dictionary* (1962). Reviews published after May 1962 are cited from the original sources.

[8]A. M. Tibbetts, "The Real Issues in the Great Language Controversy" (1966), p. 36.

[9]Mario Pei, "A Loss for Words" (1964), p. 82.

[10]Philip B. Gove, "Linguistic Advances and Lexicography" (1961), p. 8.

[11]"Nucular" is a fairly common pronunciation throughout the States (though probably *not* among physicists); it is the form President Eisenhower employed in his television broadcasts to the American public.

[12]Wilson Follett, "Grammar Is Obsolete" (1960), p. 76. In permitting a reprinting of this article, Follett changed the title to "Bargain Basement English"; see Anderson and Stageberg, eds., *Introductory Readings on Language* (1962). Follett (1887–1963) had taught English at Texas A and M, Dartmouth, and Brown before turning to a career in editing.

[13]"Grammar Is Obsolete," pp. 73, 76.

[14]Morris Bishop, "Good Usage, Bad Usage, and Usage," in *The American Heritage Dictionary of the English Language,* ed. William Morris (1969), p. xxiii.

[15]The publisher was James Parton, president of the American Heritage Publishing Company. His attempt to wrest control of the *Third* from the G. & C. Merriam Company was widely reported at the time. See, e.g., *The New York Times* for February 20, 1962, p. 32 (from which Parton is here quoted) and October 4, 1964; *Newsweek* also reported the attempted takeover in its edition of March 12, 1962, pp. 104–105.

[16]"Three Questions for Structural Linguists; Or, Webster 3 Revisited" (Postscript to Sledd and Ebbitt), p. 258.

[17]"Why Johnny Can't Write," *Newsweek* (December 8, 1975), p. 65.

[18]*Mankind, Nation and Individual* (1925; repr. 1964), p. 83.

CHAPTER II

Early British Views: From Dean Swift and Dr. Johnson to a Famous Chemist

1500–1800

". . . our language offends . . . against every Part of Grammar."
—JONATHAN SWIFT, 1712

"Perhaps he meant the grammar of some other language; if so, the charge was certainly true, but not to the purpose, since we can say with equal truth, of every language, that it offends against the grammar of every other language whatsoever."
—GEORGE CAMPBELL, 1776

"To our language may be with great justice applied the observation of Quintilian, *that speech was not formed by an analogy sent from heaven. It did not descend to us in a state of uniformity and perfection, but was produced by necessity and enlarged by accident, and is therefore composed of dissimilar parts, thrown together by negligence, by affectation, by learning, or by ignorance."*
—DR. JOHNSON, 1747

TOWARD THE END of the Middle Ages, as Latin grudgingly yielded to French, Italian, Spanish, German, and English in written discussion of learned subjects and for translations of the Bible, much of the adequacy and stability of the classical tongue, especially in vocabulary and spelling, was found wanting in its successors. Latin of course was no longer anyone's first language, and scholars prized the seeming stability and unalterability of its written form. During the Middle Ages and Renaissance, schoolmasters taught Latin grammar not as a description of classical usage but as a prescription to be followed in current writing. Grammar was the art of writing and speaking Latin correctly; "grammar" *meant* Latin grammar.

18

From the earliest analyses, grammar had been a normative art, beginning with the grammarians of Alexandria, who sought to provide "a means of analyzing classic writers and guiding contemporaries to approximate this model."[1] It was natural that similar attitudes were often transferred to the study of the vernaculars when nationalistic, religious, and political motivation prompted their increased use. Europeans hoped to establish the same kind of authoritative treatment for them that Priscian had provided for Latin in the sixth century.[2] British writers justly feared that, as the fluid and multidialectal English replaced Latin, chaos and instability could destroy the relative ease of clear and exact communication afforded by the stable classical language in universal scholarly use throughout Europe.

With the increased use of the vernaculars in learned writing on the Continent, from about the middle of the fifteenth century, interest in English as a bona fide medium of written communication among England's learned had its conscious beginning. (Its literary use, of course, was established earlier—even before Chaucer, who died in 1400.) During the sixteenth and seventeenth centuries the vocabulary was greatly expanded to fill substantial gaps as English came to function where Latin had been used before. Among learned people fear spread that the new linguistic richness could lead to ineloquent, imprecise, and ambiguous communication. Moreover, many of the innovations were judged unnecessary, ill formed, or incorrect. Principles of English needed to be established and reduced to rule. The written language was in need of standardization and codification. Divided usages were felt to need settling and the orthography had to be fixed. Scholars assumed that dictionaries could authoritatively regulate the enrichment of vocabulary, define the meanings of new words, and standardize spelling, while grammars would lend stability to the still plastic syntax and morphology. Similar problems were faced in other European countries, several of which established official academies to supervise their vernaculars—purify, standardize, and codify them—to channel their growth, if not arrest it altogether.

In 1582, the year the Italian Accademia della Crusca was founded, an Englishman named William Bullokar remarked on the "unruled" state of the English language and called for the creation of a dictionary and grammar. Four years later he published his own *Bref Grammar,* the first analysis of English now known. In 1594 Paul Greaves published an English grammar in Latin *(Grammatica Anglicana)* so as to make it available to foreign as well as British scholars. In it he accused Englishmen of speaking their own tongue ungrammatically. But the main linguistic concern in late sixteenth-century England was with the "eloquent" use of language, and especially with eloquent vocabulary. A more general interest in the grammar of the vernacular did not emerge until the middle of the following century, after English had decisively won its position as *the* written language of Britain. Ben Jonson's *English Grammar* (1640) and John Wallis's *Grammatica Linguae Anglicanae* (1653) are noteworthy examples. For the next hundred and fifty years, voices echoing Bullokar and Greaves drew attention to the "ungrammaticality" of English. In an age that prized order and regulation, English appeared chaotic in comparison with Latin and even with French and Italian, whose academies had provided authoritative dictionaries by 1694. Englishmen were appalled by the diversity of spelling practices in their country, from person to person and printer to printer.

Without codified standards for correct spelling, syntax, or accepted meanings, English authors were unsure of themselves, uneasy about the propriety of their sentences. John Dryden in 1679 expressed this feeling: "I am desirous, if it were possible, that we might all write with the same certainty of words, and purity of phrase, to which the Italians first arrived, and after them the French; at least that we might advance so far, as our tongue is capable of such a standard."[3] And in 1697 Daniel Defoe proposed an academy whose task would be "to polish and refine the *English* Tongue, and advance the so much neglected Faculty of Correct Language, to establish Purity and Propriety of Stile, and to purge it from all the Irregular Additions that Ignorance and Affectation have introduc'd. . . ."[4]

SWIFT PROPOSES, JOHNSON DISPOSES

Not until 1712 was the most famous advocacy of an English academy made, exactly a century after the Italian Accademia had published the first known monolingual dictionary. Jonathan Swift wrote in *A Proposal for Correcting, Improving and Ascertaining the English Tongue,* addressed to the Earl of Oxford, Lord High Treasurer of Great Britain: "My Lord; I do here, in the Name of all the Learned and Polite Persons of the Nation, complain to Your Lordship, as *First Minister,* that our Language is extremely imperfect; that its daily Improvements are by no means in proportion to its daily Corruptions; that the Pretenders to polish and refine it, have chiefly multiplied Abuses and Absurdities; and, that in many Instances, it offends against every Part of Grammar." Swift was enamored of the notion of a steady language—pure, regulated, and unchanging. "What I have most at Heart," he wrote, "is, that some Method should be thought on for *ascertaining* and *fixing* our Language for ever, after such Alterations are made in it as shall be thought requisite. For I am of Opinion, that it is better a Language should not be wholly perfect, than that it should be perpetually changing; and we must give over at one Time, or at length infallibly change for the worse."[5]

Unlike Italian (1582), French (1635), Spanish (1713), and Swedish (1739), English was not destined to have an authorized academy. The clamor for an official governing board lost its momentum for a variety of reasons as the eighteenth century progressed, though largely because an unofficial academy in the guise of private dictionaries and grammars supplied what the Académie française and the Accademia della Crusca had provided France and Italy. In this ersatz English academy, the two most important works were Samuel Johnson's *Dictionary of the English Language* (1755) and Robert Lowth's *Short Introduction to English Grammar* (1762).

Half a century after Dryden, Dr. Johnson voiced his own opinion about the state of English in the preface to his *Dictionary* (1755): "When I took the first survey of my undertaking, I found our speech copious without order, and energetick without rules. . . ."[6] Like other countrymen of his, he sought to "ascertain" the language—to make people confident in their use of it and to dispel doubt about its correctness. He recognized that in the absence of an academy (which he had opposed) the task of ascertaining the language would fall to independent grammarians and lexicographers. The "chief intent" of his own dictionary, as he wrote in the prospectus for it, would be "to preserve the purity and ascertain the meaning of our English idiom."[7] In this *Plan*, addressed to the Earl of Chesterfield in 1747, he explained his ambitions to settle and fix the language:

> This, my Lord, is my idea of an English dictionary, a dictionary by which the pronunciation of our language may be fixed, and its attainment facilitated; by which its purity may be preserved, its use ascertained, and its duration lengthened. And though, perhaps, to correct the language of nations by books of grammar, and amend their manners by discourses of morality, may be tasks equally difficult; yet as it is unavoidable to wish, it is natural likewise to hope, that your Lordship's patronage may not be wholly lost; that it may contribute to the preservation of antient, and the improvement of modern writers; that it may promote the reformation of those translators, who for want of understanding the characteristical difference of tongues, have formed a chaotic dialect of heterogeneous phrases; and awaken to the care of purer diction, some men of genius, whose attention to argument makes them negligent of stile, or whose rapid imagination, like the Peruvian torrents, when it brings down gold, mingles it with sand.

But as Dr. Johnson came to realize about his ambitions, they were "the dreams of a poet doomed at last to wake a lexicographer." After a decade of first-hand lexicographical enterprise, the accomplished dictionary maker of 1755, a more realistic student of language than the novice of 1747, admitted in the preface to the *Dictionary:*

> Those who have been persuaded to think well of my design, require that it should fix our language, and put a stop to those alterations which time and chance have hitherto been suffered to make in it without opposition. With this consequence I will confess that I flattered myself for a while; but now begin to fear that I have indulged expectation which neither reason nor experience can justify. When we see men grow old and die at a certain time one after another, from century to century, we laugh at the elixir that promises to prolong life to a thousand years; and with equal justice may the lexicographer be derided, who being able to produce no example of a nation that has preserved their words and phrases from mutability, shall imagine that his dictionary can embalm his language, and secure it from corruption and decay, that it is in his power to change sublunary nature, or clear the world at once from folly, vanity, and affectation.
>
> With this hope, however, academies have been instituted, to guard the avenues of their languages, to retain fugitives, and repulse intruders; but their vigilance and activity have hitherto been vain; sounds are too volatile and subtile for legal restraints; to enchain syllables, and to lash the wind, are equally the undertakings of pride, unwilling to measure its desires by its strength.

*   *   *

> If the changes that we fear be thus irresistible, what remains but to acquiesce with silence, as in the other insurmountable distresses of humanity? it remains that we retard what we cannot repel, that we palliate what we cannot cure. Life may be lengthened by care, though death cannot be ultimately defeated: tongues, like governments, have a natural tendency to degeneration; we have long preserved our constitution, let us make some struggles for our language.
>
> In hope of giving longevity to that which its own nature forbids to be immortal, I have devoted this book, the labour of years, to the honour of my country, that we may no longer yield the palm of philology to the nations of the continent.

Among the contemporary evidence that Dr. Johnson furnished the English their "academy" is a reference to his *Dictionary* in the *London Chronicle:* "he hath supplied the Want of an Academy of Belles Lettres, and performed Wonders towards fixing our Grammar, and ascertaining the determinate Meaning of Words, which are known to be in their own Nature of a very unstable and fluctuating Quality. To his Labours it may hereafter be owing that our Drydens, our Addisons, and our Popes shall not become as obsolete and unintelligible as Chaucer."[8] More striking still is the attitude expressed by the Earl of Chesterfield, counted on by Johnson as patron:

> I had long lamented that we had no lawful standard of our language set up, for those to repair to, who might chuse to speak and write it grammatically and correctly; and I have as long wished that either some one person of distinguished abilities would undertake the work singly, or that a certain number of gentlemen would form themselves, or be formed by the government, into a society for that purpose. . . .
>
> I cannot help thinking it a sort of disgrace to our nation, that hitherto we have had no such standard of our language [as the dictionaries of Italy, France, and Spain]. . . .
>
> It must be owned that our language is at present in a state of anarchy; and hitherto, perhaps, it may not have been the worse for it. . . . The time for discrimination seems to be now come. Toleration, adoption and naturalization, have run their lengths. Good order and authority are now necessary. But where shall we find them, and at the same time, the obedience due to them? We must have recourse to the old Roman expedient in times of confusion, and chuse a dictator. Upon this principle I give my vote for Mr. Johnson to fill that great and arduous post. And I hereby declare that I make a total surrender of all my rights and privileges in the English language, as a freeborn British subject, to the said Mr. Johnson, during the term of his dictatorship. Nay more; I will not only obey him, like an old Roman, as my dictator, but, like a modern Roman, I will implicitly believe in him as my pope, and hold him to be infallible while in the chair; but no longer.[9]

THE BISHOP CODIFIES

While Dr. Johnson's *Dictionary* effectively supplied England an authoritative standard for vocabulary and spelling, it barely alluded to syntax, leaving the need for grammatical codification still unsatisfied. Robert Lowth (1710–1787) complained of this in 1762: "The last *English* Grammar that hath been presented to the public, and by the Person best qualified to have given us a perfect one, comprises the whole Syntax in ten lines."[10] Thus the most famous eighteenth-century English grammarian, professor of Hebrew poetry at Oxford and later Bishop of London, prefaced his *Short Introduction to English Grammar,* an extraordinarily influential book and the forerunner of nearly all British and American school grammars since.

"The English Language hath been much cultivated during the last two hundred years," Lowth wrote. "It hath been considerably polished and refined; it hath been greatly enlarged in extent and compass; its force and energy, its variety, richness, and elegance, have been tried with good success, in verse and in prose, upon all subjects, and in every kind of style: but whatever other improvements it may have received, it hath made no advances in Grammatical accuracy." Expressing the sentiments of his contemporaries, as well as of Swift half a century earlier, Lowth claimed that "the *English* Language as it is spoken by the politest part of the nation, and as it stands in the writings of our most approved authors, oftentimes offends against every part of Grammar." Because two centuries of linguistic elaboration had enriched English, nothing inherently inferior now weakened it, and Lowth was optimistic that it could be made as regular as any learned language; but as of 1762 it had not been adequately standardized or codified: "It is not owing . . . to any peculiar irregularity or difficulty of our Language, that the general practice both of speaking and writing is chargeable with inaccuracy. It is not the Language, but the practice, that is in fault. The truth is, Grammar is very much neglected among us. . . . Much practice in the polite world, and a general acquaintance with the best authors, are good helps, but alone will hardly be sufficient. . . . It will evidently appear from these Notes, that our best Authors for want of some rudiments of grammar have sometimes fallen into mistakes, and been guilty of palpable errors in point of Grammar." To remedy such neglect Lowth offered his own codification so that Englishmen could "judge of every phrase and form of construction, whether it be right or not. The plain way of doing this, is to lay down rules, and to illustrate them by examples. But besides shewing what is right, the matter may be further explained by pointing out what is wrong."

Setting out, then, to rectify the "ungrammatical" and chaotic state of English usage, Lowth aimed to sort out what was good, proscribe "palpable errors," and prescribe rules of correct practice. Pope's fear that "such as Chaucer is, shall Dryden be" motivated him and others to ascertain the language and attempt to retard change.

Like other eighteenth-century codifiers, Lowth recognized and even endorsed the importance of linguistic custom. He declared that usage, especially older usage, governs correctness in language. But he subordinated its authority to that of logic, analogy, and the "genius of the language," and he relied on models of Latin, because it was widely thought to embody the principles of "universal grammar"—principles common to all languages. Typically, he writes (in this case speaking of "defective" or auxiliary verbs): "They are in general words of most frequent and vulgar use; in which Custom is apt to get the better of Analogy" (p. 84).

In establishing regular and authoritative rules to provide a measure of confidence to a linguistically insecure society, English grammarians not surprisingly turned to Latin grammars for answers to certain questions, discounting the fact that, unlike English, Latin was highly inflected. Moreover, some grammarians hoped a "proper" study of English grammar would facilitate the learning of Latin, and it proved tempting to let the structure of the classical language frame certain descriptions of English. A remark of Lowth's in his preface—that "if children were first taught the common principles of Grammar by some short and clear System of *English* Grammar, . . . they would have some notion of what they were going about, when they should enter into the Latin Grammar . . ."—suggests an explanation for the current suspicion that only the study of Latin has enabled some twentieth-century students to fathom some textbook formulations of English grammar.

When appeal to Latin was not suitable or fruitful in settling disputed points, grammarians like Lowth sought authority in the usage of writers. But, though generally acknowledging that usage must govern correctness, they could not agree as to *whose* usage would set the standard—a crucial issue first raised for Latin by Quintilian in the first century. And they were troubled by divided usage.

Consider Lowth's approach to past tense and past participle forms of irregular verbs. He conceded the "General bent and turn of the Language" for merging these forms. He lamented, however, that "This general inclination and tendency of the language, seems to have given occasion to the introducing of a very great Corruption; by which the Form of the Past Time is confounded with that of the Participle in these Verbs, few in proportion, which have them quite different from one another. [E.g.: *took, taken; rose, risen; went, gone; began, begun.*] This confusion prevails greatly in common discourse, and is too much authorised by the example of some of our best Writers" (pp. 85–86). Lowth cited "abuses" by Milton, Dryden, Addison, Pope, Prior, Clarendon, Gay, Bolingbroke, and even Swift, whom he revered as "one of our most correct, and perhaps our best prose writer" (p. ii)!

These are a few of his examples from "our best Writers" (pp. 86–88):

MILTON:	"have spoke" *(P.L. x. 517).*
	"had rode" *(P.R. iii 36).*
	"was took" *(Comus).*
DRYDEN:	"have began" *(Fables).*
POPE:	"The bard begun" *(Messiah).*
ADDISON:	"Mr. Milton has wrote" *(Preface to his Travels).*
	"The men begun" *(Spect. No. 434).*
SWIFT:	"had not arose" *(Tale of a Tub, Sect. x).*

"have stole" *(Ibid.).*
"have mistook" *(Ibid. Sect. ix).*

The assurance of certainty and the security that Lowth offered won the day with questioning users of English. Along with freedom from doubt and anxiety, however, they inherited his dogmatism. His statements were commonly sacrosanct even in America. In 1789, Noah Webster reported that even university graduates were apt to "read Lowth's Introduction, or some other grammatical treatment, believe what they read, without examining the grounds of the writer's opinion, and to attempt to shape their language by his rules . . . they pride themselves, for some time, in their superior learning and peculiarities; till further information, or the ridicule of the public, brings them to use the language of other people."[11]

Held in such esteem, Lowth's grammar helped establish many proscriptions still current in school grammars and stardardized tests. Prohibitions of the double negative, the objective case in *It's me,* the nominative case in *Who did you ask?,* the "confusion" of *shall* and *will* were introduced into English in the seventeenth and eighteenth centuries by codifiers like Lowth and promulgated by their imitators, notably the American-born Lindley Murray. Many such grammatical taboos have continued without significant alteration into the twentieth century, and several have determined the course of subsequent educated usage.

Eighteenth-century grammars might have been more uniform had there been an agreed-upon standard of linguistic propriety, but, with a nod to the dictum of Horace establishing usage as arbiter, each codifier elected his own authorities. All subscribed to the principle that universal usage governed correctness. But universal usages were never disputed; and the question of propriety arose only with usages that *were* disputed. Horace's oft-quoted *usus est et ius et norma loquendi* ("usage is both the rule and the norm of speaking") offered no solution. While Dr. Johnson preferred "to collect examples and authorities from writers before the restoration, whose works I regard as *the wells of English undefiled,* as the pure sources of genuine diction," Joseph Priestley found advantage citing from "modern writings, rather than from those of Swift, Addison, and others, who wrote about half a century ago." In this preference Priestley followed Quintilian, who had found it "almost laughable to prefer the language of the past to that of the present day."[12]

CAMPBELL CRITICIZES

Though it was typical, Lowth's was not the only approach to correctness in neo-classical England. George Campbell (1719–1796), the best-known rhetorician of the age, maintained that "Language is purely a species of fashion. . . ." He wrote in his *Philosophy of Rhetoric* (1776) that "It is not the business of grammar, as some critics seem preposterously to imagine, to give law to the fashions which regulate our speech"; rather, "use, or the custom of speaking, is the sole original standard of conversation . . . and the custom of writing is the sole standard of style . . . . to the tribunal of use, as to the supreme authority, and consequently, in every grammatical controversy, the last resort, we are entitled to appeal from the laws and the decisions of grammarians; and . . . this order of subordination ought never, on any account, to be reversed." Defining a grammar, Campbell wrote:

> It is no other than a collection of general observations methodically digested, and comprising all the modes previously and independently established, by which the significations, derivations, and combinations of words in that language are ascertained. It is of no consequence here to what causes originally these modes or fashions owe their existence, to imitation, to reflection, to affectation, or to caprice; they no sooner obtain and become general, than they are laws of the language, and the grammarian's only business is to note, collect, and methodize them. Nor does this truth concern only those more comprehensive analogies or rules, which affect whole classes of words, such as nouns, verbs, and the other parts of speech; but it concerns every individual word, in the inflecting or the combining of which a particular mode hath prevailed. Every single anomaly, therefore, though departing from the rule assigned to the other words of the same class, and on that account called an exception, stands on the same basis on which the rules of the tongue are founded, custom having prescribed for it a separate rule.

Campbell defined good use as "reputable," "national," and "present" use. *Reputable* he elaborated as "the practice of those who have had a liberal education" and of "authors of reputation": "The use here spoken of, implies not only *currency,* but *vogue.* It is properly *reputable custom.*" *National* he distinguished from both foreign and provincial use. And because he believed that "some time is absolutely necessary to constitute that custom of use, on which the establishment of words depends," he took his prose examples "neither from living authors, nor those who wrote before the Revolution" (the authors of the Vulgar Translation—the King James Version—were the only exception).[13]

With these explanations and modifications, Campbell's definition of good English has been widely repeated and endorsed by grammarians and rhetoricians throughout the nineteenth and twentieth centuries.

In his discussion of "the foundations and essential properties of elocution," Campbell introduced a crucial distinction between "grammarians" and "verbal critics," a distinction largely ignored subsequently. The task of a *grammarian,* he said, is solely the *description* of good use. As a grammarian, a writer cannot legitimately incorporate adjustments to the observed practice of a nation any more than the writer of a legal digest can incorporate desirable alterations of the law. As the compiler of a legal digest strives for a clear delineation of what the law actually ordains, so the grammarian should strive to describe the observed regularities and irregularities of the language as accurately and succinctly as possible.

The *verbal critic,* on the other hand, is free to suggest linguistic *improvements* on whatever basis he deems legitimate. And to this end Campbell, who did not consider himself a grammarian, offered nine "canons" to guide verbal criticism, stressing that as implying *prescription* and exhortation, his canons must be distinguished sharply from *description,* which is the essence of grammar. He voiced distress that many "grammarians" indulged in critical appraisal of the language in the guise of description, and he chided Dean Swift, Dr. Johnson, and Bishop Lowth for confusing the different undertakings.

At the heart of Campbell's philosophy of rhetoric was a belief in the possibility of improving English by criticism, and as a rhetorician-critic he allowed himself a structured freedom to evaluate English locutions. Disagreeing with Joseph Priestley's claim that the best forms of English will establish themselves in time "by their own superior excellence," Campbell claimed that the arts of verbal criticism, "by assisting to suppress every unlicensed term, and to stigmatize every improper idiom, tend to give greater precision, and consequently more perspicuity and beauty to our style." He thought it valuable that the verbal critic "seasonably notifies the abuses that are creeping in" to the language.

To settle *disputed* usages Campbell's critical canons appeal variously, and in the order given, to (1) perspicuity and variety, (2) analogy, (3) euphony, (4) simplicity and transparent etymology, and (5) ancient usage. Campbell did not judge even *established* usages worthy to be retained simply because they were established. Rather, with four more canons, he empowered the verbal critic to reject (6) anything "remarkably harsh and unharmonious, and not absolutely necessary," (7) anything whose "etymology plainly points to a signification different from that which the word commonly bears," (8) anything that has become obsolete "except as constituting part of particular phrases," and (9) anything accepted idiomatically but not conforming to current grammatical regularities (e.g., "I *had rather*" or "He *plays a good fiddle*" or "*I take it* you were sick").

His first five canons "are intended to suggest the principles by which our choice ought to be directed, in cases wherein use itself is wavering, and the four last to point out those further improvements which the critical art, without exceeding her legal powers, may assist in producing." He lamented the inclination of some critics to extend the authority of criticism "much further." But how much further than this, we must ask, could anyone have the imagination to go?

Invoking one or another of his canons, Campbell generated a list of his own preferences, a number of which have since become established custom—whether partly from his influence or not would be impossible to say. But among those that usage has not come to favor are a great many others. Invoking canon 1, he rejected *you* as the second person pronoun in the nominative plural, exhorting its restriction to the objective case, with *ye* in the nominative. Citing canon 2, he recommended discarding *he dare not go, he need not go,* and *would to God,* preferring the more analogical *he dares not, he needs not,* and *would God.* He preferred *thereabout* and *whereabout* to *thereabouts* and *whereabouts,* on the ground that English has no word *abouts* (also by canon 2). He judged *causey* and *jarter* preferable to *causeway* and *garter* by canon 5. Canon 8 entitled him to discard *lief, dint, whit, moot,* and *pro* and *con;* while by canon 9 he put aside *I had rather* and *currying favor,* this last of which he found a "vile, but common" phrase. And despite the rather broad scope allowed by his nine critical canons, he was forced to reject *dumfound, bamboozle, topsyturvy, pellmell, helterskelter,* and *hurlyburly* not on any principled basis but as "betraying some frivolous humour" in their formation!

In a chapter following the one on the principles of verbal criticism, Campbell directed himself to the question of "grammatical purity"—something quite different, it turns out, from both grammaticality and good use. Purity for Campbell was a negative virtue, noticeable more in the breach than in the observance; and there were three chief kinds: "barbarisms" (the use of entirely obsolete or entirely new words, or of good words "new-modelled"); "solecisms" ("the transgression of any syntactic rule"); and "improprieties" (misused or misapplied words or phrases). In that chapter, then, Campbell came full circle in practice, if not in theory. For he listed as offences against purity whatever offended his sense of what English ought to be. And he disliked the borrowings *opine, ignore,* and *adroitness* and urged their discontinuance, along with *analyse, connection, stoic, peripatetic, fictitious,* and *majestic*, which he saw no need for. He objected to the replacing of *dervis, Mahomet, Mussulman,* and *alcoran* by *dervish, Mohammed, Moslem,* and *Koran.* We see, then, in these matters as in so much else (though certainly not in all that he suggested), that subsequent usage has preferred the locutions Campbell sought, sometimes in a principled way, to expunge from the language. Later, verbal critics, sometimes in unprincipled ways, have also sought to rectify or purify English usage. And usage has afforded these attempted expurgations the same mixed reception it gave Campbell's. Nor is it clear, even in retrospect, why usage has favored one alternative over others.

Granting that Campbell was by his own definitions not a grammarian but a verbal critic who could therefore legitimately criticize English locutions, we see that in very large measure he failed to bring about the changes he desired. We must credit him nonetheless for his recognition that such criticism as he offered is within the province only of the critic, not of the grammarian. In practice, the role of verbal critic has often been merged into that of grammarian and lexicographer. Most discussion of English usage has been written by men with two hats—describer and prescriber—often when wearing both at once. The result for the twentieth century has been confusion and hostility.

Using Campbell's terms, it is fair to say that the role of "verbal critic" has been more attractive and profitable to writers than the role of "grammarian." In the absence of an academy, a common mode of operation has been for someone to set up as a grammarian—or, less often, lexicographer—and then, giving lip service to the supreme authority of "usage," to merge description and prescription. Many self-styled "grammarians" have "described" English as they thought it should be, offering analysis of a sometimes fictional state purporting to be reputable, national, and present use. As in Campbell's time, "grammarians" in later times have often not honored the principles they seemed to accept in theory. Nearly all have been ill at ease with divided usage and, like Campbell himself, resolved to judge one form right and others barbarous.

PRIESTLEY OBSERVES

One eighteenth-century notable, however, did apply the principle that usage governs correctness, in addition to espousing it in theory. He is Joseph Priestley (1733–1804), remembered today chiefly for his discovery of oxygen. Priestley also examined theology, politics, philosophy, and English, and his linguistic work deserves to make him, I dare say, even more famous as a grammarian than he is as a chemist.

Priestley accurately described his *Rudiments of English Grammar* (1761) as simply "a collection of observations on the structure of it, and a system of rules for the proper use of it."[14] Comparing grammar to a treatise on natural philosophy, "the one consisting of observations on the various changes, combinations, and mutual affections of words; and the other on those of the parts of nature," he recognized that "were the language of men as uniform as the works of nature, the *grammar of language* would be as indisputable in its principles as the *grammar of nature*" (1761, p. vi).

Priestley's scientific orientation made it easy for him to treat language as a phenomenon to be observed and described. "The best and the most numerous authorities [writers, not grammarians] have been carefully followed. Where they have been contradictory, recourse hath been had to analogy, as the last resource: For if this should decide for neither of two contrary practices, the thing must remain undecided, till all-governing custom shall declare in favour of the one or the other" (1761, p. vii). For Priestley, "the custom of speaking" was "the original and only just standard of any language" (p. ix). He thought that "In modern and living languages, it is absurd to pretend to set up the compositions of any persons whatsoever as the standard of writing, or their conversation as the invariable rule of speaking. With respect to customs, laws, and every thing that is changeable, the body of a people, who, in this respect, cannot but be free, will certainly assert their liberty, in making what innovations they judge to be expedient and useful. The general prevailing custom where ever it happen to be, can be the only standard for the time that it prevails."[15]

For the eighteenth-century grammarians, the task of discovering the patterns and orderliness of English was not trifling. No substantial grammatical tradition existed in England except for the centuries-old analyses of Latin; scholars were inexperienced at tackling previously uncodified languages like English. Many early English grammars resembled Latin grammars, with the Latin simply erased and the English equivalents remaining. But Priestley's grammars are remarkably independent and fresh, containing insights that have been rediscovered in the twentieth century. Unfortunately, a month after his original grammar appeared, it was overshadowed by the publication of Lowth's more decisive grammar of English, with its more familiar Latinized structures.

Priestley opposed basing grammars on Latin models. He said in the *Rudiments,* "I own I am surprised to see so much of the distribution, and technical terms of Latin grammar, retained in the grammar of our tongue; where they are exceedingly awkward and absolutely superfluous; being such as could not possibly have entered into the head of any man, who had not been previously acquainted with Latin" (1771, pp. vi-vii).

Priestley's distinction lies not only in his originality, however, but in his relatively consistent application of principles his contemporaries flouted while seeming to share them. "Of all the grammarians of this period," Albert Baugh observes, "only Priestley seems to have doubted the propriety of *ex cathedra* utterances and to have been truly humble before the facts of usage" (p. 276). Not that he lacked preferences among divided usages; but he recognized the limitations a grammarian ought reasonably to assume: "Whenever I have mentioned any variety in the grammatical forms that are used to express the same thing, I have seldom scrupled to say which of them I prefer; but this is to be understood as nothing more than a conjecture, which time must confirm or refute" (*Rudiments,* 1771, p. xvii). He had "no doubt but that the best forms of speech will, in time, establish themselves by their own superior excellence . . ." (*Rudiments,* 1761, p. vii).

On the American side of the Atlantic, Noah Webster took note of Priestley's work. When the new-world lexicographer observed in 1789 that "had the English never been acquainted with Greek and Latin, they would never have thought of one half the distinctions and rules which make up our English grammars," he echoed sentiments and phrases of the British scientist. Webster lauded Priestley for his "exceedingly judicious" linguistic criticisms and thought him "entitled to the consideration of the student, in preference to Lowth, or any other English author." He said he thought Priestley alone was "guided by just principles."[16] In 1794 Priestley emigrated from England and settled in Pennsylvania, where he died in 1804 without being naturalized as an American citizen.

With consideration of Webster and Priestley and their response to language study in England, we span the end of the eighteenth and the beginning of the nineteenth centuries and cross the Atlantic from the mother country to America and to a struggle for independence, linguistic as well as political. With Webster the early stages of America's lexical and grammatical traditions take shape. To be sure, linguistic enterprise in Europe exerted influence in America, but Americans like Webster, eager for more than political independence, were attempting to analyze and influence English from a new-world point of view.

Notes

[1] John P. Hughes, *The Science of Language* (1962), p. 41.

[2] For a more detailed treatment of the beginnings of the codification of English see Baugh and Cable, *A History of the English Language,* 3rd ed. (1978), pp. 199–294. Richard Foster Jones, *The Triumph of the English Language* (1953), treats the period 1476–1660; Sterling A. Leonard, *The Doctrine of Correctness in English Usage* (1929), treats the eighteenth century.

[3] Quoted in Baugh and Cable, p. 255.

⁴Quoted in Susie I. Tucker, ed., *English Examined* (1961), p. 59; a fuller version of Defoe's proposal is available in W. F. Bolton, ed., *The English Language: Essays by English and American Men of Letters 1490–1839* (1966), pp. 91–101.

⁵*A Proposal of Correcting . . . the English Tongue* (1712), pp. 8, 31; also available in Bolton, pp. 107–123.

⁶Samuel Johnson, A.M., *A Dictionary of the English Language . . .* (1755). The Preface to the *Dictionary* is conveniently reprinted in Bolton, pp. 129–156, and in E. L. McAdam, Jr., and George Milne, eds., *Johnson's Dictionary: A Modern Selection* (1963).

⁷*The Plan of a Dictionary . . . Addressed to the Earl of Chesterfield* (1747), p. 4.

⁸April 12–14, 1757; quoted in James H. Sledd and Gwin J. Kolb, *Dr. Johnson's Dictionary: Essays in the Biography of a Book* (1955), p. 150.

⁹*The World* (November 28, 1754); quoted in Tucker, pp. 90–91; also in Bolton, pp. 124–126. Compare Donald Greene writing in 1970: "Johnson's *Dictionary* is a very great and serious achievement in the history of the study of the English language. It is not merely a curious whim of a quaint eccentric, but a most important landmark in the development of English, from a set of unimportant local dialects spoken by a small group of islanders on the fringe of civilization, to a great world language. It represents the systematic and scientific technique of linguistic recording and investigation used earlier in the famous academic dictionaries of Italian and French, and is itself the direct ancestor of such modern scientifically compiled dictionaries as the *Oxford English Dictionary* and *Webster's New International.*"

¹⁰*A Short Introduction to English Grammar* (1762), p. v. While Lowth's remark is basically true, it is misleading in that, while Johnson's section on syntax was indeed eleven lines long, much of what other grammarians including Lowth were to put into their grammars Johnson included in fourteen long columns of discussion of "Etymology," much of which would fall under what is today called morphology.

¹¹*Dissertations on the English Language . . .* (1789), p. vii.

¹²*Institutio Oratoria,* trans. H. E. Butler (1920), vi, 43.

¹³*The Philosophy of Rhetoric,* ed. Lloyd F. Bitzer (1963), pp. 139–151: the lengthy displayed quotation is from pp. 139–140.

¹⁴*The Rudiments of English Grammar* (1771), p. 1. Other citations for the *Rudiments* are, as noted in my text, from the 1771 edition or from the Scolar Press facsimile of the original 1761 edition.

¹⁵*A Course of Lectures on the Theory of Language, and Universal Grammar* (1762), p. 184.

¹⁶*Dissertations,* pp. viii–ix; p. 206; p. 205.

CHAPTER III

Early American Grammarians: Webster and His Rivals and Successors

"Grammars . . . are compiled for boys in schools rather than for men of science, who ought to quit grammars which are the streams *and mount to the* source *of knowledge, the genuine construction of the language itself."* —NOAH WEBSTER, 1798
(Letters, ed. by H. Warfel)

"Each should ever be careful to perform his part handsomely— without drawling, omitting, stopping, hesitating, faltering, miscalling, reiterating, stuttering, hurrying, slurring, mouthing, misquoting, mispronouncing, or any of the thousand faults which render utterance disagreeable and inelegant." —GOOLD BROWN *on parsing,* 1851

THE INITIAL WIDESPREAD study of the English language in the American colonies was motivated in part by a desire to make the Scriptures widely available. As a result, until about 1720 English instruction in the new world consisted primarily of instruction in reading, with only secondary attention paid to writing and spelling. In the second and third (mightily eventful) quarters of the eighteenth century, when effective public speaking was visibly shaping a new world, and when other languages were competing for status on this side of the Atlantic, instruction in the rudiments of English grammar was increasingly encouraged throughout the colonies. To meet the demand for classroom materials, some Americans began importing English textbooks, while others more enterprising wrote their own grammars.[1]

It was apparently one Hugh Jones of Virginia who was the first American to compose a grammar. It was *A Short English Grammar: An Accidence to the English Tongue.* A mathematics professor at the College of William and Mary, Jones published his grammar in 1724—not in Boston or Baltimore but in London, where the only known copy survives in the British Museum, leaving no evidence that this first American grammar was imported into colonial schoolrooms.

An elementary text in widespread American use for some time before the Revolution was Thomas Dilworth's *New Guide to the English Tongue.* Dilworth, an Englishman, published his *Guide* in London in 1740, and it found its way to the new world as early as 1747 when it appeared in a Philadelphia edition, making Dilworth the first known author of an English grammar sent to press on this side of the Atlantic.[2] Being chiefly a speller and reader, the *Guide* presented only an abbreviated grammar of English.

More substantive in grammatical content, of course, was Lowth's *Short Introduction* (London, 1762). It saw its first American edition in 1775 and continued to serve Harvard students into the 1840s. It remains in print today, though only for historical purposes. Shamelessly imitated and copied, Lowth's book exercised far greater influence than Dilworth's. Other grammars found in the colonies before the Revolution were James Greenwood's *Essay Towards a Practical English Grammar* (London, 1711) and James Harris's philosophical *Hermes* (London, 1751).[3] Also available for classroom use were an anonymous *British Grammar* (London, 1760), probably written by James Buchanan, and John Ash's *Grammatical Institutes* (London, 1763). Ash's "Easy Introduction to Dr. Lowth's English Grammar," as he subtitled his work, appeared just a year after Lowth's book and was shipped to the colonies until it was published in New York (1774) during the Revolution. From its preface we infer Ash's desire for increased refinement among the class of people whose children, not destined for divinity or law, had little interest in and no need for classical training. Yet: "The Importance of an English Education is now pretty well understood; and it is generally acknowledged, that, not only for Ladies, but for young gentlemen designed merely for Trade, an intimate Acquaintance with the Proprieties, and Beauties of the English Tongue, would be a very desirable and necessary Attainment; far preferable to a Smattering of the learned languages."[4] From the first, then, the proprieties and beauties of the English tongue were the focus for school grammars in America.

At least four Americans wrote grammars before the War of Independence ended. There was Samuel Johnson, the first president of Columbia University, then called King's College, whose *First Easy Rudiments of Grammar,* a 36-page pamphlet, appeared in New York in 1765. Eight years later another New York teacher named Thomas Byerley put out *A Plain and Easy Introduction to English Grammar* (New York, 1773). Six years later again Abel Curtis of Dartmouth College wrote *A Compend of English Grammar* (Dresden, Vt., 1779). And there was Hugh Jones, already noted. None of the American grammars reached the popularity of Dilworth's *Guide,* however.

NOAH WEBSTER & LINDLEY MURRAY

Noah Webster

We find among the colonial teachers using Dilworth's primer a devout Anglophobe named Noah Webster, who had studied the *Guide* as a Connecticut schoolboy. A college student during the Revolution, Webster (1758–1843) graduated from Yale in 1778, then read law and was admitted to the bar. Forced to teach school by a dearth of paying legal customers, the twenty-four-year-old lawyer found the *Guide* and other textbooks unsuitable or inadequate. So he set about compiling his own speller, grammar, and reader, which he published in three parts as *A Grammatical Institute of the English Language* (I, 1783; II, 1784; III, 1785).

He then undertook a lecture tour to campaign for his system of education and to lobby for copyright laws to protect his royalties. In a score of large towns between Williamsburg, Virginia, and Portsmouth, New Hampshire, the brash Yankee told his audiences: "After all my reading and observation for the course of ten years, I have been able to unlearn a considerable part of what I learnt in early life; and at thirty years of age, can, with confidence, affirm, that our modern grammars have done much more hurt than good. The authors have labored to prove, what is obviously absurd, viz. that our language is not made right; and in pursuance of this idea, have tried to make it over again, and persuade the English to speak by Latin rules, or by arbitrary rules of their own."[5]

Favorably impressed by Lowth at this stage of his career, Webster set out in his *Grammatical Institute* to adapt to his own students' needs as much of the bishop's *Introduction* as he agreed with. He also acknowledged Ash's and Buchanan's grammars and followed them except when "warranted by the nature and idioms of the language."[6] But despite Dilworth's having provided him a partial model for his speller a year earlier, Webster had no liking for his treatment of grammar. It was "worse than none," he said, and "calculated to lead into errour" (I, p. 10); it was "not constructed upon the principles of the English language" but was a "mere Latin Grammar, very indifferently translated" (II, p. 3). To rescue pupils from this Latinized English, the young Connecticut schoolmaster designed a grammar of English "upon its true principles." "Our language has now arrived to a great degree of purity," he wrote, "and many writers of the last and present age, have, both in elegance and sublimity of style, equaled, if not surpassed the Roman authors of the Augustan age. To frame such a Grammar as to instruct our own youth, as well as foreigners, in this purity of style, is the business of a Grammarian—a business that appears to be not yet accomplished" (II, p. 4).

So he published his own primer, and schoolmasters liked it sufficiently to make it the first American grammar to attain wide circulation.[7] However, if one may judge from the recollections of the prolific "Peter Parley," recalling his own Connecticut school days around the turn of the century, even Webster's grammar (of which there were two copies in a room of perhaps forty pupils) left teachers and young scholars in the dark: "The grammar was a clever book, but I have an idea that neither Master Stebbins nor his pupils ever fathomed its depths. They floundered about in it, as if in a quagmire, and after some time came out pretty nearly where they went in, though perhaps a little obfuscated by the dim and dusky atmosphere of these labyrinths."[8] Webster's grammar was revised over the years, and passed through at least fourteen editions by 1795, but it was eventually withdrawn from the market, so much did its author's views change.

An ardent nationalist in a new nation, Webster was a vigorous and wide-ranging language planner. Single-handedly he tackled the orthographical, lexical, and grammatical codification of American English, seeking linguistic liberation from England and language uniformity throughout the States. "As an independent nation, our honor requires us to have a system of our own, in language as well as government. Great Britain . . . should no longer be *our* standard; for the taste of her writers is already corrupted, and her language on the decline" (*Dissertations,* p. 20). Seeking a basis for uniformity, Webster endorsed the "*general practice of a nation,*" claiming it the duty of grammarians "to find what the English language *is,* and not, how it *might have been made*" (*Dissertations,* pp. 24, ix). "Grammars should be formed on *practice;* for practice determines what a language is. . . . The business of a grammarian is not to examine whether or not national practice is founded on philosophical principles; but to *ascertain* the national practice, that the learner may be able to weed from his own, any local peculiarities or false idioms. If *this means* and *a means* are now, and have immemorially been, used by good authors and the nation in general, neither Johnson, Lowth, nor any other person, however learned, has a right to say that the phrases are not *good English*" (*Dissertations,* pp. 204–205).

But there was variation in the national practice and among good authors; and Webster treasured uniformity. What then did he elect as the basis for *his* rules? As legitimate standards of correctness he recommended "universal undisputed practice" and the "principle of analogy."

He need not have mentioned the first: if a usage were in universal undisputed practice, it would go unnoticed. Universal usages remain undisputed! Analogy, his second standard, could resolve some disputed usages by suggesting that one or the other item conformed to some established pattern. Frequently, however, analogy itself offers conflicting solutions, and so the choice reverts to some other criterion. Divided usage on the past tense of *dive* or *strive,* for example, might be resolved in favor of *dove* (modeled on *drove, rode, wrote*) or *dived* (analogous to *arrived, hired, piled*). Sometimes analogy yields a solution unsanctioned by educated custom, as it would in the case of *himself/hisself* and *themselves/theirselves,* where the established pattern of *ourselves, myself,* and *yourself* parallels nonstandard *theirselves* and *hisself.* In short, appeal to analogy is often barren. Moreover, the very attempt to decide between usages rests on the assumption that "custom" provides a sound basis for acceptability only when it recommends a single universal usage. For if "customary" usage sanctions alternative forms, the legislator who outlaws one of them paradoxically disregards some custom by that very act.

The tacit principle—that among variant usages if one is correct, the others must be wrong—was an invention of codifiers ill at ease with variant customs; and Webster subscribed to this principle. For example, discussing whether *European* should be stressed on the third syllable or, as he unprophetically preferred, on the second, he lamented that "The standard authors . . . very absurdly give both pronunciations, that we may take our choice. As this is a very easy method of getting over difficulties, and passing [them] along without giving offence, so it is a certain way to perpetuate differences in opinion and practice, and to prevent the establishment of any standard" (*Dissertations,* p. 119).

Webster, like others before and after him, professed a faith in democratic ideals: "While all men are upon a footing and no singularities are accounted vulgar or ridiculous, every man enjoys perfect liberty. But when a particular set of men, in exalted stations, undertake to say, 'we are the standards of propriety and elegance, and if all men do not conform to our practice, they shall be accounted vulgar and ignorant,' they take a very great liberty with the rules of the language and the rights of civility" (*Dissertations,* pp. 24–25). Nevertheless, undaunted by his own admonition, Webster took the liberty of anointing himself the standard of propriety and elegance, accounting nonconformists vulgar and ignorant. In his discussion of the "erroneous" use of *shall* and *will,* he insisted that "there is hardly a possible case, in which *will* can be properly employed to ask a question in the first person"; and with variant pronunciations he was equally uncompromising. He sought to "annihilate differences in speaking" (*Dissertations,* pp. 238, 19) and published his speller partly to correct "a vicious pronunciation, which prevailed extensively among the common people of this country" (*American Dictionary,* Preface). He even claimed to find nothing "so disagreeable as that drawling, whining cant that distinguishes a certain class of people; and too much pains cannot be taken to reform the practice" (*Dissertations,* pp. 108–109). Fearful that various immigrant groups would "retain their respective peculiarities of speaking; and . . . imperceptibly corrupt the national language," he urged teachers "to make their pupils open the teeth, and give a full clear sound to every syllable. The beauty of speaking consists in giving each letter and syllable its due proportion of sound, with a prompt articulation" (*Dissertations,* pp. 19, 109). Here we may discern Webster's hierarchy placing writing and spelling above speaking, a hierarchy characteristic of American school grammar from the beginning: the letter gives substance to the sound.

Though ostensibly descriptive, Webster frequently analyzed not what occurred in American English but what he thought ought to occur. He might have been more tolerant of alternate usages had he not committed himself to a uniform language throughout the republic. But by one principle or another he attempted to resolve variation. In his discussion of the use of past tenses and past participles, his biases surface:

> Here let it be again observed that no auxiliaries can with propriety be joined with the past time. The expressions, *I have wrote, I have bore, I have began, I have drove,* &c. which are so much in vogue, are shocking improprieties: The childish phrases, *you am, I is,* &c. are not more repugnant to the rules of Grammar. . . . An ancient Roman would be startled to hear a Latin Grammarian use *ille fuit amatus est* . . . and the most unlettered Englishman would laugh to hear another say, *he has went,* or *it will be gave;* and yet, *I have wrote, have drove,* &c. which are quite as improper, have become so familiar to our ears, that we can every hour hear them uttered by some of our best Grammarians without a smile of ridicule. *I have written, have driven,* &c. are as easy to be learned and employed as the past tense *wrote* and *drove;* and it is inexcusable to sacrifice propriety to any consideration whatever. (II, p. 60)

If the most unlettered Englishman would have laughed to hear *it will be gave,* few Americans were jarred by *I have wrote,* and fewer still took note. Even Webster (again unprophetically) accepted these castigated forms subsequently. And his disdain for them bypassed his own observation that they were the most frequent of abuses.

Again, though he found the use of *will* in first-person interrogative sentences "frequent, both in writing and conversation" in the middle and southern states, Webster rejected it: "It is impossible for a foreigner to have a just idea of the absurdity of using *will* in this manner; but a correct English ear revolts at the practice." And, deploring the neglect of the subjunctive mood, he admitted that "Numberless examples of the same kind of inaccuracy may be found in good authors." Of the "gross impropriety" of pronouncing *once* and *twice* as if they had a *t* at the end, he said he would have overlooked it "but for its prevalence among a class of very well educated people; particularly in Philadelphia and Baltimore" (*Dissertations,* pp. 238, 241, 111). In another of his *ipse dixit* pronouncements, Webster condemned the adverbial use of adjectives in phrases like *extreme cold, exceeding fine,* and *indifferent well* as "very improper and ungrammatical." But he did not explain why the same adjectives with -*ly* would be more proper and grammatical adverbs than the flat forms his pupils so often heard. Nor did he explain why *news* must be plural—why *What is the news?* is "certainly an impropriety, however authorised by custom" (II, pp. 64, 12). As codifier his *ipse dixit* must suffice; it is what he offered; and it served the insecurity of schoolmasters, however little it affected the English of school children.

America's pioneer lexicographer, then, most definitely did not regard general usage as the supreme arbiter of correctness, as he claimed he did. He had engineered a hierarchy of standards, but not even educated usage wore the crown when particular forms displeased his sense of propriety. Our greatest codifier subscribed implicitly to standards of linguistic propriety other than common usage among citizens of the first reputation; and he was not as unencumbered by familiarity with Latin as he expected Dilworth to be. Webster often fell to creating, not describing, American English—a privilege of language planners and a prerogative of poets but a practice not allowed the descriptive grammarian Webster claimed to be.

Following the lead of its predecessors, the *Institute* in its grammatical sections is larded with faulty constructions to be corrected. Webster provided abundant concoctions like these:

That books are torn.
These is a fine day.
Virtue is his own reward.
The boy, whom loves study, will be beloved by his instructor.
Philadelphia are a large city.

Unlike his predecessors', however, Webster's contrived false syntax probably did not induce imitation. Lowth and his disciples often chose examples from the best writers, and they may be accused of propagating the very forms (natural and often graceful) that they attempted to expunge from the canon of acceptable English phrases. Webster's silly fabrications only served to make grammar arcane to his students. A commentator recalling his own student days and grammar lessons of around 1790 said:

We did not dream of [finding] anything practical, or applicable to the language we were using every day, till we had "been through the grammar several times," and "parsed" several months. Why? Because we were presented at once with a complete system of definitions and rules, which might perplex a Webster or a Murray, without any development of principles, any illustrations which we could comprehend, any application of the words to objects which they represent. We supposed . . . that the dogmas of our "grammar books" were the inventions of learned men; curious contrivances, to carry the words of a sentence through a certain operation which we called parsing, rather for the gratification of curiosity, than for any practical benefit or use. . . . When we found that the nominative case did indeed govern the verb . . .—when we accidentally perceived that the rules did actually apply to sentences, and that to observe them would really make better sense than to violate them—then great was our admiration of the *inventive* powers of those great men, who had been the lights of the grammatical world.[9]

Still, to characterize Webster as subscribing to the authority of usage only in theory while ignoring it in practice is not altogether fair. He could generalize about standard usage only on the basis of personal observation. Sufficient data for sound generalization were unavailable. When he quarreled with Lowth's distinctions between modes because they were "not warranted by the present idiom of the language," his term "present idiom" referred at best to Webster's observations, at worst to his own usage. He unwittingly made this clear when he claimed never to have heard "an improper use of the verbs *will* and *shall,* among the unmixed English descendants in the eastern states" (*Dissertations,* p. 240). It is not surprising (perhaps it was natural) that so staunch a patriot sought a uniform language throughout America. Born in Connecticut and educated at Yale, his preferences naturally were governed by the customs of New England as he imagined them.

Webster's growing familiarity with educated practice modified his views. He had condemned the use of *who* in *Who did you marry?* when writing the *Grammatical Institute* (1784), but accepted it in the 1789 *Dissertations.* In a passage that simultaneously illustrates the alteration of his views and underscores his disdain for grammarians too much influenced by Latin, he wrote that *Whom do you speak to?* was "never used in speaking, as I can find, and if so, is hardly English at all." He thought only *who* had been used in asking questions "until some Latin student began to suspect it bad English, because not agreeable to the Latin rules. At any rate, *whom* do you speak *to?* is a corruption, and all the grammars that can be formed will not extend the use of the phrase beyond the walls of a college" (*Dissertations,* pp. 286–287).

By 1807, when Webster issued his *Philosophical and Practical Gram-*

mar, he had read Horne Tooke and Joseph Priestley and, swayed by their tolerant view of the force of custom and by his own greater knowledge of American English, he had become somewhat more descriptive and somewhat less prescriptive.[10] Like Dr. Johnson's mature views of correctness, Webster's are remarkable for their distance from those expressed earlier. In the 1807 grammar his commitment to the language of everyday intercourse as the basis for America's grammar triumphs:

> It struck me . . . as the most monstrous absurdity, that books should teach
> us a language altogether different from the common language of life. . . . It
> was reserved for the classical writers of the eighteenth century to lay aside the
> pedantic forms, *if he go, if it proceed, though he come,* &c. and restore the
> native idiom of the language, by writing it as men spoke it, and as they still
> speak it, unless perverted by Grammars. (p. 202)

With uncommon insight into the importance of appropriateness, he remarked that "in polite and classical language, two negatives destroy the negation and express an affirmative. . . . In popular language, two negatives are used for a negation, according to the practice of the ancient Greeks and the modern French" (pp. 191–192). More clearly than Lowth he recognized that several varieties of acceptable language exist, that what is acceptable on one occasion may not be on another. For example, he spoke of usages separating a preposition from its relative pronoun object (as in "the horse *which* I rode *on*" instead of "the horse *on which* I rode") or omitting the relative pronoun altogether (as in "the teacher I told you *about*" instead of "the teacher *about whom* I told you") as being "most common and most allowable in colloquial and epistolary language. In the grave and elevated style, they are seldom elegant . . . " (p. 193). No absolutes here—simply the observation that certain usages are "seldom elegant."

For his 1807 grammar Webster sifted through and cited the writings of the learned as the basis for accepting usages he had earlier rejected. Recalling that in 1784 he had inveighed against using the past tense form with *have* where a different past participle existed, we are surprised now by his saying that "The influence of Bishop Lowth has had some effect in preserving the use of the old participles in books, but not in oral and popular usage; and why should we retain words in writing which are not generally recognized in oral practice!" Then, citing authorities who, "coinciding with common usage, may be considered as exhibiting the true verbals and past tenses," he names Locke ("Having *spoke* of this in another place"), Milton, Dryden, Hume, Pope, Swift, Gibbon, Prior, Darwin, Bacon, Shakespeare, Burke, Bentley, Johnson, the Spectator, the Rambler, and others in support of the past participles *spoke, wove, broke, hid, shook, begot, forgot, chose, froze, stole, mistook, took, drank, writ,* and past tenses like *rung, sprung, sunk, sung, bid, forbid, begun,* and *writ* (pp. 186–189).

Dismally unprophetic in predicting which forms would survive, Webster learned to base his judgments on actual speech and the practice of established writers, not on personal predilections (as with his earlier dicta) or the writings of grammarians. Americans can take pride especially in the mature work of their first great schoolmaster, animated by the vitality and independence of the new republic and finally not intimidated by the colossal prestige of a British grammarian like Lowth. Indeed, Webster early claimed that Lowth "has criticized away more phrases of *good* English, than he has corrected of *bad.* He has not only mistaken the true construction of many phrases, but he has rejected others that have been used generally by the English nation from the earliest times, and by arbitrary rules, substituted phrases that have been rarely, or never used at all" (*Dissertations,* p. 287).

Of course, the increasingly descriptive grammarian and the nationalistic reformer wrote with the same pen. If the grammarian paid more attention to actual speech and writing over the years, the molder of American English had no dearth of ideas for improving the language. To the extent that some of his suggested spelling reforms are taken for granted in American books today, he is to be praised for urging acceptable improvements. But his ambitions for reform did not stop with orthography. For instance, he counted 177 cases of English verbs in which the past participle differed from the past tense form of the verb (as they do in *swam/swum* and *shook/shaken,* for example) and noted that his predecessors had devoted considerable attention to propping up these distinctions—often precisely because common usage tugged at bringing them into line with other verbs in using a single form for both uses (as in *swum/had swum* or *went/had went*). But, opposing the view of Lowth, Webster regretted that any verbs at all had these distinctions; it was "one of the greatest inconveniences in the language," he said, and he flatly disagreed with Lowth's claim—one made also by Johnson, Priestley, and Campbell—that we should preserve the few inflections remaining in English. Still, for all we have said, Webster is known today not for his grammars nor his views on usage but for his dictionaries, and it is to them that we now turn briefly.

After several unsuccessful efforts to return to law, Webster determined to compile the dictionaries for which he is best remembered. The first of these, *A Compendious Dictionary of the English Language* (1806), revealed a gifted definer of words. It would be exciting also to report that its author, college educated during the Revolution, an energetic reformer and ardent chauvinist, listed *bred, tru, tuf, dawter, bilt,* and *arkitect* in this dictionary, for these were the spellings he had recommended in his "Essay on a Reformed Mode of Spelling," appended to the *Dissertations* in 1789. But, tamed by pressures against spelling reform and moderated by middle age, he yielded to custom on these, though refusing to discard *doctrin, medicin, examin, determin, disciplin,* and *opak.* Moreover, he did introduce *error, favor,* and *honor,* which he had argued against in the *Grammatical Institute!* Between 1789 and 1806 he had come to acknowledge that "it would be useless to attempt any change, even if practicable, in those anomalies which form whole classes of words, and in which, change would rather perplex than ease the learner."[11] Again, we see here the language engineer compromising with tradition, if only partially and uneasily.

But the critics were not appeased. They faulted Webster for including such "vulgar" words as *advisory, presidential,* and *insubordination* and for his distressing acceptance of certain nouns as verbs (e.g., *girdle, advocate,* and *test*). Even a century and a half ago, critics damned Webster's dictionary for accepting the suffix *-ize* in words like *demoralize, Americanize,* and *deputize,* which Webster had found sufficiently widespread and reputable to include. And predictably they railed at *favor, labor,* and *honor* (where tradition preferred *-our*) and *music, logic,* and *public* (instead of the customary *-ick*). *Theater* and *center* were deemed perversely inverted variants of *theatre* and *centre,* the spellings that survive in British English.[12] All the criticism, fortunately, did not discourage him, and Webster spent the next two decades, on both sides of the Atlantic, assembling his big dictionary. In January 1825, when he was sixty-seven years old, he completed the manuscript in England and then returned home to arrange for its typesetting. The printing alone, which required the importation of type from Germany, consumed several years, so large and technical was the task.

On his seventieth birthday, two decades after the desk-size *Compendious Dictionary* appeared, Webster and his wife at last completed reading proofs for *An American Dictionary of the English Language,* a monumental work in two volumes, each the size of a 1979 Los Angeles or Chicago telephone directory, and the forerunner of the twentieth-century Merriam–Webster unabridged dictionaries. Not surprisingly, at its publication in 1828, forty-odd years after the 1785 lecture tour, the aged Yankee remained distraught over the state of grammatical and lexicographic learning in the Republic. In the dictionary front matter he says:

> . . . I am convinced [that] the dictionaries and grammars which have been used in our seminaries of learning, for the last forty or fifty years, are so in-

correct and imperfect, that they have introduced or sanctioned more errors than they have amended; in other words, had the people of England and of these States been left to learn the pronunciation and construction of their vernacular language solely by tradition, and the reading of good authors, the language would have been spoken and written with more purity than it has been and now is, by those who have learned to adjust their language by the rules which dictionaries and grammars prescribe.

Here we seem to have a reformed reformer; here finally is Webster endorsing a wholly naturalistic view of usage. And it is a view that puts the spoken language above the written as a model not only for correctness but for writing itself.

He goes on to say that the "authority of universal colloquial practice . . . I consider as the *real* and *only genuine language*. I repeat this remark, that *general and respectable* usage in *speaking* is the genuine or legitimate language of a country to which the *written* language ought to be conformed. Language is that which is uttered by the tongue, and if men do not write the language as it is *spoken* by the great body of respectable people, they do not write the *real* language."

Nevertheless, from this same preface we gain a sharp sense of Webster's ambitious lifelong goals for the American language, and it is a glimpse of a language planner at heart, not a descriptive grammarian:

> It has been my aim in this work . . . to ascertain the true principles of the language, in its orthography and structure; to purify it from some palpable errors, and reduce the number of its anomalies, thus giving it more regularity and consistency in its forms, both of words and sentences; and in this manner, to furnish a standard of our vernacular tongue, which we shall not be ashamed to bequeath to *three hundred millions of people,* who are destined to occupy, and I hope, to adorn the vast territory within our jurisdiction.

> If the language can be improved in regularity, so as to be more easily acquired by our own citizens, and by foreigners, and thus be rendered a more useful instrument for the propagation of science, arts, civilization and christianity; if it can be rescued from the mischievous influence of sciolists and that dabbling spirit of innovation which is perpetually disturbing its settled usages and filling it with anomalies; if, in short, our vernacular language can be redeemed from corruptions, and our philology and literature from degradation; it would be a source of great satisfaction to me to be one among the instruments of promoting these valuable objects.

The success of his wordbooks ultimately made the name of Webster synonymous with "dictionary" in the United States.[13] It also accounts for the chief discrepancies between current British and American orthography. But while his dictionaries carried considerable prestige and his grammars enjoyed some passing popularity, Webster's most successful endeavor was his series of spellers. The influential "Blue-Backed Speller," published first in 1783 as Part I of the *Grammatical Institute* and later officially retitled *The American Spelling Book,* sold three million copies by 1814 and perhaps a hundred million since. It is this spelling book that is credited with certain characteristic differences between British and American pronunciation, as well as for shaping the uniformity of speech throughout the States.

While his dictionaries and the speller earned Webster the title "Schoolmaster to America," his grammars exerted less influence and were eventually driven off the market. He believed it was immoral to publish "false rules and principles" and wrote in 1805 to a Philadelphia bookseller, "I have declined to permit further impressions of my *Grammar* on the ground of its imperfections."[14] In fairness to the record we should note the Lindley Murray's school grammar was selling energetically by then, and Webster may have been avoiding an embarassing competitive skirmish.

Lindley Murray

Lindley Murray (1745–1826), an American expatriate living in England, all but cornered the market during the first quarter of the nineteenth century with his *English Grammar, Adapted to the Different Classes of Learners.* Its spectacular sales record made Murray's probably the most influential grammar of its time. "On both sides of the Atlantic," one historian reports, "this man's productions were reprinted literally hundreds of times and were copied and abridged at least a score of times by other authors."[15] First published at York in 1795, the *Grammar* had its first American printing at Boston in 1800; a scant half-dozen years after its appearance in this country, it had passed through twenty-one editions in England and twice that number here. An 1807 abridgement saw thirty American and twenty British editions.[16] In all, more than three hundred editions are recorded.[17]

Murray's grammar, which sold two million copies[18] (in England, where it was written and first published, and in America, where its author was born, educated, and practiced law), had its beginning subsequent to Murray's retirement. Forced by a serious bout with illness to give up a lucrative legal practice in Philadelphia, where as a boy he had attended Benjamin Franklin's Academy,[19] Murray (apparently with loyalist leanings) determined to emigrate and sailed for England in 1784, the year that saw Webster's grammar published in Hartford. Graced with a small fortune, Murray settled in York and began a forty-year convalescence. Invited by the headmistress of a nearby school to tutor her teachers in the rudiments of grammar, he was subsequently persuaded to commit his knowledge to paper for the first-hand benefit of her students.

Not an original thinker and lacking strength to do more than assemble what others had written, Murray perused Priestley's grammar and Blair's and Campbell's rhetorics; a religious man himself, he also digested and assimilated Bishop Lowth's *Short Introduction,* sometimes incorporating whole sections of it nearly verbatim. The bishop's mission ("to teach us to express ourselves with propriety . . . and to be able to judge of every phrase and form of construction, whether it be right or not") found a willing disciple in Murray, and his gospel ("to lay down rules, and to illustrate them by examples . . . shewing what is right and pointing out what is wrong") found a zealous evangelist. Lowth had decided that the method of pointing out what is wrong was "of the two the more useful and effectual manner of instruction." The method was borrowed, of course, from Latin grammars. Murray adopted the practice with a vengeance and passed it on to amateur and professional grammarians alike. Thus the pedagogical heuristic of judging a native phrase or sentence "right" or "wrong," a practice familiar to Americans today, from school days and standardized examinations, got its germination in Lowth's grammar and its nurturing in Murray's. "From the sentiment generally admitted," Murray wrote, "that a proper selection of faulty composition is more instructive to the young grammarian, than any rules and examples of propriety that can be given, the compiler has been induced to pay peculiar attention to this part of the subject; and though the examples of false grammar . . . are numerous, it is hoped they will not be found too many, when their variety and usefulness are considered" (pp. iv–v).

Unfortunately, Murray's method of showing what is right by showing what is wrong exposed his young readers more thoroughly to "improprieties" than to those models of the best English he devoutly hoped they would emulate. Discussing double negatives, for example, where his rule legislates that "Two negatives, in English, destroy one another, or are equivalent to an affirmative," half a dozen double negatives—all with unmistakably negative force—are cited within half a page: "I never did repent for doing good, nor shall not now; Never no imitator ever grew up to his author; I cannot by no means allow him what his argument must prove"; and so on. One wonders whether exposure to such sentences might not have led to an increase rather than a decrease in their use.

Webster, as we have noted, did not share Murray's extreme predilection for teaching by analysis of bad examples, although he did use the method sometimes. And certainly Murray did not share Webster's passionate chauvinism. What the two men did share—and it pervaded their grammars—was fervent religious sentiment. Both were pious men, sensitive to a divine presence governing their lives. Murray even constructed a bridge between virtue and linguistic propriety, a link between good living and good grammar, as he confessed in his preface:

> The author has no interest in the present publication, but that of endeavouring to promote the cause of learning and virtue; and, with this view, he has been studious, through the whole of the work, not only to avoid all examples and illustrations which might have an improper effect on the minds of youth; but also to introduce, on many occasions, such as have a moral and religious tendency. This, he conceives to be a point of no small importance; and which, if scrupulously regarded in all books of education, would essentially advance the best interests of society, by cherishing the innocence and virtue of the rising generation.

Regrettably, as Allen Walker Read rightly notes, Murray's "excessive piety predisposed him to regard linguistic matters in terms of right and wrong."[20]

Two things, then, about Murray's work, besides its reliance on Lowth and its enormous popularity, should be kept in mind: its excessive employment of "unacceptable" or "wrong" English as a mode of inculcating good usage, and its religious underpinnings and motivation. As to the first, its influence can hardly be exaggerated; it molded the mental set of millions of American school children to the study of English and bears major responsibility for the widespread misconception that "grammar" is the art of adjudicating "right" and "wrong" forms among several score of divided usages. It encouraged the custom of error-hunting in English compositions, as well as in grammar and spelling lessons, and thus colored the whole subsequent history of English teaching.

As to the second point, Murray had written that "English grammar is the art of speaking and writing the English language with propriety," and two million copies of his books promoted the link he welded between linguistic propriety and religious rectitude. When one considers that two preeminently influential school grammars of English, certainly the two most prominent in the eighteenth and nineteenth centuries, were written by a bishop and a devout amateur theologian, one grows less perplexed about the association that current lore still fosters between "good grammar" and moral righteousness.[21] For many nineteenth-century English speakers, linguistic purity was next to godliness; certainly, Lindley Murray thought it so.

SAMUEL KIRKHAM & GOOLD BROWN

Besides Webster and Murray, two other very influential American school grammarians in the nineteenth century were Goold Brown (1791–1857) and Samuel Kirkham (1797–1843). These rivals, also devoutly religious men, hated one another's grammatical methods and despised one another personally. The fervent contest between them remains unmatched in the history of English grammar: they spat venomous invective at one another for many years. Kirkham called Brown "a knave, a liar, and a pedant,"[22] and Brown in turn accused Kirkham of "plagiarism" and "quackery," calling him "one of the most unscholarly and incompetent of all pretenders to grammar."[23] Brown continued: "It is cruel in any man, to look narrowly into the faults of an author who peddles a school-book for bread. The starveling wretch whose defence and plea are poverty and sickness, demands, and must have, in the name of humanity, an immunity from criticism, if not the patronage of the public." But he did not accord such immunity to his archenemy: "Under no circumstances . . . can the artifices of quackery be thought excusable in him who claims to be the very greatest of modern grammarians" (1851, pp. 28–29).

Samuel Kirkham

Perhaps Kirkham did think himself a great grammarian; the sentiments expressed in his *English Grammar* suggest he was "Content to be useful, instead of being brilliant."[24] He claimed virtually no originality for himself, acknowledging his debt to Murray, from whose popular grammar he chiefly selected his principles, adopting also "as far as consistent with his own views" the language of "that eminent philologist." Presumably, then, Kirkham—like so many others—thought Murray the greatest of grammarians.

In teaching grammar to his young readers, Kirkham aimed to ennoble them, for grammatical study "tends to adorn and dignify human nature, and meliorate the condition of man." He thought grammar "a leading branch of that learning which alone is capable of unfolding and maturing the mental powers and of elevating man to his proper rank in the scale of intellectual existence;—of that learning which lifts the soul from earth, and enables it to hold converse with a thousand worlds" (p. 13). Here again is the tie between spiritual advancement and grammatical achievement which we see in much nineteenth-century work. Not an impractical man, Kirkham sought more than spiritual benefit for his readers; he thought grammar an indispensable tool for other achievements, and said that without it no one could "think, speak, read, or write with accuracy," and that, therefore, "Nothing of a secular nature can be more worthy of your attention . . ." (p. 14). He also warned that "without the knowledge and application of grammar rules, you will often speak and write in such a manner as not to be *understood*" (p. 63).

Kirkham thought contemporary methods of teaching grammar inadequate: students should not only learn rules, as they could from a textbook like Murray's, but apply them. Combining rules with application was Kirkham's contribution to the advancement of school grammar. As a mode of application he proposed a new systematic parsing which compelled a pupil "to apply every definition and every rule that appertains to each word that he parses, without having a question put to him by the teacher; and, in so doing, he explains every word fully as he goes along." He intended his system to abolish the "absurd practice . . . of causing learners to commit and recite definitions and rules without any simultaneous application of them to practical examples" (p. 11). This was clearly a laudable aim. But his methods carried into English the centuries-old methods of studying Latin: memorizing, parsing, and correcting false syntax.[25]

By a complex system of parsing, Kirkham's students analyzed some or all words in a sentence, citing for each word first its part of speech (and why), then, for a noun, whether it was common, proper, or collective (and why), its gender, person, number, and case (and why), the rule governing its case, and then the word's full declining through "all cases." For verbs and other parts of speech the order of parsing, appropriately modified, followed the same basic system as in Latin classes. Here is a relatively simple example:

The printer prints books.

    Prints is a verb, a word that signifies to do—active, it expresses action—transitive, the action passes over from the nominative "printer" to the object "books"—third pers. sing. numb. because the nominative printer is with which it agrees. Rule 4. *The verb must agree with its nominative case in number and person.*

    Declined—1. pers. sing. I print, 2. pers. thou printest, 3. pers. he prints, or the printer prints, and so on.

    Books is a noun, the name of a thing—common, the name of a sort of things,—neut. gend. it denotes a thing without sex—third pers. spoken of—plur. num. it implies more than one—and in the objective case, it is the object of the action, expressed by the active-transitive verb "prints," and is governed by it according to Rule 20. *Active-transitive verbs govern the objective case.*

    The noun *books* is thus declined—Sing. nom. book, poss. book's, obj. book—Plur. nom. books, poss. books', obj. books.

While such exercise was not without merit and proved popular with schoolmasters, it had the detrimental effect of coloring English with hues appropriate only to highly inflected languages like Latin and of slighting the importance of English word order. Excessive attention was paid to grammatical categories like noun case, verb tense, and verb "mood" (or "mode"); and explanations for these categories—seldom manifest in the forms of English words—were based on Latin paradigms with visibly inflected forms.

In addition, following Lowth, Webster, and Murray, Kirkham overly exercised his young learners in the correction of false syntax. Though this practice persists in twentieth-century textbooks and plays a role in tests for intelligence, verbal ability, and other aptitudes, it rests on shifty ground pedagogically. Exercises in false syntax present constructions in which the student is required to spot a flaw and propose a corrected version (sometimes also specifying the governing principle). Insofar as the examples are taken from actual occurrences of language and are not concocted by compilers, they are often quite natural and their alleged errors not readily apparent.

As evidence that the benefits derived from exercises in false syntax were inestimable, Kirkham cited "the interesting and undeniable fact, that Mr. Murray's labors, in this department, have effected a complete revolution in the English language, in point of verbal accuracy. Who does not know, that the best writers of this day, are not guilty of *one* grammatical inaccuracy, where those authors who wrote before Mr. Murray flourished, are guilty of *five?*" (pp. 35–36)!

Besides selections from everyday speech, Kirkham, like Webster, invented sentences students would never possibly meet outside of class:

The fields look freshly and gayly since the rain.
An orator's tongue should be agreeable to the ear of their audience.
A circle or a square are the same in idea.
Adams and Jefferson, them who died on the fourth of July 1826, were both signers and the firm supporters of the Declaration of Independence.

And, in addition, students were challenge to detect and correct the "false syntax" of such natural constructions as these:

He bought a new pair of shoes and an elegant piece of furniture.
That is the friend who I sincerely esteem.
Who did you walk with?
He saw one or more persons enter the garden.
The enemies who we have most to fear, are those of our own hearts.
I intended to have called last week, but could not.

Education is not attended to properly in Spain.
After I visited Europe, I returned to America.
Five and eight makes thirteen.
He would not believe that honesty was the best policy.

Kirkham packed his books with such constructions, whose impropriety he challenged his students to uncover and whose repetition he hoped they would avoid. He was unconcerned about fostering these "errors" by exposing his young readers to them in his text, as they were in their lives. Nor did he fear that such sentences might raise suspicions about the propriety of other natural constructions that even he thought impeccable, as students hunted in them for "errors."

Reviewing Kirkham's false-syntax examples, we may draw one of two conclusions. Either many sentences were indeed solecisms, and exposing a hundred thousand school children to them helped propel them into today's widespread use, or these sentences were already common in his day while violating rules of a former age or a different language. A glance at nineteenth-century literature or the *OED* indicates that many expressions he cites were common in writing and, we can assume, in speech. How then did he select his examples and what criteria of correct usage did he employ?

First of all, grammar was for Kirkham "the art of speaking and writing the English language with propriety," and his standard was the "established practice of the best speakers and writers" (p. 17), by which he meant (following Campbell) reputable, national, and present use. "A usage becomes *good* and *legal,* when it has been long and generally adopted." Kirkham thus fell into the same trap that ensnared his predecessors. The "best" speakers and writers, "or such as may be considered good authority in the use of language," are "those who are deservedly in high estimation; speakers distinguished for their elocution and other literary attainments, and writers, eminent for correct taste, solid matter, and refined manner."

The circularity of the definition is apparent. He determines a standard of acceptability by ascertaining the established practice of the best speakers and writers, who in turn are chosen with criteria of literary attainment, elocution, correct taste, and refined manner. Since these must be determined by some other reference, Kirkham often applied his personal grammatical judgments.

Indeed, he did worse. Admitting his own grammar had defects, "in part, from his own want of judgment and skill," he leveled more serious blame on "the anomalies and imperfections with which the language abounds" (p. 11). Despite partial lip service to Locke's notion of

language by compact with no inherent correctness, Kirkham applied external standards to weigh the merits of English locutions and found a
plethora of anomalies and imperfections. He does not disclose how he
determined what should be, but from his rules and exercises in false syntax we can infer certain desired improvements. "In the grammar of a
perfect language, no rules should be admitted, but such as are founded
on fixed principles, arising out of the genius of that language and the
nature of things; but our language being *im*-perfect, it becomes
necessary, in a *practical* treatise, like this, to adopt some rules to direct us
in the use of speech as regulated by *custom*. If we had a permanent and
surer standard than capricious custom to regulate us in the transmission
of thought, great inconvenience would be avoided" (p. 18).

Kirkham understood Locke's view of language only with respect to
word meanings; the compact did not govern patterns for putting words
into sentences. So he applied measures he thought inherently right to
determine correct English usage. Shrewd readers would have found him
applying criteria other than "national, reputable, and present use" to
sentences whose syntax they were asked to correct. A few students may
have recognized rules appropriate to Latin structures, but we can only
guess how they resolved the dilemma of attempting to correct the "false"
syntax of English sentences common in educated usage. Perhaps they
surmised that Kirkham's sentences were not *national;* they knew they
were *current* in the speech of *reputable* citizens around them.

Kirkham lacked any sense that a usage appropriate in one context
could be inappropriate elsewhere. He admonished against certain traditional shibboleths ("Who did you walk with?" "Who did you see there?")
without recognizing that even if their use in writing was frowned on,
their acceptance in daily speech had been established for generations.
This he could have learned from Priestley, Webster, and even Lowth.

Kirkham wanted his young charges not to compromise with virtue,
and to that end he urged them to be strict with grammatical principles:
"These considerations forbid that you should ever be so unmindful of
your duty to your country, to your Creator, to yourself, and to succeeding generations, as to be content to grovel in ignorance." Cautioning
them about *grammar,* he said: "Remember that an enlightened and virtuous people can never be enslaved. . . . Become learned and virtuous,
and you will be great. Love God and serve him, and you will be happy"
(p. 15).

Kirkham's *English Grammar* might better have remained unwritten;
had it remained unread there would probably be less linguistic insecurity
among Americans today. Its mode of parsing revealed more of Latin
structure than of English, and, leaving no grey area, the citations of false

syntax colored usage black or white. Ignoring context, failing to incorporate discussion of appropriate circumstances, aware of but unable to grasp the full force of Locke's social compact, Kirkham did as much as any textbook writer in nineteenth-century America to foster an absolutist view of correct English. For teachers employing his book and for the school children drilled daily in his parsing system and false syntax, the structures of English remained opaque; linguistic insecurity flourished; and the benefits of analyzing language in context were lost entirely. A sentence was right or it was wrong; there was nothing further to say—except, if it was wrong, to diagnose the malady and prescribe the cure, producing a healthy alternative, a "correct" expression.

The connection Kirkham's books fostered between religious piety and linguistic purity gave his dicta the force of evangelical zeal, which continued to be reflected in handbooks and apparently in the public mind. "Is it not a pity," Goold Brown later asked, "that 'more than one hundred thousand children and youth' should be daily poring over language and logic like this?" (1851, p. 30).

While Brown thought only ill of Kirkham's book, the public, comforted by the security he provided, made Kirkham wealthy, and he appreciated their patronage. Effectively replying to his critic, he drew his readers into the feud: "What!" he wrote, "a book have *no merit,* and yet be called for at the rate of *sixty thousand copies a year*! What a slander is this upon the public taste! What an insult to the understanding and discrimination of the good people of these United States! According to this reasoning, all the inhabitants of our land must be fools, except one man, and that man is *Goold Brown*."[26]

Goold Brown

That one man, whatever his limitations, is of great interest to us. More extreme in his views than Kirkham, Brown was also more prolific. And to him goes the distinction of having written the densest English grammar published before or during the nineteenth century, a colossus he was to christen *The Grammar of English Grammars* when it was published in New York in 1851. An ambitious man, he described his monumental opus as "the fulfillment of a design, formed about twenty-seven years ago, of one day presenting to the world . . . something like a complete grammar of the English language" (p. iii). This "grammar of grammars," an octavo edition of more than a thousand crowded pages, is both a good deal more and a great deal less than he intended.

Born in Rhode Island, Brown absorbed his early education from a father who was financially unable to send him to college. A diligent student, he became a teacher in his father's footsteps and made his early living as a schoolmaster, though he found more satisfaction in reading and writing. "He studied grammar after his own fashion with religious fervor," one biographer tells us.[27] Another notes that, "Like Noah Webster, Brown was a New England pedagogue, albeit a very successful one, and he was as learned, perceptive, devoted, devout, indefatigable, conceited, contentious, and cantankerous as Webster himself."[28]

Like Lindley Murray, whom he judged insufficiently prepared to write a grammar and of whose grammar he said "There is no part . . . more accurate than that which he literally copied from Lowth" (1851, p. 25), Brown was a Quaker. He was also evangelically self-righteous, niggardly with praise, harshly critical of others, totally humorless, and seemingly paranoid. His grammars did not sell so well as Murray's or Kirkham's, and he became nowhere near so famous as Webster.

In title reminiscent of Webster's first grammar, Brown's earliest, *The Institutes of English Grammar,* appeared first in 1823 and reached a larger market. Particularly in the prestigious eastern academies it was favored for decades; in New York's academies Brown was the leader for over thirty years, though Kirkham prevailed in the public schools at least in the '30s and '40s. With revenue from sales of his *Institutes,* Brown continued to study, evidently limiting his scope to grammatical treatises and school books. Caught up in his determination to author the definitive English grammar, he devoted himself to the project with staggering diligence.

Skeptical of the inductive and productive systems of grammar teaching that Kirkham and others were introducing, Brown crusaded for a return to rules and parsing as the most effective pedagogy. Indeed, he thought the "only successful method of teaching grammar, is, to cause the principal definitions and rules to be committed thoroughly to memory, that they may ever afterwards be readily applied" (1851, p. 87). In an age when pedagogical experimentation was energetically pursued, he set himself staunchly against innovation.

> The vain pretensions of several modern simplifiers, contrivers of machines, charts, tables, diagrams, vincula, pictures, dialogues, familiar lectures, ocular analyses, tabular compendiums, inductive exercises, productive systems, intellectual methods, and various new theories, for the purpose of teaching grammar, may serve to deceive the ignorant, to amuse the visionary, and to excite the admiration of the credulous; . . . The definitions and rules which constitute the doctrines of grammar, may be variously expressed, arranged, illustrated, and applied . . . but no contrivance can ever relieve the pupil from the necessity of committing them thoroughly to

memory. . . . in teaching grammar, to desert the plain didactic method of definition and example, rule and praxis, and to pretend to lead children by philosophic induction into a knowledge of words, is to throw down the ladder of learning, that boys may imagine themselves to ascend it, while they are merely stilting over the low level upon which its fragments are cast. (1851, pp. 91–92)

While resisting innovation Brown was nevertheless paradoxically distressed by the lack of original analysis in the treatises of others. He campaigned for a fresh look at English, damned the mimics, and called for an honorable vindication of independent thinkers. So self-righteous was he that no grammarian escaped the scourge of his pen, though a few, long since buried, suffered no outrage. "A grammarian," he said, "must be a writer, an author, a man who observes and thinks for himself; and not a mere compiler, abridger, modifier, copyist, or plagiarist" (1851, p. 17). Taking the real and imagined faults of earlier grammars as personal affronts, Brown wrote:

English grammar is still in its infancy; and even bears, to the imagination of some, the appearance of a deformed and ugly dwarf among the liberal arts. Treatises are multiplied almost innumerably, but still the old errors survive. Names are rapidly added to our list of authors, while little or nothing is done for the science. Nay, while new blunders have been committed in every new book, old ones have been allowed to stand as by prescriptive right; and positions that were never true, and sentences that were never good English, have been published and republished under different names, till in our language grammar has become the most ungrammatical of all studies! (1851, p. 12)

Referring to Murray's grammar—the "Great Compiler's code"—he continued:

Were this a place for minute criticism, blemishes almost innumerable might be pointed out. It might easily be shown that almost every rule laid down in the book for the observance of the learner, was repeatedly violated by the hand of the master. Nor is there among all those who have since abridged or modified the work, an abler grammarian than he who compiled it. Who will pretend that Flint, Alden, Comly, Jaudon, Russell, Bacon, Lyon, Miller, Alger, Maltby, Ingersoll, Fisk, Greenleaf, Merchant, Kirkham, Cooper, R. G. Greene, Woodworth, Smith, or Frost, has exhibited greater skill? . . . No man professing to have copied and improved Murray, can rationally be supposed to have greatly excelled him; for to pretend to have produced an *improved copy of a compilation,* is to claim a sort of authorship, even inferior to his, and utterly unworthy of any man who is able to prescribe and elucidate the principles of English grammar. (1851, pp. 25–26)

What Brown had set out to construct, then, was an ideal grammar, superior to Murray's but independent of it. The resulting "grammar of grammars" was one of the most self-serving books on English ever to find its way into print, given Brown's overriding determination to evaluate the justness of fame accorded other grammarians. From an earlier remark of his, we learn something of Brown's psychology:

> To most persons grammar seems a dry and difficult subject; but there is a disposition of mind, to which what is arduous, is for that very reason alluring. The difficulties encountered in boyhood from the use of a miserable epitome, and the deep impression of a few mortifying blunders made in public, first gave the author a fondness for grammar; circumstances having since favoured this turn of his genius, he has voluntarily pursued the study, with an assiduity which no man will ever imitate for the sake of pecuniary recompense.[29]

One might wish that Brown had written more for the sake of pecuniary recompense than from the overzealous grammatical morality that seems so out of place in discussions of language.

In the *Grammar of English Grammars* Brown selected his countless examples of false syntax from the writings of other grammarians. They were intended not only to provide raw material for his human parsing machines but simultaneously to discredit the respectability of every competitor. While delight at finding others with their pants down has characterized the grammatical musings of English speakers for centuries, no one shades Goold Brown in this respect. He in fact justified the activity on principle, as an inevitable by-product of grammatical sensitivity and insight: "it is the great end of grammar, to secure the power of apt expression, by causing the principles on which language is constructed . . . to pass through [the mind] more rapidly than either pen or voice can utter words. And where this power resides, there cannot but be a proportionate degree of critical skill, or of ability to judge of the language of others" (1851, p. iv).

Ironically, more than any other grammarian, Brown frustrated part of his own design by parading before his readers a long, colorful line of the very usages he hoped to annihilate. Though he did not launch the practice of error hunting in English grammar, he did as much to propagate it as anyone. And every time a writer quotes a supposed grammatical infelicity, the number of occurrences of that "error" is thereby added to, and its likelihood of further occurrence possibly increased with increased exposure to it.[30]

The significance of Goold Brown for our purposes lies in his expressed attitudes concerning divided usage and the authority of custom, the relationship between speech and writing, and the link between grammar and morality. His views survive in many attitudes of the twentieth century.

A victim of the so-called classical fallacy, Brown as grammarian had no use for the spoken language; the written word alone was worthy of his analysis and of imitation. He believed that the oft-cited definition of grammar—*recte scribendi atque loquendi ars* ("the art of writing and speaking correctly") "not improperly placed writing first, as being that with which grammar is primarily concerned," and he claimed that "over any fugitive colloquial dialect, which has never been fixed by visible signs, grammar has no control" and that "the speaking which the art or science of grammar teaches, is exclusively that which has reference to a knowledge of letters" (1851, pp. 2–3). Further, he proclaimed that "It is the certain tendency of writing, to improve speech. And in proportion as books are multiplied, and the knowledge of written language is diffused, local dialects, which are beneath the dignity of grammar, will always be found to grow fewer, and their differences less" (p. 3). He ignorantly asserted that "'the nations of unlettered men' are among that portion of the earth's population, upon whose language the genius of grammar has never yet condescended to look down!" (p. 14). While "first in the order of nature," he said baldly, speech is "last with reference to grammar" (p. 5).

As to choosing between alternative locutions, Brown acknowledged a limited role for usage but reserved to himself the prerogative of choosing just whose usage was preferred. Nearly alone among grammarians, he did not subscribe to the importance of custom even in theory; in practice, his work blatantly denies it any significance. He denied explicitly the social-compact theory of language, believing rather that language derived directly from the Deity. Approvingly he cited classical authors to the effect that names and words subsist by nature and not from art, and agreed with what Sanctius (a sixteenth-century grammarian of Latin) had written: "For those who contend that names were made by chance, are no less audacious than if they would endeavour to persuade us, that the whole order of the universe was framed together fortuitously" (1851, p. 7). Given that the true meanings and uses of words are inherent in nature (i.e., God-given?), it followed for Brown that the more ancient usages are to be preferred: "Etymology and custom are seldom at odds; and where they are so, the latter can hardly be deemed infallible" (p. 10). Thus, he totally rejected Kirkham's view that a grammarian "is bound to take words and explain them as he finds them in his day, *without any regard to their ancient construction and application*" (p. 10).

If language was divinely instituted and humanly perverted, then mere custom could not be authoritative; and Brown deemed it necessary for some Solomon-like grammarian, elevated above others, to resolve points of disagreement and decide among the array of interpretations that lesser grammarians had generated. Throughout his work, therefore, an "important purpose . . . borne constantly in mind, and judged worthy of very particular attention, was the attempt to settle, so far as the most patient investigation and the fullest exhibition of proofs could do it, the multitudinous and vexatious disputes which have hitherto divided the sentiments of teachers, and made the study of English grammar so uninviting, unsatisfactory, and unprofitable, to the student whose taste demands a reasonable degree of certainty" (1851, p. iv).

Finally, having furnished Americans their definitive *Grammar of English Grammars,* this guru sat confident that his views would prevail. For by his prescriptions was the acceptability of English to be judged, and the allegiance due his rules was allied to the obedience due other commandments. For Brown, "The grammatical use of language is in sweet alliance with the moral" (1851, p. 94), and he therefore had every reason to expect decent readers to honor the grammatical morality he revealed.

The memorization of rules of grammar, like memorization of the Ten Commandments, the Pater Noster, or the Pledge of Allegiance, suggests a fixed state, an unchangeable formula, a liturgy whose effectiveness is vitiated if the ritual is altered. The same applies to spelling and derives support from spelling rules (such as "*i* before *e,* except after *c* . . .") and from spelling bees, where to vary once from the norm is to disqualify oneself absolutely and forever from winning the prize.

As Charlton Laird has observed, "Samuel Kirkham and Goold Brown did much to fasten upon the minds of American youth the conviction that the first of the deadly sins is grammatical impropriety, and that salvation is to be sought through the repetition of rules. If prissiness and pedantry have dogged the use of language in the United States, part of the cause is apparently to be sought in the cult of parsing, where Samuel Kirkham and Goold Brown are among the patron saints."[31]

Notes

[1]Though I have made corrections where I know him to be wrong, my discussion of the earliest American grammars draws on Rollo LaVerne Lyman, *English Grammar in American Schools before 1850* (1922), pp. 16, 33–36.

[2]The *Guide* may have had a colonial printing seven years earlier still, for in 1740, the year of its initial London printing, Benjamin Franklin, regularly importing books from

England at the time and responsible for printing the 1747 *Guide,* published a work called *A New and Complete Guide to the English Tongue* by an anonymous writer who bibliographers suspect was Thomas Dilworth.

³After a reprinting in Philadelphia by Benjamin Franklin, Harris's *Hermes, or a Philosophical Inquiry Concerning Universal Grammar* was translated into French for a Paris edition and into German for publication in Halle—not surprising for a grammar that was, according to Lowth, "the most beautiful and perfect example of analysis that has been exhibited since the days of *Aristotle.*" It was not, however, a textbook for students. Greenwood's *Essay* was largely a translation of the English grammar that John Wallis had written in Latin in 1653.

⁴John Ash, *Grammatical Institutes,* 4th ed. (1763), p. iii. Besides the 1774 New York edition, others followed at Philadelphia (1778 and 1788) Worcester (1785), New York (1788), and Boston (1794).

⁵*Dissertations on the English Language* (Boston, 1789), p. vii. For his subsequent role in getting a federal copyright law passed in 1790, Webster has been called the "father of American copyright."

⁶*A Grammatical Institute of the English Language,* Part I, pp. 4–5. Henceforth, citing Part I or Part II of the *Institute,* I shall use the abbreviations "I" and "II."

⁷Lyman, pp. 77–78.

⁸Samuel G. Goodrich (1793–1860) was the pseudonymous Peter Parley, whose recollections were reprinted in the *American Journal of Education,* XXX (1863), 139.

⁹Asa Rand, *American Annals of Education and Instruction,* III (1833), 161–162.

¹⁰John Horne Tooke (1736–1812) was a British politician sympathetic to the American cause and a learned philologist. His *Diversions of Purley* (London, 1786) was an original grammar of English intended for a scholarly audience.

¹¹*Compendious Dictionary,* p. x. Webster did italicize an unnecessary letter here and there so as to indicate its vacuous function in the spelling and to suggest its omissibility.

¹²Bergen Evans, "Noah Webster Had the Same Troubles" (1962), pp. 77, 79.

¹³Webster was not the only important lexicographer in America in the mid-nineteenth century. Certainly his chief competitor, Joseph Worcester, warrants attention, but not in the matter of usage. For the fullest treatment, see Joseph H. Friend, *The Development of American Lexicography: 1798–1864* (1967). We can mention here, however, that in some quarters the dislike for Webster's dictionaries was fanatical. Bergen Evans reports in "Noah Webster Had the Same Troubles" (1962, p. 80) that William Cullen Bryant, editor of *The New York Evening Post* in 1856, was so pleased with a scathing review of Webster's dictionary that he volunteered to help fund a project that would provide for having the denunciation read twice a year in every schoolhouse in America!

¹⁴Letter to Mathew Carey dated June 14, 1805; in Harry R. Warfel, ed., *Letters of Noah Webster* (1953), pp. 262–263. His moderate success with textbooks gained Webster seventeen competitors, British and American, in the eleven years between the appearance of his grammar in 1784 and Murray's in 1795.

¹⁵Lyman, pp. 79–80.

¹⁶*Ibid.*

¹⁷R. C. Alston, "Note" in the Scolar Press facsimile edition of Murray's 1795 *English Grammar.*

¹⁸Murray's success attracted competitors to the expanding marketplace. Fourteen new grammars appeared in America between 1801 and 1810, and the decade between 1811 and 1820 saw a tripling of that figure to 41, which doubled to 84 in the '20s. Still Murray led the field, not reaching his peak in New York, for example, until 1829; only in the '30s was he outdistanced there by Samuel Kirkham, Goold Brown, and others. As late as 1833 in the public schools of New York, Murray's was the text being used in 459 towns, while Kirkham, soon to supersede him, was studied in 179 towns. By 1836 Kirkham took the lead, with 371

towns to Murray's 294. In neighboring Massachusetts, Roswell Smith led by 1837, when Murray's grammars were carried home from the schoolrooms of only 104 towns. The situation differed in New York's academies, where Murray yielded the palm briefly to Kirkham, Goold Brown reigning as undisputed master between 1842 and 1873, having jostled Kirkham out of first place in the '30s. Data from Lyman, pp. 83, 84, 86, 95.

[19]Lyman, p. 54.

[20]"The Motivation of Lindley Murray's Grammatical Work" (1939), p. 531.

[21]A hint of how Murray engaged his mind during his early recuperation and of what preoccupied him throughout his later life can be found in the end pages of his *Grammar,* which contain an advertisement for another book of his called *The Power of Religion on the Mind, in Retirement, Affliction and at the Approach of Death,* popular enough to be in its sixth edition by 1795, still more than three decades before his death.

[22]*The Knickerbocker* (October 1837); quoted by Brown, in *The Grammar of English Grammars* (1851), p. 36, fn.

[23]*The Grammar of English Grammars* (1851), p. 29. Cited hereafter as "1851."

[24]Samuel Kirkham, *English Grammar, in Familiar Lectures* (1829), p. 10. Later Kirkham quotes, cited by page number only, are from this volume.

[25]Lyman, p. 120.

[26]*The Knickerbocker* (October 1837), p. 361; cited by Brown (1851), p. 31, fn.

[27]George Harvey Genzmer in the *Dictionary of American Biography.*

[28]Charlton Laird, *Language in America* (1970; repr. 1972), p. 301.

[29]*The Institutes of English Grammar,* p. v.

[30]Studies of language errors in the twentieth century indicate that "the errors actually increase in number and proportion in the later grades after teachers have made an attack upon them. . . ." See Charles C. Fries, *American English Grammar* (1940), p. 284.

[31]Laird, p. 307.

CHAPTER IV

Pioneer Linguists and Amateur Philologians: 1786–1875

"There is a misuse of words which can be justified by no authority, however great, by no usage, however general."
—RICHARD GRANT WHITE, 1870

BESIDE THE WORK of the schoolbook writers, two other forces in the late eighteenth and early nineteenth centuries helped shape American linguistic attitudes. One was the development of scientific linguistics in Europe, the other the writings of American and British amateur philologians. But these two influences pulled in opposite directions.

It is convenient to call 1786 the date for the beginning of modern linguistics, for in India that year an Englishman named Sir William Jones announced his discovery that the Sanskrit language bore a "stronger affinity" to Latin and Greek "than could possibly have been produced by accident; so strong, indeed, that no philologer could examine all three without believing them to have sprung from some common source which, perhaps, no longer exists."[1] This germinal recognition of an Indo-European family of languages inspired a conscious sophistication of approach to comparative and historical linguistics, and the mythical Tower of Babel began to crumble. European philologists methodically compared one language with another, and current forms of a language with its earlier stages. Their investigations revealed a good deal about the historical development of languages and the relationships among them, and also about the structures of language and the general principles of their evolution. The conviction grew that linguistic change, natural and inevitable, followed describable patterns.[2]

After nearly half a century of comparative linguistic investigation on the Continent, however, little had been done to spread knowledge of this new science in Britain or America.[3] By 1828, when Noah Webster's *American Dictionary* appeared, European scholars had gained substantial insight into the development of the Germanic languages, including

62

English. Had Webster known Jacob Grimm's monumental *Deutsche Grammatik,* which had appeared in 1822 in its second edition, he would have relinquished his belief that all languages derive from Biblical Aramaic ("Chaldee," as he called it). But awareness of European linguistic scholarship was rare in mid-nineteenth-century America, and news of German discoveries was not always welcome.

Ironically, James Gates Percival (1795–1856), retained by Webster to read proofs for the *American Dictionary,* was himself a student of German linguistic science. But Webster, approaching seventy in 1828, refused to consider Percival's suggestions for revision in line with Grimm's discoveries; and he was unsympathetic when Percival cited errors in the dictionary "such as will strike a tyro." Webster remained unwilling to read Grimm, as he was urged to do in 1830 by an Englishman eager to publish the *Dictionary* abroad. In 1833 he still balked, and in 1842, twenty years after Grimm's work and only months before his own death, Webster proclaimed that "my researches render it certain that in etymology the Germans are in darkness." George Philip Krapp's assessment is essentially correct about Webster's etymologies: ". . . it was really spiritual, not phonological truth in which Webster was primarily interested . . .," and this is what produced such "etymological crudities."[4]

As the bulky *Dictionary* went to press, a few Americans were toting linguistics treatises home from German universities. Especially at Harvard and Yale, knowledge of the new science was taking root. But no major treatment of linguistics was available in English until 1861, when the German-born scholar F. Max Müller published his *Lectures on the Science of Language* at Oxford.

William Dwight Whitney

A few years later, on this side of the Atlantic, William Dwight Whitney (1827–1894) published a dozen lectures on the principles of the new science; his *Language and the Study of Language* (first published in 1867 and still in print!) introduced linguistics to a larger American audience. Some of the lectures had been presented at the Smithsonian Institution and the Lowell Institute. Whitney's later volume *The Life and Growth of Language* (1875) dealt with much the same subject matter.

As a youth Whitney had intended to become a natural scientist, but while on a geological survey of the United States, a chance browsing in his brother Josiah's Sanskrit grammar enticed him to linguistic study. (Strangely enough, his brother achieved distinction as a professor of geology at Harvard.) From Edward Elbridge Salisbury at Yale and from others in Germany Whitney grasped the principles of a science he imparted to Yale students for forty years, from 1854 to the end of his career, principles that later provided the foundation for his work as editor of the great ten-volume *Century Dictionary and Cyclopedia* (1887–1891).

The principles infusing Whitney's work form the cornerstone of the relativistic position of usage which has been endorsed, elaborated, and refined by succeeding American linguists. Maintaining that "speech is a thing of far nearer and higher importance" than writing (p. 45); that language is arbitrary and conventional (pp. 32, 35), changing all the time (pp. 24, 32–34), and varying from place to place and time to time (p. 153),[5] he articulated the view to which all modern linguists subscribe. He taught that usage is the supreme authority in ascertaining correctness, the speakers of a tongue constituting "a republic, or rather, a democracy, in which authority is conferred only by general suffrage and for due cause, and is exercised under constant supervision and control" (p. 38). Horace's maxim that usage is the rule of speech he regarded as "of supreme and uncontrolled validity in every part and parcel of every human tongue" (p. 40). Whitney recognized that "each individual can make his fellows talk and write as he does just in proportion to the influence which they are disposed to concede to him" (p. 40).

In *Essentials of English Grammar,* a school text, Whitney maintained that "Grammar does not at all make rules and laws for language; it only reports the facts of good language, and in an orderly way. . . ."[6] And report the facts in an orderly way is what his grammars do. He discusses debatable items of usage only when they fit into general patterns, as with *shall* and *will* as parts of the verb phrase. Paramount in his work was this view of a grammarian—"that he is simply a recorder and arranger of the usages of language, and in no manner or degree a lawgiver; hardly even an arbiter or critic" (1877, p. v). Opposing the notion that the chief goal of grammar is to inculcate correct use of English, he advised teachers to be cognizant of the limits of linguistics and warned that improvement in writing is only "a secondary or subordinate" purpose in studying grammar, though not an unimportant one (1877, p. iii).

Typical of Whitney's approach is his discussion of whether the objective or possessive case is "preferred" before an *-ing* word (e.g., pardon *me* or *my* blushing): "There are cases where both are equally proper; but even among good writers (and yet more among careless ones), the one is occasionally found where more approved usage would favor the other . . ." (1877, p. 223). In referring to "more approved" usage Whitney, like Webster, Lowth, and Priestley, skirted recognition of levels of usage, a concept that was only later to emerge. He described good English as "those words, and those meanings of them, and those ways of putting them together, which are used by the best speakers, the people of best education"; and in terms unusual for the nineteenth century, he defined bad English in reference to those who avoid it: "bad English is simply that which is not approved and accepted by good and careful speakers" (1877, p. 3). His failure to identify good and careful speakers is less noteworthy than the fact that his criterion for "bad" usage is sociological and not inherently linguistic. For the first time, an American broke loose from the circularity of preferring the usage of the best speakers and writers while identifying such models by the character of their English.

Whitney also perceived the existence of functional varieties of English, recognizing that forms appropriate for one occasion may not be universally suitable. For example, he observed that "In poetry, especially, the use of an adjective as adverb directly, without any [-ly] ending, is very common," citing *clear, scarce, free,* and *soft* as frequently accepted poetic specimens of "flat" adverbs (1877, p. 139).

Yet even Whitney, a notable spokesman for the science of language and the most gifted American linguist in his century, occasionally proved to be what some have called prescriptive[7] in his analysis of specific English usages. In *Essentials,* though he could acknowledge without regret that "the subjunctive, as a separate mode, is almost lost and out of mind in our language" (1877, p. 194), he withheld approbation from certain common usages of the future auxiliaries. He accused the Irish and the Scots of having "long been inaccurate in their use" of *shall* and *will,* "putting *will* often where the cultivated and approved idiom requires *shall,*" and he lamented that "the inaccuracy has recently been greatly increasing in the United States" (1877, pp. 120f.). Reminiscent of Webster, he elsewhere suggested that in his native New England "the proper distinction of *shall* and *will* was as strictly maintained, and a slip in the use of the one for the other as rare, and as immediately noticeable and offensive . . ., as in the best society of London."[8] Thus, though he certainly accepted Locke's view of linguistic conventionality, his talk of "inaccuracy" and "proper distinction" perhaps reveals a notion of inherent linguistic correctness, something his principles disallowed.

Whitney also deplored the approval conferred by some contemporary books on *It is me:* "It may well enough be that 'it is *me*' is now already so firmly established in colloquial usage, and even in written, that the attempt to oust it will be vain; but the expression is none the less in its origin a simple blunder, a popular inaccuracy. It is neither to be justified nor palliated by theoretical considerations . . . ."[9] Thus, while usage reigned supreme in Whitney's theory, analogy and personal preference sometimes triumphed in his practice. His devotion to scientific observation and his conviction that language is arbitrary and conventional did not prevent biased conservative judgments about specific points of disputed usage. A distinguished theoretical linguist, he was nevertheless an amateur philologian in the realm of English usage.

Still, *Language and the Science of Language* and *Essentials of English Grammar* set forth certain fundamental principles of linguistic science and laid a theoretical foundation for grammars based on current appropriate usage. Republished after his death, Whitney's works continue to advance our understanding of language.

But the effect of such linguistic science on school grammars was not sufficient to overcome the momentum of the eighteenth-century authoritarian approach—not even in the English grammar Whitney wrote himself. Conservative and authoritarian views continued to dominate discussion of school grammar.

George Perkins Marsh

Prominent among Americans whose conservative views influenced popular opinion and typified school texts was George Perkins Marsh (1801–1882). A native Vermonter educated at Dartmouth, he taught school and practiced law before he was elected to Congress and appointed to the diplomatic corps; later he produced valuable work in geography. During the 1858–59 academic year Marsh delivered a series of postgraduate lectures at New York's Columbia College. Subsequently published as *Lectures on the English Language*,[10] they demonstrate the total unacceptability of usage as a standard of correctness for well-educated and prominent mid-nineteenth-century Americans.

From the linguistic scholarship of his day Marsh knew that the English language had always been changing and would continue to change. He confessed that "our speech must bow" to the law of change; but he bowed reluctantly. Like Dr. Johnson, Marsh hoped that we would "avail ourselves of a great variety of means and circumstances peculiar to modern society, to retard the decay of our tongue, and to prevent its dissipation into a multitude of independent dialects" (p. 679). Like most eighteenth- and nineteenth-century grammarians, he accepted the authority of usage in principle but disregarded it when its conclusions ran counter to his own preferences.

Languages could be corrupted, Marsh believed, and he leveled scathing criticisms against one Robert Latham for confusing "the progress of natural linguistic change, which is inevitable, [with] the deterioration arising from accidental or local causes, which may be resisted" (p. 645). Latham, a British physician and later student of the

English language, had proclaimed that in language "not only whatever *is* is right, but also that in many cases *whatever was was wrong.*"[11] Indignant, Marsh exposed the logical flaw in the second part of the remark and summarily dismissed the first: "To deny that language is susceptible of corruption is to deny that races or nations are susceptible of depravation; and to treat all its changes as normal, is to confound things as distinct as health and disease" (p. 649).

In this opaque distinction between inevitable and accidental change, between normality and depravity, we see the association of morality and grammaticality which has infused American attitudes toward usage. As the fall of Adam taints us with sin and inclines us to evil, so the effects of Babel permit language to be corrupted. Webster, Murray, Kirkham, and Brown were all touched in varying degrees by this belief. But none was so fanatic in zeal or harsh in judgment as Marsh. For him linguistic propriety was *chiefly* a moral question. He was convinced that "The wanton abuse of words by writers . . . of popular imaginative literature has been productive of very serious injury in language and in ethics" (p. 258). Concerning supposed atrocities like the pronunciation of *Ohio* and *Mississippi* as "Ohiuh" and "Mississippuh," he preached this: "To pillory such offences, to point out their absurdity, to detect and expose the moral obliquity which too often lurks beneath them, is the sacred duty of every scholar . . . who knows how nearly purity of speech, like personal cleanliness, is allied with purity of thought and rectitude of action" (pp. 644-645). Such a fanciful creed is woven into the fabric of American thought about grammatical correctness and, as in the reactions to *Webster's Third* and the Winston cigarette ad, continue to color the yarn of linguistic criticism.

Perhaps a distrust of the lower classes, especially among recent immigrants,[12] prompted Marsh to deny the conventionality and arbitrariness of language. His condemnation of the Italians and their language is revealing:

A bold and manly and generous and truthful people certainly would not choose to say *umiliare una supplica,* to humiliate a supplication, for, to present a memorial; to style the strength which awes, and the finesse which deceives, alike, *onestà,* honesty or respectability; to speak of taking human life by poison, not as a crime, but simply as a mode of facilitating death, *ajutare la morte;* to employ *pellegrino,* foreign, for admirable; . . . to apply to a small garden and a cottage the title of *un podere,* a power; to call every house with a large door, *un palazzo,* a palace . . . .[13]

Not surprisingly, he saw as a "general law" the supposition that there exists "a natural connection between the sound and the thing signified and consequently, that the forms of language . . . are natural and necessary products of the organization, faculties, and condition of men" (p. 37). The dispute between conventionalists and naturalists, at least as old as Plato, remained unsettled in 1860. A very influential American writer on language upheld and propagated views that linguists like Whitney already regarded as myth and poppycock.

Marsh cannot readily be characterized. He did claim that English had no grammar (that is, no regularity) and that if there were only half a dozen persons in Europe who knew French, there were still fewer in America who knew English. Flouting consistency, however, he also condemned lexicographers who fail to "present the language as it is, as the conjoined influence of uncontrollable circumstances and learned labor has made it," but who instead present their own "crude notions" of what it ought to be (pp. 13, 99, 420).

Marsh's ambivalence was typical of his age. Some grammarians reluctantly accepted the emerging principles of linguistic science, but the implications of these ran counter to national and class prejudices. Principle urged grammarians to approve what a touch of xenophobia prompted them to disdain. It was not difficult to reject in practice what they espoused in theory when faced with language forms associated with social characteristics for which they had little tolerance. Guilt by association contaminated linguistic items that some acknowledged could have no intrinsic fault of their own. Nor was it uncommon to associate correct grammatical usage with an upright life, as Marsh did, with the result that defending language from the onslaughts of impurity became an ethical imperative. Inspired to restore English to its putative God-given pristine state, many took to pointing up errors and inconsistencies in linguistic enemies and social inferiors. Inevitably the prescriptions of one traditionalist became the proscriptions of another, and public feuds flared between amateur grammarians.

Henry Alford & George Washington Moon

The pious rancor between Henry Alford (1810–1871), Dean of Canterbury, and George Washington Moon (1823–1909), an American living in England, proved entertaining (if not terribly instructive) to the literate public for a quarter-century. British and American presses published the rival works, and the numerous copies lining the shelves of second-hand bookshops in America testify to the controversy's considerable following. In 1863 Alford penned a series of magazine articles entitled "A Plea for the Queen's English." Moon, deliberately misconstruing that title, countered with *A Defense of the Queen's English*. The next year, his essays gathered into one volume, Alford devilishly retitled them *The Queen's English,* tempting people to interpret Moon's *Defense of the Queen's English* as support for Alford's book. The ruse provoked Moon into calling his next edition *The Dean's English,* in which he ridiculed Dean Alford for violating his own rules.[14]

What had moved Alford in the first place was his conviction "that most of the grammars, and rules, and applications of rules, now so commonly made for our language, are in reality not contributions to its purity, but main instruments of its deterioration" (p. xiv). In customary British fashion, and to demonstrate that purity of language was an important matter, he directed attention to the shortcomings of Americans: "Look at those phrases which so amuse us in their speech and books; at their reckless exaggeration, and contempt for congruity; and then compare the character and history of the nation—its blunted sense of moral obligation and duty to man; . . . and, I may now say, its reckless and fruitless maintenance of the most cruel and unprincipled war in the history of the world" (p. 6). How the "amusing phrases" gave rise to or stemmed from the same causes as the Civil War, Alford left to his readers' imaginations. His fear that the proliferation of Americanisms would ruin the English language was widely shared in England and only slightly less so among America's literati.

Nevertheless, Alford's frankly prescriptive notes on speaking and spelling are generally sane and cool. If his manual lacks the realistic judgments that additional information might have led to, it is not nearly so dogmatic as others of its day. More realistic than Whitney, for example, Alford sanctioned *It is me* because it was "an expression which everyone uses." While recommending that people write much as they speak, he also recognized that we must distinguish spoken and written English (pp. 154, 279, 74).

Apart from his skirmishes with Alford, George Moon took aim at the grammatical naughtiness of his American countrymen, including Lindley Murray: ". . . I cannot resist the temptation to take up the pen against him, and to repay him for the terror of his name in my school days, by showing that, in the very volume in which he laid down his rules, he frequently expressed himself ungrammatically."[15]

Moon's attack on the usage of Alford, Murray, Marsh, and their fellow purists was a natural result of the kinds of grammar teaching that characterized nineteenth-century schools. Exercises in false syntax fostered the error-hunting syndrome. And in this preoccupation, initiated by Lowth and Murray, the habits of Americans were formed. Today, an editorial or newspaper column lamenting the state of the language hardly ever fails to prompt outcries that the condemnation itself is faulty. Such rebuttals in turn, if made public, prompt another wave of accusations. It is an occupational hazard among language guardians that standards are never sufficiently strict to ward off criticism from other language guardians.

Richard Grant White & William Mathews

The battle of the books attracted considerable attention, but interest in Moon's activities after Alford's death was eclipsed by the enormous popularity of a famous New Yorker named Richard Grant White (1821-1885). His *Words and Their Uses*[16] first appeared in 1870, saw thirty-three editions by the turn of the century, and was being copyrighted in a revised edition as late as 1927. In it White flatly denied the absolute authority of general usage or even the usage of great writers: "There is a misuse of words which can be justified by no authority, however great, by no usage, however general" (p. 24). His chapter entitled "Jus Et Norma Loquendi" is a thirty-page brief explicitly denying validity to Horace's oft-quoted dictum on the power of usage and implicitly questioning Locke's social contract.

Like so many others, White was ill at ease with divided usage among reputable authors; his view of language seemed to preclude the possibility of multiple acceptable usages. Even if fifty instances of *both* applied to three things could be discovered—in Milton, Shakespeare, Spenser, and Chaucer ("To whom bothe heven and erthe and see is seene")—that use could not be justified in terms of the word's etymology and its usage elsewhere (p. 400). If *both* properly relates two countable items, he argued, then it must be degenerate to force it to relate more than two—Chaucer, Milton, and Shakespeare be damned: "it is impossible that the same word can mean two and three!"

White's lambasting of "words that are not words" demonstrates the futility of opposing usage by logic, etymology, or esthetics. Among the condemned locutions he exhorted people to reject were the verbs *donate, jeopardize, resurrect,* and *initiate;* the nouns *practitioner, photographer, pants, conversationalist,* and *standpoint;* the adjectives *presidential, gubernatorial, shamefaced,* and *reliable.* He preferred *enthusiasmed* to *enthused, telegraphist* to *telegrapher, washing-tubs* and *shoeing-horn* to *wash-tubs* and *shoe-horn.* He penned a lengthy chapter against the "incongruous and ridiculous" use of the progressive passive verb form as in *is being done* and *is being built.* With Marsh and other amateur philologians, White favored the more traditional *The house is building* over *The house is being built,* though he feared (correctly) that the latter would prevail.

White's view was what Alford had described as the fallacy of believing that "of two modes of expression, if one be shown to be right, the other must necessarily be wrong." This position was widely adhered to in nineteenth-century America, especially among the philologians who did most to propagate an authoritarian approach to grammatical propriety. George McKnight observes that "Americans then . . . in the lack of training in good English from social experience, welcomed positive directions, and these they found in the dogmatic, often perverse, assertions of White."[17]

White's opposition to the authority of usage was ringingly condemned by the distinguished linguist-lexicographer Fitzedward Hall, in a book entitled *Recent Exemplifications of False Philology* (1872). But White's *Words and Their Uses* was generally applauded,[18] and his attitudes influenced handbook writers and the general public and pervaded schools and colleges. Leonard Bloomfield, one of the most influential American linguists in the first half of the twentieth century, recalled that his undergraduate instructors at Harvard recommended White's book—and never mentioned Whitney.[19]

Another popular American writer on language was William Mathews (1818-1909), a New Englander encouraged by the success of his prescriptive writings to give up his professorship of rhetoric and English at the University of Chicago. Unlike White, but like most popularizers at the time, Mathews acknowledged the power of usage in deciding linguistic correctness. "They that will fight custom with grammar are fools," he remarked, quoting Montaigne's aphorism; they are even more foolish "who triumphantly appeal against custom to the dictionary." Critics "who seek by philological bulls to check its growth . . . do not see that the immobility of language would be the immobility of history. They forget that many of the purest words in our language were at one time startling novelties, and that even the dainty terms in which they challenge each new-comer . . . had to fight their way inch by inch."

In the familiar pattern, however, Mathews treated usage inconsistently. As with Whitney, it requires considerable juggling to reconcile his sober general remarks with particular ones like that which solemnly pontificates that "there is no such word as banister" after pointing out that "hundreds of educated people . . . speak of the banister of a staircase when they mean *balustrade* or *baluster*."[20]

Like Marsh and Alford, Mathews surmised that the putative corruption and debasement of a language reflected the moral state of its speakers: "Could anything be more significant of the profound degradation of a people than the abject character of the complimentary and social dialect of the Italians, and the pompous appellations with which they dignify things in themselves insignificant . . . ?'' (p. 61). He expressed equal disdain for French: ''Can we properly hate or abhor any wicked act till we have given it a specific objective existence by giving it a name which shall at once designate and condemn it? The *pot-de-vin,* and other jesting phrases which the French have coined to denote bribery, can have no effect but to encourage this wrong [because such phrases are not suitably disagreeable]'' (p. 63). Persuaded that the ''corrupter of a language stabs straight at the very heart of his country,'' he lamented that ''the prose of the leading English authors . . . exhibits more slovenliness and looseness of diction, than is found in any other literature'' (pp. 91, 327). Damning ''all inaccuracies of speech, whether offenses against etymology, lexicography or syntax,'' he railed: ''To pillory such offenses, to point out the damage which they inflict upon our language, and to expose the moral obliquity which often lurks beneath them, is, we believe, the duty of every scholar who knows how purity of speech, like personal cleanliness, is allied to purity of thought and rectitude of action'' (p. 335). Mathews' words, it may be recalled, were borrowed from Marsh; the sentiments expressed were widespread. For most Americans, moral and grammatical delinquency were synonymous.

Along with inconsistency between theory and practice, one of the most notable characteristics in the thinking of nineteenth-century grammarians was their conviction that particular linguistic forms possess *inherent* goodness or badness. Marsh, White, and Mathews rejected outright the intrinsic arbitrariness of linguistic symbols and the conventionality of usage. Their remarks recall the view of Plato's Cratylus, who believed ''that everything has a right name of its own, which comes by nature, and that a name is not whatever people call a thing by agreement, just a piece of their own voice applied to the thing, but that there is a kind of inherent correctness in names, which is the same for all men, both Greeks and barbarians.'' For Marsh, White, and Mathews, Locke's linguistic compact had no merit.

Before 1875, grammatical popularizers commonly regarded usage items as intrinsically right or wrong; they did not formally recognize that circumstances alter cases. That appropriateness to an occasion ultimately governs linguistic propriety escaped them. Whitney alone grasped this insight, though his formulation failed to achieve useful explicitness. Americans had been nurtured on the absolutist dogmas of Murray, exercised in Brown's false syntax, and disciplined by Webster's spelling books and dictionaries. No one had articulated a concept of functional varieties or classified their significance in determining correctness. Apparently, no one had sought, in examining English, to establish its varieties with their social, functional, and regional correlates. The notion of a monolithic grammatical English with bastardized offspring continued to prevail.

Notes

[1]Quoted in Louis H. Gray, *Foundations of Language* (1939), pp. 435–436.

[2]For a detailed history of linguistics in this period, see Holger Pedersen, *The Discovery of Language* (1931; repr. 1962).

[3]For the information in this and the following paragraph, I rely on Allen Walker Read, "The Spread of German Linguistic Learning in New England during the Lifetime of Noah Webster" (1966). See also Franklin Edgerton, "Notes on Early American Work in Linguistics" (1943).

[4]*The English Language in America* (1925), I, p. 365.

[5]All page references in this paragraph are to *Language and the Study of Language* (1867).

[6]*Essentials of English Grammar* (1877), p. 4. Cited hereafter as "1877."

[7]Charles V. Hartung, in "The Persistence of Tradition in Grammar" (1962), claims that Whitney "judged goodness and orderliness by degree of adherence to the standard rules." See also Karl W. Dykema, "The Grammar of Spoken English" (1958).

[8]*Oriental and Linguistic Studies: Second Series* (1874), p. 203.

[9]*Ibid.,* p. 173.

[10]George Perkins Marsh, *Lectures on the English Language* (1860). All citations from Marsh are to this work.

[11]Robert Gordon Latham (1812–1888), in the preface to the 2nd ed. of *The English Language* (1848; 1st ed., 1841). Latham dropped the offensive preface from the fourth edition, which had appeared five years before Marsh berated the second edition. I have seen very few statements that echo Latham's; among them are: (1) Raven I. McDavid's "Essentially, in the usage of native speakers, whatever is, is right; but some usages may be more appropriate than others, at least socially," ("Usage, Dialects, and Functional Varieties" (1966, p. xxi), and (2) Samuel Ramsey's "Grammar, like botany or mineralogy, is a purely descriptive science. . . . What is true of nothing else is true of language, that whatever is is right" (*The English Language and English Grammar,* 1892, p. 51).

[12]John Higham says that "the major ideological outlines of American nativism"—the anti-Catholic, anti-radical, and Anglo-Saxon traditions—had been established by the middle of the nineteenth century. See *Strangers in the Land* (1963), p. 11.

[13]Pp. 224–225. About a year after these remarks were made, Marsh was appointed first U.S. Minister to Italy, a post he held until his death in 1882.

[14]Henry Alford, *A Plea for the Queen's English,* repr. from the 2nd London ed. G. Washington Moon, *The Dean's English,* 4th ed. References in my text are to these editions unless otherwise noted.

[15]George Washington Moon, *The Bad English of Lindley Murray and Other Writers on the English Language,* 3rd ed. (1869), p. xxv.

[16]Richard Grant White, *Words and Their Uses* (1870). Citations are from the "Thirty-first edition, revised and corrected."

[17]George H. McKnight, *Modern English in the Making* (1928), p. 536.

[18]See, e.g., *The Atlantic Monthly* (1871), 394–395. The anonymous reviewer found White an exception among "Writers on etiquette and deportment," among "men who would not fall into the blunders of Shakespeare, Addison, and Thackeray." McKnight is probably

correct in attributing the general neglect of Hall's condemnation to his polemic tone and "the assemblage of dry facts with which he supported his judgements" (*Modern English in the Making,* p. 536).

[19]Leonard Bloomfield, "Secondary and Tertiary Responses to Language" (1944).

[20]William Mathews, *Words; Their Use and Abuse* (1876), pp. 330–332.

CHAPTER V

Scholarly Views and Systematic Surveys of Usage in America: 1875-1952

"It is the practice and consent of the great authors that determine correctness of speech."
—THOMAS R. LOUNSBURY, 1908

"Standard English is the customary use of a community when it is recognized and accepted as the customary use of the community. Beyond this . . . is the larger field of good English, any English that justifies itself by accomplishing its end, by hitting the mark."
—GEORGE PHILIP KRAPP, 1909

"We set up as the best language that which is found in the best writers, and count as the best writers those that best write the language. We are therefore no further advanced than before."
—OTTO JESPERSEN, 1925

IN THE FINAL quarter of the nineteenth century, an increasing number of scholars and teachers were recognizing the disparity between educated American usage and the English described in grammars and taught in schools. The founding of the American Philological Association in 1869 and the Modern Language Association in 1883 provided some impetus for the pursuit of accurate information about current English usage. Then during the first quarter of the twentieth century both the National Council of Teachers of English (1911) and the Linguistic Society of America (1924) were founded and added to that impetus.

In the twentieth century the most powerful and influential force in promulgating a realistic view of correctness has been the NCTE, whose annual meetings and publications fostered examination of the function of English grammar in the schools, as well as the forms of suitable pedagogical grammars and methods of teaching. Still, little enough had been accomplished by 1924 that the distinguished linguist Leonard

Bloomfield lamented that "Our schools are conducted by persons who, from professors of education down to teachers in the classroom, know nothing of the results of linguistic science, not even the relation of writing to speech or of standard language to dialect. In short, they do not know what language is, and yet must teach it . . . ."[1]

SCHOLARS BEGIN TO FACE FACTS

Starting about 1875, however, some scholars had attempted to apply the insights of linguistics to English teaching and to keep teachers informed about these applications. Not only by lecturing and writing but also by organizing professional societies, these men made some headway in understanding the varieties of English and promoting recognition of their existence.

The 1899 presidential address to the Modern Language Association treated "Philology and Purism."[2] In it Professor H. C. G. von Jagemann asserted that "the chief task of philology is to record and explain, not to prophesy or to legislate" (p. 74). He ventured that "Philology cannot expect to influence contemporary speech without recognition and consistent application of the principle that the living languages are for the living and the usage of each generation is a law unto itself" (p. 88). The authority of past and present writers was overrated and so, reminiscent of earlier appeals for an academy, von Jagemann called for a class of philologist-purists to balance the forces of usage with hoped-for changes.[3] The questions to be raised should relate to the hold of present usage on speakers and to the advantages and disadvantages of a particular adoption or rejection. Such a suggestion—that particular locutions be evaluated for their utility—is extremely rare in the history of discussion of language correctness, where either *ipse dixit* pronouncements or purely descriptive statements have held sway. It is of course the position assumed by national academies charged with evaluation.

In another MLA address two years later, president E. S. Sheldon spoke about "Practical Philology."[4] He wanted philologists' views on grammars, dictionaries, and language in general to become more widely known, and he urged acceptance of the principle that "good usage is decisive" *regardless* of its historical or logical basis. Thus, within two years, we see differences of opinion among philologists themselves on the matter of correctness—von Jagemann calling for balanced reform as a basis for standards, Sheldon advocating a *laissez faire* approach. Sheldon did acknowledge, nevertheless, the dilemma of the school teacher, who was expected to know and practice the teachings of linguists and yet be responsible for improving students' English.

The attention of teachers was indeed being drawn to the need for basing grammar on actual usage. In 1887, Edward A. Allen, professor of English at the University of Missouri, published in the journal *Education* a stout condemnation of the writers of grammar texts. He unflatteringly noted among such compilers "a real fascination" for surrounding themselves "with a few hundred of the existing grammars and picking about among them for material to arrange in an odd way." Poking fun at the attempts of many such grammarians to "fit all English to ingeniously devised diagrams," he observed virtually no reliance on usage in their determination of the rules. Because "language precedes grammar and dictates its laws," he insisted that "the facts which the grammarian records be real, such as he sees in language, not such as exist in other languages, and which he imagines must also exist in English."[5]

Thomas Lounsbury

One of the most distinguished American scholars who first recognized the chasm between educated usage and the prescriptions of amateur philologians and school grammarians was Thomas Lounsbury (1838–1915). In 1859 Lounsbury graduated from Yale, the original home of scientific linguistics in America, where he was influenced by William Dwight Whitney. After the Civil War, Lounsbury became professor of English in Yale's Sheffield Scientific School, whose department of modern languages Whitney had organized; and for some time Whitney and his protégé constituted the major faculty for Yale's philology program. In 1879, Lounsbury's excellent *History of the English Language* appeared. Revised several times over the next thirty years, it was widely studied by students of English in American colleges and universities.

For his later book, *The Standard of Usage in English* (1908), comprising articles previously published in *Harper's Magazine,* Lounsbury's mastery of the history of English supplied him abundant examples and saved him from those dogmatic condemnations and assertions that actual usage subsequently makes foolish. Following "all the great authorities who from remotest antiquity have treated this subject," his essays had "for their common aim the maintenance of the doctrine that the best, and indeed the only proper, usage is the usage of the best, and that any rules or injunctions not based upon the practice of the best speakers and writers neither require nor deserve attention, no matter how loudly they are proclaimed or how generally taught."[6]

Lounsbury recognized that the chief faults of grammarians since the mid-eighteenth century had been unfamiliarity with the practice of the best writers and ignorance of the development of the language. He was less anxious about the freedom allowed to the man in the street than about the peril stemming from the authority exercised by "amateur champions of propriety," whom he found "ensconced at every fireside." Their rules, he said, based on what they think usage ought to be, generate a "fictitious standard" of correctness, whereas the legitimate standard is actual usage. Appeals to reason, etymology, or "universal grammar" are irrelevant. Typically light in its handling was his analysis of the word *manoeuvre,* which "in all its existing senses . . . refers to actions which are the result of the operations of the mind," but which etymologically refers only to work with the hand. As though that were insufficient to reveal "the worthlessness of relying upon derivation as a final authority for present meaning," he off-handedly mentions that "*manoeuvre* and *manure* are precisely the same word, so far as their origin is concerned" (p. 154).

Like the mature Dr. Johnson, Lounsbury expressed contempt for the futile hope of fixing the language: "in order to have a language become fixed, it is first necessary that those who speak it should become dead . . ." (p. 71)! Because language changes, the best usage of a past generation may cease to be acceptable. Hence, the sole authoritative standard of propriety is present good usage.

Unlike most grammarians before him, Lounsbury attempted to delimit *whose* usage set the standard. He agreed with Horace that usage is the deciding authority and judged that he meant the usage of the best speakers and writers. He saw Horace's *usus* as "precisely the same as Quintilian's *consensus eruditorum*—the agreement of the cultivated" (p. 89). His interpretation of the classical authors led Lounsbury to define good usage as that of the "intellectually good," the "cultivated."

> Such men are the absolute dictators of language. They are lawgivers whose edicts it is the duty of the grammarian to record. What they agree upon is correct; what they shun it is expedient to shun, even if not wrong in itself to employ. Words coined by those outside of the class to which these men belong do not pass into the language as a constituent part of it until sanctioned by their approbation and use. Their authority, both as regards the reception or rejection of locutions of any sort, is final. It hardly needs to be said that "the man in the street" is not only no dictator of usage, but that he has no direct influence upon the preservation of the life of any word or phrase. This depends entirely upon its adoption by great writers. If these fail to accept a new locution, it is certain to die eventually and as a general rule very speedily. (p. 97)

The way to knowledge of good usage is "by associating in life with the best speakers or in literature with the best writers." As to deciding on the best speakers and writers, however, Lounsbury failed to provide an explicit solution. Perhaps for him the answer was obvious; or perhaps he felt as Paul Roberts claimed to teach, fifty years later—that correct English is the English used by himself and his friends.[7]

If we compare Lounsbury's "good" usage with Campbell's "reputable," his position is not as refined as the Scottish rhetorician's; Campbell defined standard as present, reputable, and national, whereas Lounsbury played down the value of national usage. More significantly, he emphasized the written word more than his predecessors did. As George Krapp noted when he reviewed *The Standard of Usage,* the chief difficulty with Lounsbury's ideas lay in his insistence on calling only literary usage standard. Krapp objected to "the imposing of this authority of literary speech upon the actual, living, creating processes of present speech. It puts the cart before the horse." He feared that the authority of great authors would prove stifling and noted that such a standard has never governed "the really creative minds in the use of English speech."

Lounsbury's literary standard also failed to recognize that various kinds of English could be correct, depending on circumstances; it wrongly made cultivated written usage the measure of correctness for all varieties and seemed to suggest that spoken use derives from written. "Authority there must surely be somewhere," he said. "Did it not exist, there would be a reign of license in which each man, no matter how incompetent, would be a law unto himself. . . . If the best speakers and writers are not guides, to what quarter can we repair in cases of doubt or difficulty?" (p. 91).

Brander Matthews

Brander Matthews (1852-1929), though influenced by Lounsbury's view of linguistic propriety, eventually provided a radically different answer to the question of standards. Columbia graduated Matthews in 1871 and later awarded him a law degree. For two decades dozens of his articles appeared in *Galaxy, Nation, Critic, Saturday Review of Literature,* and elsewhere. Many addressed drama, his first love, but others revealed his keen interest in standards of correctness and in spelling reform. As president of the Modern Language Association, chairman of the Simplified Spelling Board, member of the American Academy of Arts and Letters, and professor of English at Columbia, Matthews played a key role in scholarly discussion of linguistic correctness in his day, while his magazine pieces broadcast his notions more widely.

The linguistic essays, collected in *Parts of Speech* (1901) and *Essays on*

English (1921), indicate that Matthews⸱ was not free of idiosyncratic biases. Despite a personal preference for using new, usually shorter, spellings like *tho, altho, thoro, thoroly, fonetic,* and *thruout,* he found certain clipped forms like *pants* and *gents* abhorrent and detested back-formations like the verb *enthuse;* it struck him as "vulgar and uncouth, bearing the bend sinister of offensive illegitimacy."[8]

But Matthews also expressed uncommon linguistic tolerance. Personal distaste for a usage did not prompt him to condemn it in others: "When we have once possessed ourselves of the inexorable fact that it is not in our power to warp the development of our language by any conscious effort, we can listen with amused toleration to the excited outcries of those who are constantly protesting against this or that word or phrase or usage which may seem to them new and therefore unjustifiable."[9] Following Dr. Johnson, he too knew that "to 'fix' a living language . . . is an idle dream" and that *purity* was a "chameleon word," changing meaning with its surroundings. Before the American Academy of Arts and Letters, he defended the state of the language, vigorously disputing charges that it was becoming debased and degenerate. Echoing Lounsbury, he said that the history of any language is a history of corruption and that growth and improvement presuppose change. To preserve "the purity and beauty of the English language" and to foster a suitably high respect for its simplicity and complexity, he urged the Academy to "aid in arousing a livelier interest [in it] and to help in the dissemination of sounder knowledge."[10]

Putting aside the written standard urged by Lounsbury, Matthews looked to speech as a standard of correctness. Listen to the drama critic: "The real language of a people is the spoken word, not the written. Language lives on the tongue and in the ear; there it was born, and there it grows"; English "belongs to the peoples who speak it"; it is "their own precious possession, to deal with at their pleasure and at their peril" (*Speech,* p. 71 and Prefatory Note). Theater was his love, while Lounsbury's was written history.

Matthews was glad the language was not entrusted to the care of even "the most competent scholars." He feared that "In the hands of no class would it be enfeebled sooner than if it were given to the guardianship of the pedants and the pedagogs." He found most popular books on grammatical usage "grotesque in their ignorance," even the best of them assuming that English, like Latin, is dead and permanently fixed. The only valid function he allowed writers of guidebooks and grammars was to record usage and "discover the principles which may underlie the incessant development of our common speech" (*Speech,* pp. 212, 221, 220).

He believed that "In language, as in politics, the people at large are in the long run better judges of their own needs than any specialist can be" (*Speech,* p. 212). Questioning the efficacy of an academy, he said language is "governed not by elected representatives but by a direct democracy, by the people as a whole assembled in town-meeting." By a simple show of hands is "the irrevocable decision of the community . . . rendered." "The only tribunal whose judgment is final" in the matter of correct usage is "the next generation" (*Essays,* pp. 9, 28).

Brander Matthews thus provided the most democratic response to the question of *whose usage* determines linguistic correctness. For him language and politics go hand in hand; it is a simple matter of majority rule. His view of usage, then, is the most extreme in the authoritative place it assigns to the ordinary use of English by ordinary users.

Despite the fact that both Lounsbury and Matthews placed usage in the position of supreme arbiter of linguistic correctness, their views represent opposite extremes in interpretation of "usage." We see in Lounsbury the classical, perhaps aristocratic, conviction that the usage of the best authors sets the standard, whereas in Matthews a fully democratic view prevails. Leaving aside some important political and social questions involved here, we may make two criticisms. First, insofar as the determination of the "most cultivated" writers is a subjective matter, Lounsbury's standard necessitates using personal preference, something he disallowed in principle. Matthews, on the other hand, overlooked the fact that the majority does not necessarily trust in the correctness of its *own* language use, even—or perhaps especially—in a democracy.

The essays of Matthews and Lounsbury shared the informality and popularity of the less learned discussions of the amateur philologians. But in addition they had scholarly content and appeal that set the stage for concerted academic interest in defining standard English, partly by elucidating the history of language standards. It was perhaps inevitable that other scholarly attitudes that would emerge in the twentieth century would be neither as democratically indiscriminate nor as aristocratically selective as those we have just examined.

J. Lesslie Hall

The work of John Lesslie Hall (1856–1928), another advocate of literary usage as standard, was most directly akin to the program Lounsbury had suggested. Prompted by Lounsbury's *Standard of Usage* and read by him in manuscript, Hall's *English Usage* (1917) was the product of a determination "to search the literature and see how far some of the disputed words and phrases" had been employed by "reputable authors." Initiating a claim that some linguists still maintain, Hall felt that "purists" were putting teachers, students, and the general public in "straight jackets" (p. 5). In revolt against the "distinguished grammarians and eminent rhetorical scholars" who condemned locutions frequently used by "eminent writers" and "attractive speakers," Hall gathered from 75,000 pages of English and American literature instances of about 125 usages "condemned more or less vehemently by purists, pedants, verbalists, grammarians, and professors of rhetoric." He devoted a chapter each to such things as the difference between *continually* and *constantly,* whether *athletics* is singular or plural, and *dove* versus *dived.* It was not his intention to recommend particular locutions but only to point out "the authorities *pro* and *con* . . . and leave the reader to draw his own conclusions."

Hall's approach had two virtues. It recorded actual usage, and it limited its discussion solely to that record. But in implementing the literary standard Lounsbury had advocated, it did not avoid difficulties that George Krapp had warned about—and would elaborate. In the tradition of the absolutists, though on the liberal side of the fence, Hall paid insufficient attention to a locution's *appropriateness.* After determining whether a usage had been employed by respected authors, his judgments implied a simple-minded dichotomy. If he could document a locution's use by reputable authors, it was good; otherwise not. Hall missed a crucial distinction—noted and articulated earlier by a contemporary, namely Krapp—between *standard* usage and *good* usage. Consequently, his handbook—more tolerant than any till then—was as misleading as any. Traditionalists like Richard Grant White, who judged certain usages wrong no matter how they were employed or by whom, were in some ways no farther afield than Hall, who implied that a locution's use by reputable authors made it acceptable English in any circumstances. Hall's seemingly liberal view flew in the face of some contemporary insights.

George Philip Krapp

In 1909, a year after reviewing Lounsbury's book, George Krapp (1872–1934) published *Modern English,* the first major work of his own distinguished career. He had earned a doctorate from the young Johns Hopkins University, which gave full academic recognition to modern languages and stimulated original research by stressing scientific investigation with special emphasis on observation.[11] After teaching at

Columbia University from 1897 until 1907, he spent two years at the University of Cincinnati, then rejoined Matthews at Columbia and remained in New York until the end of his career. Perhaps the greatest contribution Brander Matthews made to the usage movement was his influence on the astute and very learned George Philip Krapp.

Modern English, dedicated to Matthews, articulated the first cogent view of the *relativity* of correctness. In it Krapp delineated an elementary exposition of levels and functional varieties of English, recognizing among the "kinds of English" popular, colloquial, and formal or literary. He also explained that several "manners" of formal English exist, e.g., pulpit speaking and public lecturing. Though Krapp later refined his view, *Modern English* can be credited with instigating a systematic understanding of the varieties of English.

Spoken language was of the greatest importance for Krapp, and he thought it "a false standard of values to assume that the test of highest excellence is to be found only in printed and written words."[12] He claimed with Matthews that "the real guide to good grammar, to good English in all respects, is to be found in the living speech" from which literary language derives its vitality. Citing Walt Whitman, he said that language "is something arising out of the work, needs, ties, joys, affections, tastes, of long generations of humanity, and has its bases broad and low, close to the ground. Its final decisions are made by the masses, people nearest the concrete, having most to do with actual land and sea" (*Modern English,* pp. 328–329).

Like many grammarians before him, Krapp saw that "the laws of language are not based on theory, but arise from actual use" and that, therefore, "the grammarian has no more power of legislating in the rules of grammar than the scientist has in the physical laws of nature" (*Modern English,* pp. 158–159, 322). But he also recognized and articulated the real problem of settling on a standard: it lay, he said, not in deciding between popular, illiterate speech and educated, cultivated speech but "in determining just who are the cultivated and refined speakers whom we are willing to regard as affording the model or laws of the correct or standard speech" (*Modern English,* pp. 159–160). Thus Krapp again addressed the central issue for a doctrine of usage: *Whose* usage is standard?

Krapp identified *good* English as English that "hits the mark," and he distinguished it sharply from *standard,* or conventional, English. Laying heavy stress on *appropriateness* and *effectiveness* as the measures of good English, he made a case against the very notion of an absolute or uniform standard.

The only way in which language grows, the only way in which it could have grown in the past, is by the creation of individuals, who thus established a trend or tendency or law of the language. . . . It follows, therefore, unless we suppose that language has reached its ultimate degree of expressiveness, that all future progress in language depends upon individual initiative. The conception of society in which there is no differentiation of individual from individual, but an absolute regularity of impulse and achievement, a complacent acquiescence in a codified and established system of human activity, whether possible as an actuality or not, cannot arouse much enthusiasm as an ideal. . . . Divergences and irregularity, provincialisms, localisms, and even vulgarisms . . . would be virtues, if they were the expressions of real characteristics, the sincere expression of people who lived their lives in such surroundings and conditions as nature had placed them.[13]

The "chief province of education in language," Krapp said, was in helping a speaker or writer "realize what the expressive value of his speech is to the public . . . he is addressing [and] what the general social trend or tendency is." "The best language is that . . . which functions to its environment," and whatever makes language "less effective is wrong." Summing up his views, he wrote: "The true road towards community sympathy, towards community efficiency, in language as in all other social institutions, is through the recognition of the value, of the right, even of the duty, of individual variation based on the principle of truth to individual character and environment" (*Authority*, pp. 23, 26).

In other words, Krapp saw that *standard* or conventional English is not necessarily *good* English. Standard English is "customary use raised to the position of conscious legalized use." But the most favorable set of circumstances for a vital and effective language involves the interplay between the forces of standardization and the force of inventiveness: "standard English must continually refresh itself by accepting the creations of good English. . . . If the standardizing tendency were carried to its fullest extent, it would result in a complete fixity of language" (*Modern English*, p. 333). Complementing the standardizing tendency is the ideal of English that hits its mark. "Poets and prose writers, lively imaginations of all kinds, in speech as in literature, are continually widening the bounds of the conventional and standard language by adding to it something that was not there before. They must do so if speech is ever to rise above the dead level of the commonplace" (*Modern English*, pp. 333–334). Consequently Krapp urged Americans to recognize "the lesson of the complete relativity of the value of language, that there is no such thing as an absolute English, but that language is valuable only as it effects the purposes one wishes to attain, that what is good at one time may be bad at another, and what is bad at one time may be good at another" (*Modern English,* p. 330). For him it was a "purely utilitarian and practical" matter to determine good English: "The purpose of language being the satisfactory communication of thought and feeling, that is good English which performs this function satisfactorily." Thus, good English is defined "without reference to any theoretical and abstract conceptions of its value or significance" (*Modern English,* p. 326).

In Krapp's early books, then—*Modern English* (1909) and *The Authority of Law in Language* (1908)—he attempted to define levels of usage and sketched the contours of what we can call a doctrine of appropriate usage. Later he contributed three additional studies in which he laid out a program for pursuing American speechways and filling in the outline of "appropriateness."

In his scholarly two-volume history of *The English Language in America* (1925), Krapp argued that "speech is standard when it passes current in actual usage among persons who must be accounted as among the conservers and representatives of the approved social traditions of a community" (II, p. 7). It is noteworthy that he placed the emphasis on the *users* rather than the *forms* of language, and that the standard users are defined conservatively. Democratic leveling, as per Matthews, is not in the picture.

A description of the language of socially acceptable Americans by definition codifies socially acceptable American English; for socially acceptable persons speak in socially acceptable ways. To determine acceptable American English, therefore, one need only record the usages of socially acceptable Americans. To do otherwise, namely to define socially acceptable people by their use of certain predetermined language forms and then produce a grammar of standard English based on the usage of a group so defined, is circular and begs the question. As we have noted, Krapp acknowledged in 1909 the great difficulty of determining "just who are the cultivated and refined speakers."

More important than his *English Language in America* for their contribution to the usage movement are Krapp's *Knowledge of English* (1927) and *Comprehensive Guide to Good English* (1927). In them, too, he stressed appropriateness as the first requirement but added speaker comfort as the second: "To be good, English must not only meet the practical demands of utility, it must also satisfy the inner sense of goodness of the speaker or writer," who needs "the assurance that he has honorably exercised his privileges and his obligations as a free citizen in the commonwealth of the English language."[14] Insisting that "the only sound test of the goodness of a linguistic action is to be found within the action itself" (*Knowledge,* p. 5), he nevertheless denied that the "seat of authority" rests solely with "the individual impulse" (*Knowledge,* p. 182). Krapp was fully cognizant that for reasons of "self-defense, every person is compelled to take account of the social demands and penalties" involved in the use of language (*Knowledge,* pp. 175–176).

The major theme of Krapp's program was that mature students should observe for themselves how language can best be used. His *Comprehensive Guide* is a reference book, arranged like a dictionary, that discusses points of usage he considered debatable in terms of "many different aspects of the life and practice of the English language." He used various labels (including *literary, local, dialect, colloquial, low colloquial, vulgar,* and *ungrammatical*) and many additional adjectives (e.g., *careful, crude, incorrect, offensive, proper, feminine*) to classify and describe usages. But his primary purpose in the *Guide* was "to encourage direct observation of the varied possibilities of English speech as it appears in living use, spoken and written, and, as a consequence of such observation, to enable readers to make for themselves independent and sensible judgments in the practical use of the English language" (p. ix.).

This call to train people to observe for themselves how language functions came to be a rallying cry of leaders in the English teaching profession during the second quarter of the century, though it was not much favored by an insecure rank and file. Professional language guardians were predictably critical.

During the fifty years preceding the founding of the Linguistic Society of America in 1924, dozens of works by respected American linguists and historians of English appeared. Scholars of other nations also published the results of their influential research into the history and structure of English.

The outstanding linguistic event of the last quarter of the nineteenth century in the English-speaking world was the publication of the first volumes of the *Oxford English Dictionary,* known initially as *A New English Dictionary on Historical Principles.* Under the auspices of the Philological Society of London and the editorship of Sir James Murray, the *OED* began appearing in 1884 and directed attention to the history of words and their past usage. Completed in 1928, under Sir William Craigie, it furnished scholars with a still unsurpassed wealth of reference to the literature of every age in which an English usage had occurred. As Krapp said of it, it held a mirror up to nature!

In the first quarter of the twentieth century general linguistic works, especially those by the Americans Bloomfield, Sapir, and Sturtevant, gave scientific linguistics a good foundation in this country.[15] Not directly concerned with the correctness controversy, they nevertheless provided a framework for discussion among linguists. Though they merely alluded to a basis for standards of correctness, all implicitly affirmed the principles of a doctrine of usage: that linguistic change is natural, speech primary, meaning conventional, grammar dependent on usage, and linguistic correctness relative. While the works of these linguists directly influenced only a few English teachers, they helped kindle wholesale re-evaluation of programs among leaders of the English teaching profession.

For linguists the debate over standards of correctness seemed won, and one sanguine scholar expressed genuine unconcern about the forces of "purism." George McKnight, writing in *English Words and Their Background* (1923), pointed to the "gradual yielding of purism before the tide of prevailing usage," and against the position of one celebrated purist he opposed the combined convictions of "the most influential students of language of the present day." Naively convinced of the inevitable acceptance of the doctrine of usage, McKnight felt no need to defend it from the purists and off-handedly remarked that "in the formation of the language felicitous results have frequently been reached by processes which might be called 'muddling through' " (pp. 410–411, 191). (Nonchalant acceptance of such views had flavored the reception of Krapp's *Modern English* in some quarters as early as 1909. William A. Read, for example, had found Krapp's emphases on the principles of usage almost "tiresome" except that they were so well expressed.)

By 1925, the greatest dictionary ever produced in any language was nearing completion for English; professors of education and a few well-known language scholars had condemned the doctrine of correctness and had taken the initial steps toward implementing a relativistic view in the schools; some very influential linguistic treatises had appeared; and the professional organizations that were to do most to foster the relativity of correctness had been founded. A few professors of English, notably Lounsbury, Matthews, and Krapp, had written eloquently of the need to base grammar on usage, though they disagreed about the relative authority of written and spoken varieties. Matthews had voiced the negative implications of a doctrine of correctness for a democratic society. Following his lead, Krapp had explored usage levels and functional varieties, recognizing their relevance in a pluralistic democracy; and he distinguished "good" English from "standard" English.

Still, during the final quarter of the last century and first quarter of this one, while preparation for implementing a relativistic doctrine of usage was under way, little effect in school books or schools was noticeable. Teachers continued drilling the prescriptions of Lowth, Murray, and White, and the error-hunting syndrome of American school grammars flourished. The gap between the views of the linguists and the traditional grammarians had never been wider. There was need for intermediaries to apply to school grammars the approach that the linguists were developing. And, with the founding of the National Council of Teachers of English in 1911, the task fell to its leaders.

NCTE USAGE STUDIES

In this section we will examine early NCTE history and analyze the various documents that gave spirit to the linguistic content of the 1952 publication called *The English Language Arts,* which represents the NCTE view of language study as it evolved over the first half of the century.

In 1911 the National Education Association's English Round Table requested the Committee on College-Entrance Requirements to institute a national society of English teachers. A group of English instructors met in Chicago in December, and some sixty-five delegates founded the National Council of Teachers of English. Fred Newton Scott of the University of Michigan was elected president and James Fleming Hosic of Chicago Teachers College became secretary. The objective of the new organization was "to increase the effectiveness of school and college work in English," and one step taken to implement this goal was the establishment of *The English Journal,* an official NCTE organ. From the outset editor Hosic aimed to be "progressive," articulating his policy in the first volume: "We do not wish to root out, tear up, and overthrow, but we are eager to move steadily forward. The *Journal* does not worship at the shrine of tradition; it does not prize school practices merely because they are old. Social conditions change, and schools must change with them."[16]

Indeed, at the turn of the century social conditions were altering American schools. In 1890 only 68.9 percent of the five-to-seventeen-year-old population was enrolled in school; this figure grew to over 81 percent by 1922. Between 1890 and 1930 the number of students graduating from college increased by 800 percent, graduates from high school by 1500 percent.[17] Such dramatic growth in secondary schools and colleges brought about significant adjustment in the average social standing of students and a distinct shift of goals. The function of high schools became diluted as streams of non-college-bound students poured in. Teachers could no longer assume their students came from homes where standard English was spoken.

The Council's founding members were aware of these changing social patterns. The secretary commented thus on the tone of the organizational meeting: "The emphasis so strongly placed upon the necessity of adapting the work of the school to the needs and capacity of the student is significant. It means that practical and cultural, and not merely academic, ideals are to control . . . ."[18] The progressive concerns of the Council leadership and their awareness of school realities and social conditions so caught the attention of teachers that within a year NCTE membership grew to about 750, with an additional 10,000 teachers in fifty affiliated organizations. Before the 1929 Depression *The English Journal* was the most widely circulated periodical in the field of secondary education.[19]

Wilbur Hatfield, Council secretary for over thirty years, raised provocative and important questions in the *Journal's* pages. "Do we not too often assume that certain phases of literacy—spelling, grammatical correctness, and even sentence-sense—are the necessary equipment for a useful life? Ought we not, rather, to survey the uses the citizen actually makes of spoken and written language and then to teach our youngsters the commoner types of speaking and writing?" He pointed out that such reasoning "led the National Council to invest thousands of dollars in an investigation of *The Place of English in American Life,*" and he hoped a perusal of it would lead every English teacher "a long day's journey toward the genuine socialization of school composition."[20] This emphasis on the social functions of language characterizes much discussion in Council circles both in the early years and recently.

Judging from the *Journal,* the primary concerns of early NCTE members were spelling reform, uniform grammatical terminology, and college-entrance requirements. Little dissatisfaction with the pronouncements on usage in grammar textbooks appears for the first few years after 1911.[21] As one member put it, "the rules of English composition are quite as easily explained, and consequently imitated, as are the rules of mathematics," and hence there was no excuse for teachers to treat errors in student compositions in a coddling manner.[22] Still, at a national meeting only five years after the Council's founding, Fred Newton Scott questioned the logic of current standards of correctness, concluding that teachers and texts were unreasonably strict in judging supposed errors of grammar.[23]

Convinced by the work of historical linguists that a fixed standard is untenable in theory and practice, Scott maintained that "If any considerable body of educated Americans in any part of the country is using seriously a peculiar form of English for transacting the business of life, that form of English is good American and has a chance of becoming our national speech" (p. 6). That no universally recognized standard of pronunciation prevailed in America did not make him (or most Americans) uneasy, and he felt no compulsion to settle other questions of divided usage. Taking the relativity of linguistic correctness for granted, he insisted that the implementation of a doctrine of usage would instigate neither chaos nor anarchy. He repeated the ritual reminders that "the laws of good English are after all only the observed uniformities in the serious speech of large bodies of intelligent and cultured users of the language" (p. 6) and that the purpose of dictionaries and grammars is solely to record such uniformities.

After Scott's paper appeared in the *Journal,* kindred articles cropped up. In "The Improvement of American Speech" (1918), George Krapp pointed to the discrepancy between actual usage and textbook rules. Sterling Leonard's "Old Purist Junk" (1918) sneeringly condemned the "purist dementia" of some textbooks and suggested that

> . . . for a very considerable part of the actual difficulties and regrettable ill successes of our English teaching—I know at least that it is true of my own—the blind leading of purists is responsible.
>
> If this is indeed true, the remedy is surprisingly simple. It is merely to make no alteration whatever in the conventional details of children's expression—grammatical forms, idiomatic phrasing, or choice and pronunciation of words—except in complete certainty, based on real authority and not on an uninformed and arbitrary dictum in some handbook, that the emendation is both true to present usage *and also essential.* (pp. 296-297)

Leonard cited a good many usages condemned in current textbooks but reputably illustrated in the *OED.* He and Krapp urged investigation of American speech habits to determine actual practice. In 1924 the *Journal* published a statistical survey of current pronunciation, and other statistical studies followed. The next year Charles Fries asked "What Is Good English?" (1925) and in his answer stressed usage as the foundation.

In 1927 Leonard and a colleague published preliminary results of probably the first study of *attitudes* toward certain usages prominent in textbook discussion. Allowing that "The place and value of intelligent purism are by no means to be questioned," they submitted that their study and that of citation dictionaries like the *OED* would define purists—in a "correct light"—as *reformers:*

> Instead of being announcers of what really is good usage, as they assume, purists are actually proponents of reform in language. If one is convinced that the expressions accepted as "cultivated informal" usage should not be so accepted, one must adopt the position of the reformed speller or the advocate of any other rectification of conduct, and should make one's appeal on that ground, not by promulgating as facts unsound statements of what usage is.[24]

Subsequently Leonard, then a past president of the Council, published a history of the beginnings of the doctrine of correctness, a subject suggested for his doctoral dissertation at Columbia by Professor Krapp.[25] He tried to demonstrate that twentieth-century school grammar was rooted in the rationalism of the eighteenth century, with its insistence on order, logic, and consistency. He showed that the early grammars were too reliant on Latin and not sufficiently attentive to contemporary English.[26]

By about 1930 so much had been done to spread the gospel of usage that a more flexible approach to correctness and more reliance on actual usage characterized the view of Council leaders and the articles in *The English Journal*. Between 1911 and 1930, a Council historian records, "the NCTE attitude toward language was one of an open-minded willingness to listen to all viewpoints, to undertake investigations when called for, and to make recommendations based upon their findings."[27]

In 1929 an NCTE committee recommended as part of normal teacher-training programs in English the study of grammar and phonetics from a linguistic point of view. This should not suggest that great changes occurred in textbooks or in teacher education. Little was done for or by classroom teachers to align prescriptions with actual language practice. While the Council provided an atmosphere of open inquiry and a platform from which to urge and implement change, the activities of the leadership bore fruit chiefly among a few college instructors; the great majority of elementary and secondary school teachers continued propagating rigid grammatical prescriptions.

Sterling Leonard: Current English Usage

Between 1931 and 1940 three very significant usage studies appeared under the auspices of the Council, all written by its past or future presidents.[28] *Current English Usage* (1932), the first of them, was begun by Sterling Leonard (1888-1931) and completed by colleagues after his untimely death. It fell into two parts, one on punctuation and one on grammar. Attention here will be limited to the controversial grammar section.

Leonard sent a ballot of 102 debated usage items to seven juries: linguistic experts (Krapp, Jespersen, Sapir, William Ellery Leonard, and a score of others); leading businessmen; authors (Churchill, Leacock, Lindsay, Bennett, Wells—22 in all); editors of influential publications; NCTE members; MLA members; and teachers of speech. In all, 229 ballots were returned. The largest number of responses came from MLA and NCTE members with about 50 each; there were a score from businessmen and almost two dozen from authors. A second ballot of 130 additional items was submitted to two of the groups, and 17 linguists and 32 NCTE members replied. On both ballots judges were asked to rate "according to your observation of what is actual usage rather than your opinion of what usage should be." Of the four categories described, three are of interest to us: (1) literary, or formally correct, English; (2) standard, cultivated colloquial English ("fully acceptable English for informal conversation, correspondence, and all other writings of well-bred ease; not wholly appropriate for occasions of literary dignity"); and (3) naive, popular, uncultivated English ("popular or illiterate speech, not used by persons who wish to pass as cultivated, save to represent uneducated speech, or to be jocose; here taken to include slang or argot, and dialect forms not admissible to the standard or cultivated area; usually called 'vulgar English,' but with no implication necessarily of the current meaning of vulgar"). (The fourth category of commercial, foreign, scientific, or other technical uses did not figure significantly in the evaluations of the judges.)

In the analysis of responses Leonard regarded the first two categories as "allowable for use by educated people, whether formally or colloquially." Items in category 3 he deemed unacceptable. As an indication of their "probable usage status" he labeled items *established* if at least 75 percent of the judges approved them (i.e., rated them 1 or 2), *illiterate* if approved by fewer than 25 percent, *disputable* if approved by at least 25 percent but fewer than 75 percent of the judges.

Leonard found the following usages, among others, judged *illiterate:*

The *data is* often inaccurate.
John *had awoken* much earlier than usual.

Though disapproved generally in contemporary texts, he found these *established* in good usage:

It says in the book that . . . .
None of them *are* here.
Everyone was here, but *they* all went home early.
It is *me.*
Invite *whoever* you like to the party.
Who are you looking for?
That's a dangerous curve; you'd better go *slow.*

The judges disagreed sufficiently about some items that Leonard classed them *disputable;* for example:

Everybody bought *their* own ticket.
He *dove* off the pier.
It *don't* make any difference what you think.
Martha *don't* sew as well as she used to.

As expected, Leonard's opinion survey documented a conservative bent in contemporary texts. Many items condemned in the books were judged to be in acceptable use by distinguished speakers of English, and educated opinion about others was far from unanimous. In teaching about the disputable items, "dogmatism is unjustified," said Leonard; and "no class time should henceforth be wasted in an effort to eradicate any construction here listed as established—no matter what the personal preference of the instructor or the dictum of the adopted text." He felt his analysis reconfirmed that educated speech habits do change and that grammar books must keep pace.

Despite the relative modesty of the results, despite the NCTE's publishing it with commendation and with a foreword by a past president, *Current English Usage* received an unfavorable press.[29] Members of the Council had been prepared by articles in the *Journal,* but the educated public at large found the study "extreme and in complete violation of the cherished stereotype of the English teacher."[30] Surprisingly, one reviewer thought it "not so revolutionary as its compilers appear to think it—unless one is to go further than the judges and approve and adopt usages which are here left disputable."[31] Krapp objected that insofar as it represented "an appeal to authority to find a ground for decision, . . . it does not differ from previous discussions of usage." He claimed that "There is . . . no other way to answer questions of usage than that of practice and authority, the important point being the character of the authority one calls in for aid."[32] At least there could be no question about Leonard's authorities; his study was authoritative, and the pages of *The English Journal* reflected its impact. *Current English Usage* prompted a rash of articles urging teachers to become more liberal in the classroom. One observer felt this impetus "ended the age of certainty for the teacher and ushered in the age of anxiety."[33]

Apprehension sparked by the survey was fanned to anxiety by overinterpreting the results, for Leonard (or the colleagues who completed the work) deduced more from the survey than the data warranted. Given his impressive list of judges, readers were misled by not questioning how validly Leonard's results followed from his evidence. Thus, he speaks of his judges as approving or disapproving the debated items. Of "*Yourself* and your guests are invited," for example, he writes: "This expression is approved by a majority of the linguists, disapproved by a majority of the English teachers"; of *"Everyone* was here, but *they* all went home early": "138 out of about 200 judges approve this as colloquial usage . . . ." In short, he analyzed the returns as if they represented the judges' personal opinions of the items, whereas they had been explicitly directed *not* to judge personally.[34]

After one reviewer suggested the judges be asked whether they thought the ballots had been misused, a linguist so polled replied that the criticisms were "theoretically sound" but did not "essentially invalidate the practical effect" of the study.[35] He felt that, while Leonard should not have referred to the judges as approving or disapproving, he was nevertheless not far wrong in assuming that their evaluations did represent at least implicit judgments rather than observations. In light of the linguist's response, the following appraisal, which was not a solitary one, may be fair: "Usually it is the purist who pushes his virtues so far that they become vices. In this instance the virtue of tolerance is in danger of being carried so far that it leads to the vice of slovenliness."[36]

To suppose that some of Leonard's observers acted instead as judges is doubtless correct. The directions were broad enough to elicit personal evaluations, and Leonard might have anticipated confusion no matter what the instructions. A more helpful survey could have been produced if the referees had been expressly directed to judge the items personally. Then, at least, teachers would have possessed a unique report on the favor or disfavor in which items of dubious stature were regarded by respected users of English around 1930.

Marckwardt & Walcott: Facts About Current English Usage

Not until long after its appearance did discussion of *Current English Usage* subside. By late 1937 both Fred Walcott and Albert Marckwardt had analyzed it at NCTE meetings. Reflecting upon an earlier publication of Leonard's, they concluded that he had intended ultimately to compare his survey of opinion with actual recorded usage. So Marckwardt and Walcott proposed to do just that, by surveying the recorded usage of Leonard's items, chiefly in the *OED*. At the suggestion of NCTE president Holland Roberts, the two of them collaborated on a unified study that the Council published as *Facts About Current English Usage* (1938).

Facts took issue with the methods and implications of Leonard's study. In particular, it focused on Leonard's 121 "disputable" items. Marckwardt and Walcott pointed out that *disputable* could not represent a level of usage. A locution could be established, popular, regional, or upper or lower class; but only opinion could be disputable. They did not quarrel with Leonard's use of the term but questioned its value for classroom teachers faced with the task of correcting themes. After checking usages of each item as recorded in the *OED* and elsewhere,[37] they recast all of Leonard's items into six usage categories: *literary, American literary, colloquial, American colloquial, dialect,* and *archaic.*

They found 50 of Leonard's 121 "disputable" items recorded in *literary* English; for example:

A treaty was concluded *between the four* powers.
One rarely likes to do as *he* is told.
Neither of your reasons *are* really valid.
The British look at this *differently than* we do.
She *sung* very well.

An additional 43 were found in good *colloquial* usage, and 13 more in *American literary* English. While no attempt could be made to assess the frequency of such usages, *Facts* reported the status labels assigned by the dictionaries and listed several of the authors cited. That 106 of Leonard's 121 "disputable" items occurred in standard literary or colloquial use, as Marckwardt and Walcott interpreted the published citations, demonstrated "how much more conservative a survey of opinion about language is apt to be than the facts of language actually warrant" (pp. 50–51).

More strikingly, they discovered 5 of Leonard's 38 "illiterate" items in *literary* or *American literary* usage:

John *had awoken* much earlier than usual.
A woman *whom* I know *was* my friend spoke next.
I enjoy wandering *among* a library.
They *swang* their partners in the reel.
Both leaves of the drawbridge *raise* at once. (American)

Another 8 were in standard *colloquial* usage; for example:

A light *complected* girl passed.
I want *for you to come* at once.

And 20 were in *dialect* or *archaic* use. A mere 5 were not recorded in the sources at all. In other words, 13 of Leonard's 38 "illiterate" items were recorded in literary or current standard practice as defined by Marckwardt and Walcott. They concluded that, contrary to Leonard's supposition, recorded usage in dictionaries outpaces educated opinion on it.

Marckwardt and Walcott were making the same point as Leonard—

textbooks are too conservative in matters of usage—but they made it more strongly and supported it with facts, not opinions, about usage. Some critics had no questions about the methodology of *Facts* or the importance of its findings and reviewed it favorably.[38] But several questioned the insubstantial support offered for certain assertions, citing, for example, the reclassification of "I *can't help but* eat it" from "disputable" to *literary* English as based on insufficient evidence.[39] Actually, the only evidence is that the *OED* records its occurrence once in 1894. Since Marckwardt and Walcott classified as *literary* any expression cited at least once from the nineteenth century without a limiting label, *can't help but* satisfied their criteria. But they were unrealistic to hope that teachers and critics would modify their evaluation on the basis of such evidence. Trained to eschew an expression, teachers might appreciate documentation of its use by masters, but they could sometimes justifiably ignore such flimsy demonstration of its "literary" character as *Facts* offered.

Had they wanted to, reviewers could also have discovered examples of Leonard's "illiterate" expressions reclassified as *literary* English, again on sometimes meager evidence. For "They *swang* their partners in the reel," *Facts* cited *Webster's* label (archaic past tense) and Curme's description (older literary form). It also reported that the *OED* describes the form as "rarely" used, though its use is illustrated between the years 1000 and 1912. But because a citation exists after 1800, *Facts* elevated *swang* to *literary* English, though "archaic" would certainly have been more helpful to teachers faced with the task of correcting themes.[40]

Marckwardt and Walcott explained their procedures clearly, followed them carefully, and observed strict objectivity in their application. Still, the adequacy of their criteria as guidelines for teachers is questionable. As a compilation of the recorded usage of debated items, *Facts* is useful. But its labeling of these items, especially as literary, could mislead. The teacher using it might do better judging the data anew than accepting its classifications.

Leonard's monograph and the Marckwardt-Walcott follow-up irrefutably demonstrated the conservatism not only of handbooks and school grammars but also of current, seemingly liberal, opinion. They acquainted teachers with the possibility of a fresh view of usage and prepared the way for a new kind of grammatical analysis, which was, shortly to appear.

Charles C. Fries: **American English Grammar**

In 1940 a work revolutionary in its approach and radical in its conclusions appeared under NCTE auspices with support from the Modern

Language Association and the Linguistic Society of America. It was the *American English Grammar* of Charles Carpenter Fries, a work that crowned two decades of investigation.

With a 1925 dissertation on the periphrastic future with *shall* and *will,* Fries (1887–1967) began a productive and very influential career. He was a founding member of the Linguistic Society of America and later served as president of that organization and vice-president of the Modern Language Association. As NCTE president in 1927 and an active committee member after that, and as a professor at the University of Michigan for over thirty years, he inculcated in countless teachers a scientific view of language. In a 1927 sketch of the rise of prescriptivism in the eighteenth century, he discussed standards for pronunciation, grammar, and vocabulary, insisting of course that the only standard of acceptable English of any kind is usage: "usage is the final arbiter of all the correctness there can be in English."[41] He believed that to be taught effectively, grammar must be taught inductively (1927, p. 158). Like Krapp before him, Fries urged that students be trained to observe the practice of people carrying on the affairs of the English-speaking world. Echoing the refrains of progressive education, he stressed that students need reinforcement outside the classroom and argued that such support would exist only if teaching reflected current informal usage among educated Americans. Comparing the laws of biology and physics with the rules of grammar, he proposed that if the facts of usage were "not in harmony with the rules or generalizations we have had in our grammars hitherto, then these rules must be restated and expanded to include all the facts. There can thus never be in grammar an error that is both very bad and very common. The more common it is, the nearer it comes to being the best of grammar" (1927, pp. 33–34).

Fries, like Krapp, espoused the principle of appropriate usage. But, more sensitive than his predecessors to the desirability of relative standards of linguistic correctness in a democracy, he denied flatly that only the speech of the socially acceptable was correct. Fries claimed a correctness for *all* social varieties: "One speaks correctly the dialect of the socially acceptable when he uses accurately the speech habits common to that group. . . . Likewise, one speaks the dialect of 'vulgar' English correctly when he uses accurately the speech habits of those whose language it is; he speaks 'vulgar' English incorrectly when he introduces language forms not current in that dialect" (1927, p. 133). He called for "a grammar that records the facts of the actual usage of those who are carrying on the affairs of English-speaking people and does not falsify the account in accord with a make-believe standard of 'school-mastered' speech . . ." (1927, p. 44).

To obtain a natural corpus of current English for analysis, Fries had persuaded the LSA to join with the NCTE and the MLA in seeking from the federal government portions of its correspondence with citizens; and letters written to Washington in the 1920s and earlier were made available. This was the material analyzed in *American English Grammar* (1940).

Besides its compilation of actual American usage, the importance of this research lies in its methodology, for only *after* he sorted the writers into social groupings on nonlinguistic grounds did Fries investigate their language usage. The vicious circle of defining correct English as the usage of the cultured and defining the cultured by their usage was finally broken. His study assumed that the only method to master "effective language nicely adapted in both denotation and connotation to the circumstances of the occasion and the demands of both the speaker and hearer" is "constant observation of the actual practice of the users of the language together with *a sensitiveness to the suggestions inevitably attached to words and constructions.*" Hence, it strove "to present the material so organized as to provide the tools for further observation, classification, and interpretation; to show certain tendencies and patterns . . .; to provide a method and outline for *continual* filling in on the part of . . . the student." Very significantly, it attempted to identify "the important matters of American English that . . . have distinct social class connotations." Fries stressed that "the most important facts concerning any words, forms, or constructions of language are the circumstances in which they are usually used, because these words, forms, or constructions will inevitably suggest these circumstances" (p. 24).

Scrupulous in his selection of material to be analyzed, Fries excluded all typewritten letters to help ensure that each sample was written by the signer. The place and date of birth of the writers, and also of their parents, and the history of the letter writers' schooling and employment were known. All selections—2,000 complete letters and 1,000 additional excerpts—were written by native Americans of at least three generations' standing.

Into group III, speakers of "Vulgar English," went persons who had not passed beyond eighth grade and whose occupations were strictly manual or unskilled, earning them not more than $90 per month. In selecting members of this group Fries also relied on certain "definite, formal, non-linguistic matters" such as spelling, capitalization, and end-punctuation when they clearly indicated that the writer was semi-illiterate.

At the other end of the social scale in group I, he placed speakers of "Standard English"—college graduates engaged in professions: professors, physicians, lawyers, judges, Army officers above the rank of lieutenant, and, from cities of more than 25,000 people, superintendents of schools and newspaper editors.

As speakers of "Common English," group II, he selected people who had completed between one year in high school and one year in college or technical school, neither professionals nor strictly unskilled laborers. This group included businessmen, electricians, foremen of large shops, superintendents of mills, police chiefs, undertakers, Red Cross workers, nurses, and noncommissioned Army officers of the grade of sergeant. Their letters conformed to conventional practices of capitalization and end-punctuation. While occasional misspellings of words did not exclude a writer from this group, habitual misspelling of common words did. To ensure the validity of this middle category, borderline cases were excluded. About 300 writers finally fell into each group.

Because *American English Grammar* was a big step toward an actual grammar of English, my singling out of its treatment of the kinds of questions that occupied Leonard, Marckwardt, and Walcott will of course not do it justice. Five of its eleven chapters describe the materials, the method of investigation, and the implications of the study; the other six, over 80 percent of the book, form the heart of the grammar proper, and the entire work is rich in historical detail. Fries organized his observations into three categories, in terms of word *forms, function* words, and word *order*. The findings I report are mostly in the first category.

The chief current English inflections are those for number (in noun, pronoun, and verb) and those for tense. There was relatively little said by Leonard or Marckwardt and Walcott about the uses of tense, because there was little disagreement about the status of such forms—however common—as *he done it* and *they have went*. (This has been true in general in disputes about "usage," and accordingly such forms rarely figure in my discussions.) But many usages treated by the previous NCTE studies were matters of number (especially agreement of number between subject and verb), and I will mention Fries's findings for a few of these.

All three groups of writers in Fries's final sample used singular introductory formulas *(there is, there was, there has)* before plural nouns.

Don't appeared with a third-person singular subject *(she don't, it don't)* in group II (about 30 percent of the possible cases) and in group III (where *doesn't* was "exceedingly rare"), but not once in the letters of group I. Nor did *we was, you was,* or *they was* occur in any Standard English letter.

These kind of . . . and *those sort of . . .* , which Leonard labeled Disputable and Marckwardt and Walcott found in Colloquial usage,

Fries found "primarily" in his Standard English letters, while his group III preferred *them kind of books,* for example. (Group II, which Fries doesn't discuss on this matter, presumably combined the group I and group III preferences, as on so many other items.)

The use of a singular collective noun (like *family* or *majority*) or a pronoun like *none, everyone,* or *everybody* with a plural reference pronoun or a plural verb (e.g., "*None* of the married children *are* in a position to assist" or "The family *were* very fine people") was characteristic of the Standard English group but seldom appeared in the letters of Vulgar English. Better-educated subjects paid more attention to semantic number than to formal grammatical number, whereas the Vulgar English letters attended less to semantic number and tended to generalize *they, their,* and *them* as forms for common number (as in "After a Mother and Father suffer to raise *a Boy* to become the age of 17 *they* should be some help to *their* parents"). Only a single example of an indefinite pronoun with a singular verb occurred in the letters of Standard English ("numerous affidavits were brought in but *none was* sufficient to prove"). Leonard judged "*None* of them *are* here" and "*Everyone* was here but *they* all went home early" Established. He labeled "*Everybody* bought *their* own ticket" Disputable, which Marckwardt and Walcott raised to Literary after they found it in Ruskin and other writers.

The four minor English inflections dealt with in Fries's study are genitive (commonly called possessive), dative-accusative (commonly called objective), adjective comparison, and verb mood forms. His findings about some of these forms are summarized here.

Fries found only one case of a genitive noun (with *'s* or *s'*) before a gerund in any letter, despite the large number of nouns preceding gerunds in the sample. Curiously enough, on the other hand, 52 percent of the Standard English cases used the genitive form for pronouns before gerunds. In other words, Standard English writers did not use phrases like "on account of their *father's being* sick" but did have a slight preference for "on account of *his being* sick" over "on account of *him being* sick." *Facts* labeled "What was the reason for *Bennett making* that disturbance?" as Literary (Leonard found it Established) and "What are the chances of *them being* found out?" as Colloquial, along with "That was the reason for *me leaving* school" (both Disputable for Leonard).

Surprisingly, Fries discovered not a single example of *whom* used as an interrogative. Leonard had found "*Who* are you looking for?" acceptable, though "most authorities do not approve it for written English." Then Marckwardt and Walcott, noting its use by Shakespeare, Southey, and Hardy, labeled it good Colloquial practice. Thus, in all three surveys, sentences like "*Who* did you apply to?" are more characteristic of educated usage than the traditionally preferred "*Whom* did you apply to?" Fries rightly observed that "the 'subjective' territory in which the interrogative stands seemed to have more force in determining the form than the 'objective' relationship of the word." On the other hand, in the case of *who/whom* as relative pronouns (as in "I have one child *whom* I have not seen . . ."), the Standard English writers of group I used *whom* in about two thirds of the cases in which traditional grammar would call for it, *who* the rest of the time. (And, of course, in both the Standard and Vulgar English letters there were also hyperurban or hypercorrect uses of *whom* where *who* would traditionally be expected.)

With respect to verb moods, Fries found that for nonfactual conditions and *that* clauses after verbs of asking and suggesting, the subjunctive form was absent from both Standard and Vulgar English. Leonard labeled "I *wish I was* . . ." Established, while Marckwardt and Walcott, finding it in Defoe, Swift, Fielding, Dickens, and Hardy, called it Literary.

Also in harmony with both previous NCTE studies was Fries's finding in all the letters only 20 cases of a split infinitive, 18 of them in the Standard English materials (e.g., "*to adequately prepare* myself for this examination"); in all the letters, 98 percent (869 cases) of the infinitives occurring with *to* had them immediately adjacent to one another (as in "to prepare"). Clearly, split infinitives were not characteristic of Common English, nor indeed of Vulgar English.

In concluding his report, Fries maintained that "a study of the real grammar of present-day English has never been used in the schools . . ." (p. 285) and reiterated what he and Krapp had advocated earlier—that students should be taught a sensitivity to the actual usage of educated persons. He even asserted that consciousness of the abstract rules "deadens" students' sensitivity to their speech environment and turns them "away from the only path to real knowledge" (p. 24). He recommended teaching according to the three kinds of grammatical devices (inflections, word order, function words) that actually operate in English, a method that would facilitate continual assimilation of observed language data. Students should watch for the real differences between varieties of English and have confidence as judges, basing decisons on their observations. Through such organizations as the MLA and the NCTE, English teachers should ensure that surveys of current written and spoken English are conducted and the results made available regularly. "We must agree to base our teaching upon an accurate, realistic description of the actual practices of informal Standard English and eliminate from our language programs all those matters of dispute for which there is any considerable usage in informal Standard English" (p. 290).

Instructors reading Fries's critical evaluation of decades of English teaching were doubtless affronted by his conclusion that despite "all their efforts and the huge expenditure of teaching time and resources in the schools, there is hardly a single item of the grammar of our language that has been affected. . . . The experience of at least two hundred years shows that we cannot hope to change the practices of a language; we can only help students to learn what those practices are." Citing the confusion of *lie* and *lay* despite the prodigious energy allotted to sorting them out, he said, "We may not like it, but we can do absolutely nothing effective about it" (pp. 289–290). He continued to claim that, as he and Bloomfield had both argued in the 1920s, ignorance of linguistics among teachers contributed to the propagation of an eighteenth-century viewpoint.

Fries's critical remarks also displeased some scholars, including George McKnight, who, as we saw earlier, had nonchalantly assumed the triumph of a doctrine of usage. Unhappy at Fries's "defeatest attitude," he verbalized the wince of writing teachers facing an unsympathetic and unencouraging assessment. Indeed, McKnight poked at the very foundation of a doctrine of usage in the schools and, by inquiring after the "justification for limiting the function of the grammarian to the registering of the facts of usage," voiced a refrain that came to be repeated often in the decades to follow. Prescriptive grammarians *can* accomplish certain desirable things, McKnight claimed, and he asked whether the differences that *do* exist between the language practices of educated and uneducated speakers might not "provide illustration of the effects of school efforts toward elimination of 'errors'." Like a good many others, but unlike most historians of English, he seemed convinced that often his efforts to teach "correct English" were successful.[42] Probably like most English teachers, he was skeptical of the value of Fries's radical proposals.

McKnight also questioned the "breadth of the basis for the generalizations regarding the 'standard' English represented by Group I," an issue other critics also raised, including one enthusiastic enough about *AEG* to call its publication "an event for rejoicing." Since Fries knew little, if anything, about the education and occupations of the parents and grandparents of his educated speakers, the latter might have been first-generation holders of socially respected positions, while still maintaining speech characteristics of their parents—who would not have satisfied the criteria for inclusion in group I.[43] The logic of this argument is interesting because it indicates, if valid, that mastery of standard English is not a prerequisite to social or educational advancement, something that has been persistently assumed by both traditionalists and linguists. And it also suggests, if true, that mastery of standard English might not follow from associating with standard speakers—an assumption that has not been tested. In any case, McKnight's criticisms about Fries's research are valuable in suggesting improved methodologies and additional questions about relationships between social status and language use.

But in questioning the role of grammarian as *describer* of usage, McKnight flew in the face of the entire tradition of grammatical and rhetorical analysis. His demurral harks back to Cratylus in ancient Greece and to Richard Grant White in nineteenth-century America. It has been at the heart of our survey and deserves serious consideration; for related to this criticism was a sensational one leveled by Harry Warfel, evaluating *AEG* twelve years after its publication. Warfel objected head-on to Fries's classification of language on the basis of the user's education. "Obviously," he wrote, "any classification of language should be made on the basis of language and not so superficial a device as a person's years in school."[44]

First, let us dismiss the incorrect allegation that Fries divided his letter writers solely on the basis of education. But, far more important, insofar as he did rely partly on education to classify his subjects, he did so precisely because, as an objective criterion, it helped break the unenlightening circle previously criticized by Krapp but now being run around again by Warfel. More than a hundred years of tortuous struggle had enabled grammarians and linguists to recognize in a practical way that judgments about correctness of language must follow, not precede, analysis of samples. The great Danish linguist Otto Jespersen had already addressed the difficulty of following suggestions like Warfel's: "We set up as the best language that which is found in the best writers, and count as the best writers those that best write the language. We are therefore no further advanced than before."[45] Generations of struggling to break this unenlightening circle were beginning to bear fruit in the work of Fries; but clearly that advancement was either not understood by or not acceptable to a good many traditionalist grammarians.

Despite some reservations, critical reaction to *AEG* was generally favorable. On Fries's claim that "usage or practice is the basis of all the *correctness* there can be in language," *The Nation* commented that this view was "always held by sensible people but [was] only just dawning on most teachers of English."[46] *The Nation*'s attitude characterized the reception in similar publications. Professor Raven McDavid's more recent remark that Fries's work "deserves serious rereading every few years by every conscientious teacher" suggests the esteem in which linguists hold *AEG*.[47]

Several years after *AEG* appeared, John Kenyon, professor of English at Hiram College, proposed a major refinement in the notion of levels of usage. He pointed out that the concept of "levels," as commonly employed in discussions of good English, merged cultural *levels* with various *functions*—a confusion particularly apparent in contrasts between the Colloquial "level" and the Standard or Literary "level." The frequent grouping of "levels" like Literary, Colloquial, and Illiterate leads people to suppose that just as Illiterate is culturally below Colloquial, so Colloquial is culturally below Literary. Kenyon urged attention to the distinction between *cultural levels* (standard vs. substandard) and *functional varieties* (colloquial, literary, scientific). Then it would be clear that different varieties of English are equally good when used for their respective *functions*. The functional variety called Colloquial might be standard or substandard, like any other functional variety, but the term Colloquial itself would not refer to a cultural level.[48]

Attempts to have school grammars mirror usage are not an isolated current in the history of American education. Early in the century educators commonly tried to make the curriculum reflect life. The ideas of John Dewey in this regard are sufficiently well known in American educational circles not to need rehearsal here. While Dewey did not write about the doctrine of usage, the realism of its relativistic view harmonized with his educational philosophy. His stress on correlating school and home, theory and practice, learning and living, parallels the attention to everyday usage advocated by Krapp, Leonard, and Fries.

Dewey described his philosophy as a system "based on experience as the ultimate authority in knowledge and conduct." The consonance between his view and that of the supporters of the relativity of good usage, especially Krapp, Leonard, and Fries, is not a mere coincidence. Dewey taught at the University of Michigan from 1884 to 1888 and again from 1889 to 1895, after which he moved to the University of Chicago until 1904 and then to Columbia University where he retired in 1930. Fries attended Chicago in 1910 and received all his other graduate training at Michigan. Leonard took his doctorate from Columbia while Dewey was teaching there; after he had taken his A.B. (1908) and A.M. (1909) from Michigan, he taught in Milwaukee. Later, while Dewey was at Columbia, he headed the English department at New York's Lincoln School, which operated under the auspices of Columbia's Teachers College. Fred Newton Scott, the first NCTE president and one of Fries's teachers, took his degrees from Michigan (A.B. 1884, A.M. 1888, Ph.D. 1889) and spent his entire academic career there. Furthermore, George Krapp, who influenced Leonard, taught at Columbia during Dewey's tenure there. In *English Composition as a Social Problem,* Leonard acknowledged his great indebtedness to Dewey; and Fries refers to various works of Dewey in *The Teaching of the English Language.* It is no accident that Scott, Leonard, and Fries did so much to keep the NCTE attentive to the shifting social character of students.

Curriculum Commission: The English Language Arts

The National Council has consistently sought, by encouraging curriculum reform, to keep pace with the changing constituency of the schools and the varying needs of pupils. In 1945, a commission was appointed to "study the place of the language arts in life today, to examine the needs and methods of learning for children and youth, and to prepare a series of volumes on the English curriculum based on sound democratic principles and the most adequate research concerning how powers in the language arts can best be developed."[49] Six years later the commission put forth *The English Language Arts,* the first of five projected volumes. This comprehensive report covered all phases of the English curriculum, but the chapter on "The Modern View of Grammar and Linguistics," which attained some notoriety, is most pertinent here. In it the commissioners recommended that five basic principles evolved by linguists should provide "the foundation of the current attitude toward any teaching of the language today":

1. Language changes constantly.
2. Change is normal.
3. Spoken language is the language.
4. Correctness rests upon usage.
5. All usage is relative.

In elaboration of principle three, the commission stated that "the language of today is not to be identified with that found in books but is to be chiefly found upon the lips of people who are currently speaking it." In this it followed the recommendations of Matthews, Krapp, Leonard, and especially Fries.

Concerning the relativity of usage, it endorsed the position of the contemporary linguist, who "does not employ the terms 'good English' and 'bad English' except in a purely relative sense. He recognizes the fact that language is governed by the situation in which it occurs." Hence: Good English is defined as " 'that form of speech which is appropriate to the purpose of the speaker, true to the language as it is, and comfortable to speaker and listener. It is the product of custom, neither cramped by rule nor freed from all constraint; it is never fixed, but changes with the organic life of the language'."[50] "Bad English is that use of language which is unclear, ineffective, and inappropriate to the linguistic occasion, no matter how traditional, 'correct' or elegant the words or phrases employed."

Because this theory of usage judges correctness by appropriateness, it "leads to the recognition of *levels of usage* rather than a single standard of usage." Unmistakably echoing the refrain of Krapp and Fries, the commissioners urged teachers to develop in pupils "the same sensitivity to the appropriateness of language in each situation" as they possessed themselves. They stressed that study of grammar is not equally valuable for all pupils, that maturing language habits depend as much on desirable attitudes as on technical knowledge, and that ability to use a language must be distinguished from mastery of its rules. It is regrettable that they referred to "levels" of usage instead of to levels and varieties, because levels suggest higher and lower, good and bad.

The commission's statements, none of them new in Council circles, were the product of six years' investigation and deliberation by thirty-one respected educators drawing upon a hundred fifty years of research by philologists and linguists. The chair of the commission, Dora V. Smith, professor of education at the University of Minnesota, was aided by three associate directors; several professors of education, psychology, and English; college deans and a college president; and a number of secondary and elementary school teachers and supervisors. Though Fries was not a member of the commission, his influence is discernible throughout the report.

No surprise to teachers familiar with other Council documents before 1952, *The English Language Arts* nevertheless unleashed a barrage of criticism. Teachers and reviewers vigorously opposed the commission's view of language correctness; and the struggle between the proponents and the antagonists of usage extended far beyond the Council's walls.

Notes

[1] "Why a Linguistic Society?" (1925), p. 5.

[2] "Philology and Purism" (1900), pp. 74–96.

[3] For a discussion of attempts to initiate an academy for American English, see Allen Walker Read, "American Projects for an Academy to Regulate Speech" (1936).

[4] "Practical Philology" (1902), pp. 91–104. Albert H. Marckwardt discusses von Jagemann and Sheldon in *Language and Language Learning* (1968).

[5] "English Grammar, Viewed from All Sides" (1887), p. 465.

[6] *The Standard of Usage in English* (1908), pp. viii, vi. Unless otherwise noted, citations from Lounsbury are to this work.

[7] Roberts has reported that when a student asks him about the correctness of a certain usage, he answers "according to the only principle I know—the usage of the best people, i.e., my friends and me." If the student persists, insisting that what Roberts and his friends

say is irrelevant, Roberts "can only suppose him to be asking what God says." See "The Relation of Linguistics to the Teaching of English" (1960); repr. in and cited from Harold B. Allen, ed., *Readings in Applied English Linguistics,* 2nd ed. (1964), p. 401.

[8]*Essays on English* (1921), p. 110. Cited hereafter as *Essays.*

[9]*Parts of Speech* (1901), pp. 130-131. Cited hereafter as *Speech.*

[10]"The English Language and the American Academy" (1925), p. 91.

[11]See C. Alphonso Smith, "The Work of the Modern Language Association of America" (1899), pp. 252-253.

[12]*Modern English* (1909), p. 14.

[13]*The Authority of Law in Language* (1908), pp. 24-25. Cited hereafter as *Authority.*

[14]*Knowledge of English* (1927), pp. 178, 182. Cited hereafter as *Knowledge.*

[15]See, e.g.: Leonard Bloomfield, *An Introduction to the Study of Language* (1914); Edgar Sturtevant, *Linguistic Change* (1917); Edward Sapir, *Language* (1921).

[16]Hosic, "Editorial: The Policy of the 'English Journal'" (1912), p. 375.

[17]Statistics taken from *Historical Statistics of the United States, Colonial Times to 1957* (U.S. Bureau of the Census, Washington, D.C., 1960).

[18]Hosic, "Editorial: The Significance of the Organization of the National Council" (1912), p. 47.

[19]Reported in *English Journal,* XXV (1936), 826.

[20]Hatfield, "Editorial" (1927), pp. 238f.

[21]See Betty Gawthrop's review of Council attitudes between 1911 and 1929 in *An Examination of the Attitudes of the NCTE toward Language,* ed. Raven I. McDavid, Jr. (1965), pp. 7-15. I rely on Gawthrop's analysis of the articles on grammar that appeared in the *Journal* through 1929.

[22]Paxton Simmons, "Coddling in English" (1916), p. 664.

[23]"The Standard of American Speech," *English Journal,* VI (1917), 1-11. My citations are to the reprint in Scott's *The Standard of American Speech and Other Papers* (1926).

[24]S. A. Leonard and H. Y. Moffett, "Current Definitions of Levels in English Usage" (1927), p. 358.

[25]*The Doctrine of Correctness in English Usage, 1700-1800* (1929). Krapp suggested the study with a reference to W. F. Bryan's "Notes on the Founders of Prescriptive English Grammar" (1923) and supervised the dissertation.

[26]Mildred E. Hergenhan, one of Leonard's students, demonstrated in her dissertation (1938) that the momentum given to prescriptive English grammar in the eighteenth century propelled it through nineteenth-century school texts virtually unaltered. After Leonard drowned in 1931 while boating with I. A. Richards, William Ellery Leonard (no relation) directed Hergenhan's study.

[27]Gawthrop, p. 15.

[28]Leonard 1926; Fries 1927; Marckwardt 1967. Fries (1939) and Marckwardt (1962) also served terms as president of the Linguistic Society of America.

[29]Even the sanity of its authors was questioned, according to Marckwardt and Walcott, *Facts About Current English Usage* (1938), p. 1.

[30]C. Michael Lightner, "1930-1945," in McDavid, ed., *An Examination of the Attitudes of the NCTE toward Language* (1965), p. 19.

[31]Hoyt H. Hudson (1933), p. 585.

[32]Krapp (1933), p. 46.

[33]Charles V. Hartung, "Doctrines of English Usage" (1956).

[34]Several reviewers also seem to have interpreted Leonard's ballot as one that elicited personal approval or disapproval; see, e.g.: *Educational Method,* XII (1934), 234; *Quarterly Journal of Speech,* XIX (1933), 585.

[35]William Ellery Leonard (1933); the reviewer was Bentley—cf. note 36 below.

[36]Harold W. Bentley (1933).

[37]For some items *Webster's New International Dictionary* (1934) was consulted. Where appropriate the authors also consulted H. W. Horwill, *A Dictionary of Modern American Usage* (Oxford, 1935); Otto Jespersen, *A Modern English Grammar* (Heidelberg, 1928-1931); George O. Curme, *Syntax* and *Parts of Speech and Accidence* (Boston, 1931, 1935); J. Lesslie Hall, *English Usage* (Chicago, 1917).

[38]See, e.g., *The New York Times* (February 26, 1939) and Robert T. Oliver (1939).

[39]See, e.g., I. Willis Russell, "Prescription and Description in English Usage" (1939).

[40]*Webster's Third New International Dictionary* (1961) labels *swang* "chiefly dialectal." *The Random House Dictionary of the English Language* (1966) labels it Archaic and Dialect, as does *Webster's New World Dictionary of the American Language,* College ed. (1953).

[41]*The Teaching of the English Language* (1927), p. 102. Cited hereafter as "1927."

[42]McKnight (1941).

[43]I. Willis Russell (1941).

[44]*Who Killed Grammar?* (1952), p. 12.

[45]Jespersen, *Mankind, Nation and Individual* (1925; repr. 1964), p. 91.

[46]Anon., January 4, 1941, p. 26.

[47]Intro., McDavid, ed. *An Examination of the Attitudes of the NCTE toward Language* (1965), p. 1.

[48]"Cultural Levels and Functional Varieties of English" (1948). This paper has been reprinted frequently.

[49]The Commission on the English Curriculum of the National Council of Teachers of English, *The English Language Arts* (1952), p. vii.

[50]The commission quoted this definition from Robert C. Pooley, *Grammar and Usage in Textbooks on English* (1933), p. 155.

CHAPTER VI

Science, Nonsense, and *Webster's Third:* The Storm Breaks

"Grammarians have ever disputed, and often with more acrimony than discretion." —GOOLD BROWN, 1851

"Barbarisms and solecisms have not been rebuked away as they deserve to be." —GOOLD BROWN, 1851

"While men are paying fifty dollars for this new dictionary, the Samuel Johnson lexicon remains out of print and virtually unobtainable." —GARRY WILLS, 1962

THE YEAR 1952 can be regarded as a high-water mark for half a century of growing "liberality" in the attitudes of teachers toward usage, if the NCTE adequately represents its constituency. For *The English Language Arts,* published that year by the Council's Commission on the English Curriculum, embodied the ideas promulgated by the advocates of a relativistic view of linguistic correctness. Succeeding volumes by the commission applied to various educational levels the principles articulated in this initial work. Such was the protest against *The English Language Arts,* however, so truculent and widespread the dissent, that we may seriously question whether the influence of Council leaders reached significantly into the membership ranks; and if it did, then we must doubt that these teachers transferred their views to their students.

Before proceeding to review the critical reception of *The English Language Arts* (and of *Webster's Third,* nine years later), it will be useful to consider where the NCTE's 1952 doctrine of usage had come from. We have seen that from the early grammars of English nearly all writers had acknowledged the importance of usage. We saw it in Dr. Johnson, Bishop Lowth, Joseph Priestley, Noah Webster, William Dwight Whitney, and even Lindley Murray. In quite different degrees, according to their information and inclinations, these grammarians and lex-

109

icographers described, prescribed, or proscribed usage. Some invoked principles they valued higher; and some disregarded usage and substituted their own personal preferences or those of their favorite predecessors. In the nineteenth century, a few grammarians disputed the authority of usage, and Richard Grant White's words are worth recalling: "There is a misuse of words which can be justified by no authority, however great, by no usage, however general"!

In the twentieth century, Lounsbury placed literary usage at the pinnacle of authority, and his precepts were put into practice by Hall, who deemed it sufficient merely to point out what usages the great writers had in fact employed. But Lounsbury's view was rejected by Brander Matthews, who instead placed spoken English on a pedestal and declared that the usage of the majority should reign. Then came Krapp, who recognized the functioning of various kinds of English, declared that a monolithic standard of correctness dulls sensitivity to good usage, and urged that students be aware of the users and uses of the varieties of English. Teachers were urged to inculcate ability to use English that "hits the mark," adapting itself to speaker, addressee, and the purpose of the communication. Finally, Fries advanced the notion that only objective analysis correlating social class with language use could reveal the facts of English that are necessary to establish a program for the schools. He maintained that in a democratic society no group's English should be considered superior to other varieties, though he did suggest as a basis for schools the actual language used by people carrying out the important affairs of everyday life. Fries claimed "a correctness" for each kind of English—namely, the correctness attendant upon its appropriate use in its own environment. Denying that any form of English could be inherently better or worse than others, he nevertheless recommended a middle road that accepts neither literary nor majority usage as the basis of school grammar. He thought his view suitable for a pluralistic democracy tolerant of diversity but needing at least one language variety adequately normed and widespread to ensure communication among the members of a diverse citizenry. Americans comfortably accept diverse regional pronunciations and vocabulary, and English speakers throughout the world tolerate national differences in pronunciation, vocabulary, and spelling. Fries therefore urged teachers to extend greater tolerance to diverse grammatical and lexical usages.

If the first half of the century witnessed vigorous exploration and propagation of the doctrine of usage in English grammar, however, the period since then must be described as one of extreme hostility to it. Culminating in a torrent of criticism against *Webster's Third New International Dictionary,* a storm of resentment was signaled by the threatening criticism of *The English Language Arts.* During the decade preceding 1961 and since then, many teachers and various commentators have explicitly and vehemently opposed the assumptions of this view of usage. More has been revealed than simple intellectual disagreement; deep-seated emotional convictions of several kinds underlie the bitterness that has surfaced.

Gathering Clouds: Reactions to The English Language Arts

An early and vociferous critic of *The English Language Arts* was Professor Harry Warfel, who the same year presented his small book *Who Killed Grammar?* as "a minority report" on the relevant chapter. Appalled by the "decline in reputation of the teaching of grammar in American schools," he laid the responsibility "chiefly at the door of the linguists themselves" and blamed his former professor Fries as "the 'villain' in this 'murder' story" (p.v).[1] Dismayed at the "non-science and non-sense" in the NCTE, Warfel wrote:

> The worst feature of the non-sense of the "new" linguists is its "book-burning" quality. By shaking faith in the correctness of a few items in grammars of the English language, these detractors have destroyed faith in every book on the subject. (p. 59)

> By focusing attention on "it is me," "who are you with," "none are," "data is," *shall* and *will,* and similar instances of divided usage, these self-called "descriptive" grammarians have hooted at "prescriptive" grammars and have created in educational circles a thoroughly rebellious attitude toward all formal study of the English language. . . . They assert that they have standards, but they have not defined these standards in precise terms. . . . They have done untold harm, and, except as they have added a few facts to the record, they have done almost no good. (p. 18)

Who Killed Grammar? did not quite typify antagonism to the commission's relativistic approach to usage; most of the criticism was less histrionic. Yet the reaction of one of America's most distinguished educators nearly surpassed Warfel's.

Jacques Barzun, Columbia University historian and administrator, warned the public against an insidious influence. "To appreciate the extent of the intellectual disaster brought on by the liquidation of grammar and to gauge the fanaticism, the bad reasoning, the incapacity to come to a point, the self-righteousness of the antigrammarians," he directed people to the commission's report: "The volume is one long demonstration of the authors' unfitness to tell anybody anything about English. Their great maxim, an act of faith in the teeth of the evidence, is that 'change in language is not corruption but improvement . . .'."[2] Barzun deemed the changes he saw overtaking English "not simplification and clarification but obscurity, pretension, and pedantry" (p. 243); and he too blamed the putative decadence on the linguists:

> For the state of the language as we find it in the centers of culture, certain modern linguists bear a grave responsibility. In wanting to prove their studies scientific, they went out of their way to impress the public with a pose and a set of principles that they thought becoming: a true science, they argued, only records, classifies, and notes relations; it never prescribes. Hence, the old grammar was sinful and must be harried out of the schools. It was unscientific, dangerous, and—they added irrelevantly—it was impossible to teach it to the majority. The campaign succeeded. The graduate of an elementary school today cannot with certainty be accused of knowing any given subject, but he can be guaranteed to know no grammar. In one generation grammar has been uprooted and pedantic fantasies about teaching the mother tongue have been made to seem liberal and advanced. (p. 240)

> Frivolously, the would-be scientists argued . . . that democracy and their science alike called for a policy of 'Hands Off.' As scientists they maintained that the speech of any group is good speech for that group; as democrats and progressives they maintained that the child should not be made to feel inferior (or superior) by changing his speech. 'There can . . . never be in grammar an error that is both very bad and very common.' Thus spoke Charles Carpenter Fries, the theorist who engineered the demise of grammar in the American schools. Yet this doctrine and his crusade were not, as he thought, objective and detached in the spirit of science. Rather, philanthropy and egalitarianism inspired him. To teach one kind of usage, pronunciation, and grammar seemed to him tantamount to reintroducing social distinctions of the most artificial kind. Wanting the opposite gave him his first principle: Accept what comes and in time we shall have a classless speech corresponding to the usage of the most numerous. (p. 241)

Imagining thus that the aim of linguists like Fries was "a classless speech corresponding to the usage of the most numerous," Barzun inveighed against their call for students to be taught to observe language customs for themselves. This, he said, combined "the affectation of science with the 'progressive' principle of learning by doing, here carried to a ludicrous extreme" (p. 241). He seemingly approved the use of objective methods only in the natural sciences—and certainly not in the study of language.

> This pseudo-scientific pedantry has obscured the important fact of the willful inexactitude of science, that is, its deliberate refusal to grasp the in-

dividual and relate him to its models and systems. Not to know this results, for the whole realm of learning outside natural science, in a superstitious reliance on figures, graphs, and labels. Give a man a rating on a scale, call him a something-or-other, and no amount of direct evidence will erase the suspicion that he is what he has 'scientifically' been called. Hence the modern abdication of direct, responsible judgment by human beings. (pp. 244–245)

The jeremiads of Warfel and Barzun pit them against "descriptive linguistics," an approach to language study which, through the efforts of NCTE leaders, was indeed changing the old school grammar.

Following the appearance of the commission's first volume, discussion of "new grammar" and "new grammarians" proliferated. There was wholesale expression of consternation at the passing of the "old grammar." Traditionalists distrusted the objectivity and scientific bias, the progressivism and egalitarianism of the new grammar. In 1960 John C. Sherwood, director of freshman composition at the University of Oregon, assembled his view of the miscellaneous virtues of the old grammar and the evils of the new. Collating the tenets of the "old grammar," Professor Sherwood proclaimed:

It stands for order, logic, and consistency; for the supremacy of the written language and of the literate classes in setting linguistic standards; for continuity, tradition, and universality—for what is common to older and modern, British and American English, to the whole body of European languages rather than for what is local and singular; for discipline and self-control; for the practice of an art, a system developed by tradition and the authority of masters rather than statistical study. It is aristocratic only in the sense of following Jefferson's "natural aristocracy," valuing the language of the leaders of the community, and accepting the right of these to give the law to those who are less skilled; it is snobbish only as all education must be snobbish, as implying the transmission of wisdom from those who possess it to those who do not. It values the language of momentous and dignified occasions over casual talk, language that comes from premeditation and thought rather than spontaneous expression. It is a grammar for the idealistic, for Ortega y Gasset's "select man," who is willing to live up to higher standards than the generality are willing to impose upon themselves. . . . Loving logic and order, it opposes oddity and irregularity, and at times may have the coldness that goes with order and regularity. It is not resigned to the chaos of experience but wishes to impose its own order upon it; it believes, with Orwell, in man's power to master his linguistic environment. It may recognize . . . language levels but attaches little importance to the lower levels; it attempts to raise the illiterate to the level of the literate, not to average everyone out to a common level. It is best to think of it not as Platonic, dwelling in a realm apart from concrete reality, but as Aristotelian,

the "form" of reality, what reality would be shorn of the anomalous and accidental, what reality at its best tends to be. It is usage, but usage ordered by
reflection.[3]

Sherwood's eulogy identified "old grammar" as that generally presented
in English classes by teachers concerned primarily with traditionally correct and persuasive language, hoping indeed to inspire students "to live
up to higher standards." Trained in literary analysis, these teachers professionally value "the language of the momentous and dignified occasions over casual talk, language that comes from premeditation and
thought rather than spontaneous expression." To encourage in students
facility with such language is a commonly accepted duty of English
teachers, and the accomplishment of this task is indeed one reason for
which a community employs them.

Instruction in language of "higher standards than the generality are
willing to impose upon themselves" is often referred to simply as teaching
grammar or teaching English, but its subject matter is more properly
regarded as rhetoric. Children normally master the sound patterns and
basic sentence structures of their language before arriving in school,
where they spend the first years learning to read and write sentences they
can already understand and speak. Subsequent attention is directed
toward acquiring more complex communication skills and at developing
effective and persuasive English, especially in its written form. As Sherwood's "old grammarians" function in departments of English, they
teach students to write effectively, focusing on connotations and denotations of words, concerned primarily with the external functioning of
language, with how it affects others. Traditionally their subject matter is
regarded as an art—the art of effective writing—and as such it tends to
be prescriptive. Its teachers are the prescribers of what is correct and effective in written communication; prescribing is part of their role.

The "new grammar," on the other hand, represented for Sherwood
"some things which are good and many things which are questionable in
modern life and thought":

> . . . it stands for democracy; for spontaneity, self-expression, and per-
> missiveness; for nominalism; for skepticism; for a social-scientific view of
> life; for progress and modernity; for nationalism and regionalism. It is
> "other-directed," seeing the proper standard of conduct as conformity to the
> mores of the group. It represents a linguistic Rousseauism, a belief that
> man's language is best and most real when most spontaneous and un-
> premeditated and that it is somehow tainted by the efforts of educational
> systems to order and regularize it. Just as the old grammar tried to take its
> values from above, the new tries to deduce them, in the manner of Dr.
> Kinsey, from the facts. (p. 277)

Because the label "grammarian" is commonly associated with teachers of composition and rhetoric, "new grammarians" ought to have a different name. Traditionally "grammar" has meant correctness; "rhetoric," effectiveness. But, as rhetorician Edward Corbett has noted, "What we mean—or what we should mean—when we say that grammar is concerned with 'correctness' is that grammar is preoccupied with how a particular language works—how words are formed and how words can be put together in phrases and clauses."[4] As we have seen, students of grammar in that sense are today called linguists. Sherwood's descriptions of "old" and "new" grammar reveal historical and philosophical commitments too disparate to share the same umbrella term; as he acknowledged, "What the two grammars really reflect is two ways of looking at language, two ideals of language, and perhaps in the end two ways of life" (p. 276).

While a fitter label for "new grammarian" is "linguist," Sherwood had in mind professors of English who, like Fries, were influenced by linguistic science and attempted to spread this view throughout the English teaching profession. In this sense "linguists" refers to scholars conducting research into the structure and history of English—its systematic patterns of sound, word, and sentence formation.[5] They analyze how language functions internally and how its grammatical subsystems evolve historically. Unlike the traditional grammarians and rhetoricians, their subject matter is not an art, and when they analyze writing they are not concerned with distinguishing well-written prose from prose that is simply adequate for communication. They are not lackadaisical about effective communication, however, and remain persuaded of the value of fine writing, there being no difference between "old" and "new" grammarians in this matter. As the traditionalists have noted, the writing styles of Krapp, Leonard, Fries, and Marckwardt are as orthodox as other English professors'. Nevertheless, the attempts of these linguists to undermine the time-honored approach to "good grammar" struck fear and resentment into a substantial segment of the English teaching profession. Given that the "old grammarians" were almost by definition prescribers of what is good in English, it is not surprising that the linguists and the NCTE were viewed as traitors to the written word and even as threats to the traditional employment of English teachers.

While it is clear who his "new grammarians" are, then, Sherwood's description betrays mistaken notions about their tenets. It is wrong to think that linguists like Fries believe the best language is spontaneous and unpremeditated, that education merely taints it. If their being professors of English does not belie such misapprehension, their writings on grammar and usage do.

Two notes in Sherwood's descriptions echo familiar refrains—the elitist disdain for genuine democracy and the association of linguistics with moral waywardness and political decadence. The snobbishness and natural aristocracy of the "old grammar" is granted a legitimate place in the teaching of native English. As for the implied obliquity of the "new grammar," the associating of Fries's research with that of Kinsey suggests that language scientists were viewed as advocating linguistic abandon. Fries did claim that anything very common (in grammar!) cannot be very wrong. Kinsey, it may be noted, did not draw corresponding conclusions from his observations; but the popular view of his findings did infer tacit approval for sexual promiscuity. The eighteenth- and nineteenth-century linkage between profligacy and "bad grammar" continued, in some quarters, in the twentieth century.

Possibly Fries took delight in being compared with Kinsey. Both men certainly subscribed to the value of candid description. Fries, in any case, saw the doctrine of usage not as inculcating linguistic promiscuity but, on the contrary, as infusing students with the powerful check of sensitivity to the nuances of current English use.

Thunder and Lightning: The **Third** as Radical Document

During the decade after 1952, the turbulent reaction to the influence of a scientific approach to English instruction, as represented mainly by *The English Language Arts,* should have warned lexicographers about popular unreceptiveness to the views of linguists. In America, in addition to politics, religion, and sex—the trinity of topics cultured persons avoid in peaceable discussion—the subject of correct grammar was of utmost delicacy. But despite the forecast, the most respected American dictionary makers of that time misjudged public sentiment and provoked a surly storm.

After Noah Webster's death in 1843, the brothers George and Charles Merriam had bought from Webster's heirs the remaining copies of the second edition of the *American Dictionary* and the rights to publish subsequent revisions of it. In 1847 the first "Merriam-Webster" dictionary appeared, and several others were subsequently published. In 1934 the G. & C. Merriam Company published a second edition of *Webster's New International Dictionary,* "successor" to Webster's original, and this dictionary earned a reputation as an authoritative source of information about the language. Many Americans came to regard it (or any "college" or other abridged edition "based on" it) as *the authority* on matters of spelling, meaning, and usage.

Then, after twenty-seven years of work recording the changes in

English since 1934, the Merriam Company staff produced a new, completely revised, unabridged dictionary. With three and a half million dollars invested in the best scholarship, Merriam's lexicographers and business executives were eager for their new dictionary to make its way in the world. In brochures announcing its advent, in the fall of 1961, the customer relations office was prodigal in its praise of the mammoth work: *"Webster's Third New International Dictionary* presents the English language in a new, modern way giving you the most useful, understandable, and authoritative fund of word information ever available and covering every area of human thought." Apparently hoping to place the $50 "unabridged" alongside the Bible in every American home, the publicists boasted that "Special attention was given to the language of tax forms, game laws, insurance policies, instruction booklets for everything from automobile maintenance to the putting together of children's toys, legal contracts and wills, as well as the colorful vocabularies of such fields as show business, sports, retailing, and fashion and the technical terms of science, agriculture, and industry." They vaunted the fact that, besides such highly regarded sources as Joseph Conrad and Bernard Shaw, the editors had culled passages from the *Annual Report of J. C. Penney Co.,* the *Boy Scout Handbook,* the *Marine Corps Manual,* and the *Ford Times.* More politic, they might have forestalled censure as Dr. Johnson had in 1755 by conceding that "Some of the examples have been taken from writers who were never mentioned as masters of elegance or models of stile; but words must be sought where they are used; and in what pages, eminent for purity, can terms of manufacture or agriculture be found?" But they did not. To discover the spoken variants of the word *vaudeville,* the editors drew on pronunciations of Gypsy Rose Lee, Mickey Rooney, George Gobel, and Bob Hope. With such citations Merriam's public relations office sought to indicate that their lexicon was "the most complete, authoritative, and up-to-date unabridged dictionary available today to meet the needs of the Space Age and to present accurately our language as it is spoken and written." Proudly (but perplexingly, given the input), they promoted this "final word authority" as "one of the most remarkable *literary* achievements of all time" (emphasis added).

While these brochures circulated to catch the attention of aspiring households, the dictionary's chief editor, Philip B. Gove, penned for more scholarly audiences a description of the principles governing the dictionary's production:

> Within the lifetime of nearly all who are teaching today . . . the study of
> the English language has been deeply affected by the emergence of linguistics

as a science. Some of the conclusions clearly arrived at have been occasionally received with strenuous objections especially from teachers with established routines sometimes based on what was traditional at the turn of the
century. Although some resistance remains, acceptance of the basic tenets of
this new science is hardly any longer a matter of opinion. It is a matter of
demonstrable fact now set forth in scores of reliable books and hundreds of
articles in learned journals and repeatedly being orally dispersed in an increasing number of classrooms and meetings of linguistic groups. . . . The
fundamental step in setting down postulates for descriptive linguistics is
observing precisely what happens when native speakers speak. This is the
essential first step required by scientific method. Its obviousness and
simplicity are deceptive, however, for its application calls for a radical
change in analytical method. Instead of observing a language in terms of its
past, specifically in its relations to Latin grammar, the linguist must first
observe only the relationships of its own elements to each other.[6]

Persuaded that linguistic principles should be taught in school to provide an adequate understanding of language and a suitable use of and
appreciation for dictionaries, Dr. Gove suggested as a starting point the
by-then familiar pentalogue of NCTE maxims: language changes constantly, linguistic change is normal, spoken language is the language,
correctness rests upon usage, and all usage is relative.

To avoid the appearance of radicalism, he denied that descriptive
linguistics had contributed much to the new dictionary's treatment of
spelling, etymology, meaning, or vocabulary—though its influence on
pronunciation was "profound and exciting," especially in the information collected for the *Linguistic Atlas of the United States*. As they applied to pronunciation, Gove said, the five precepts of *The English
Language Arts* were already explicit in the 1934 edition of the dictionary—which by 1961 was revered—though techniques had not been
refined enough in 1934 to yield the current results. And he went on to
say:

Lexicography is not yet a science. It may never be. It is an intricate and
subtle and sometimes overpowering art, requiring subjective analysis, arbitrary decisions, and intuitive reasoning. It often uses analogy, precedent,
and probability, and it constantly has to distinguish between the typical and
the atypical on the basis of knowledge and experience. It has no reason to
scorn sprachgefühl, or to apologize for depending on it. But it should have
no traffic with guesswork, prejudice, or bias or with artificial notions of correctness and superiority. It must be descriptive and not prescriptive. . . . If a
dictionary should neglect the obligation to act as a faithful recorder and interpreter of usage . . . it cannot expect to be any longer appealed to as an
authority. When the semantic center of gravity appears to have moved far

enough, when the drift of pronunciation is ascertainable, when a new science makes new knowledge and new methods available, then revision of the affected parts of a dictionary becomes the conscientious duty of the lexicographer. It is in the execution of this duty that Merriam-Webster dictionaries have begun a new series suitable to a new age.

The editor in chief of *Webster's Third* clearly regarded his dictionary's prime task as the accurate recording of actual usage in spelling, pronunciation, and meaning. He and his associate editors, developing the tradition of drawing upon the principles of linguistics, borrowed whatever could serve them while adhering to the lexicographic creed that had earned Merriam-Webster dictionaries their honor in the past. In both respects they unabashedly, if equivocally, endorsed a doctrine of usage.

When advance copies of the dictionary reached reviewers, the gnashing of teeth that ensued demonstrated unequivocally that the views expressed in *The English Language Arts* had not won over the influential commentators on wordbooks. The very titles of the critics' tirades convey the discordant reception: "The Death of Meaning," "Madness in Their Method," "The String Untuned," "Sabotage in Springfield," "Say It 'Ain't' So!"

Writing for *The Atlantic,* Wilson Follett claimed that "it costs only minutes" to discover that the *Third* is "in many crucial particulars a very great calamity." Especially grieved by its treatment of the "fundamental English" which "belongs to all of us," wherein it had "thrust upon us a dismaying assortment of the questionable, the perverse, the unworthy, and the downright outrageous," he was aghast at what he saw as the *Third*'s aim "to destroy . . . every surviving influence that makes for the upholding of standards, every criterion for distinguishing between better usages and worse. . . . With but slight exaggeration we can say that if an expression can be shown to have been used in print by some jaded reporter, some candidate for office or his speech writer, some potboiling minor novelist, it is well enough credentialed for the full blessing of the new lexicography." Follett's overall evaluation can be inferred from his interpretation of the dictionary's purpose: "To erode and undermine [the traditional controls] is to convert the language into a confusion of unchanneled, incalculable williwaws, a capricious wind blowing whithersoever it listeth. And that, if we are to judge by the total effect of the pages under scrutiny . . . is exactly what is wanted by the patient and dedicated saboteurs in Springfield."[7]

No wonder, given such views of its purpose, the new wordbook was a "disappointment" and a "shock," "a scandal and a disaster," "a fighting document." But the jeremiads are well documented; there is no need to rehearse them further. It will prove more instructive to analyze the sources and causes of the attacks on the dictionary.

One of the most noteworthy aspects of the hubbub was the assumption by many of the discussants that the new dictionary was the product of modern linguistics. For a generation resentment had been building up toward the "infection" that linguists were thought to be spreading. This resentment simply exploded when the *Third* appeared to be a carrier of that infection. The fact that the dictionary seemed to give approbation to scores of nonstandard usages accepted by linguists helped establish that connection, as did the use of phonetic notations and the absence of the label "colloquial"; so, what was deemed bad in linguistics tarnished the reputation of the dictionary. Observers in business, education, publishing, law, and journalism suspected that grammar teaching had foundered during the three decades preceding the dictionary, because even college graduates could not demonstrate language ability suitable for the jobs they sought. And accompanying the alleged easing of instruction in composition, as many knew, was a nascent respect for linguistics among leaders in the English teaching profession. No one really documented a tie between linguistics and the enfeebling of composition, and informed observers knew that the young science had not become potent enough in classrooms or textbooks to have a major impact; but its ascent in the NCTE and the putative decline in writing skills were taken for cause and effect. Many thought the new dictionary attested to the coup linguists had been suspected of engineering for a generation. The dictionary was thought a "hostage" of the new science. Professor Barzun discovered a "theology" of linguistics embodied in it. Professor Mario Pei, writing in *Saturday Review* a year after the dictionary was published, voiced a similar suspicion:

> The appearance of the new Webster's International . . . has for the first time brought forth, into the view of the general public, those who are primarily responsible for the shift in attitude and point of view in matters of language—not the ordinary classroom teachers of English, not the educationists of the teachers colleges, but the followers of the American, anthropological, descriptive, structuralistic school of linguistics, a school which for decades has been preaching that one form of language is as good as another; that there is no such thing as correct or incorrect so far as native speakers of the language are concerned; that at the age of five anyone who is not deaf or idiotic has gained a full mastery of his language; that we must not try to correct or improve language, but must leave it alone; that the only language activity worthy of the name is speech on the colloquial, slangy, even illiterate plane; that writing is a secondary, unimportant activity which cannot be dignified with the name of language; that systems of writing serve

only to disguise the true nature of language; and that it would be well if we completely refrained from teaching spelling for a number of years.[8]

If Pei's depiction represents what educated Americans imagined of descriptive linguistics, it is not puzzling that such an outcry greeted its supposed contagion of American lexicography. But his caricature misses the spirit of what linguists attempted and ignores earlier denials of allegations.[9] What the linguists wanted to achieve, as the works of Leonard, Krapp, and Fries reveal, was innocuous enough as they perceived it. Pei's tactics in this manner made of him a scaremonger.

Follett's appraisal in *The Atlantic* followed the lead of two widely read and influential publications. Editors at *The New York Times* on October 12, 1961, said *Webster's* had "surrendered to the permissive school that has been busily extending its beachhead on English instruction in the schools," a development they found "disastrous because, intentionally or unintentionally, it serves to reinforce the notion that good English is whatever is popular." A fortnight later *Life's* editors lamented that *Webster's* had joined "the say-as-you-go school of permissive English" and had "all but abandoned any effort to distinguish between good and bad usage—between the King's English, say, and the fishwife's." To damn editorially the major publishing venture of such a distinguished firm after allowing so little time for the public to grow familiar with it suggests a view of the *Third* as political document rather than scholarly enterprise. But the editors at *Life* and *The New York Times* were keeping distinguished company in their rush to excoriate the dictionary. "When it came up as a subject of interest at a meeting of the board of *The American Scholar*," Professor Barzun reports, "everyone present felt that its importance warranted notice"; and he "was delegated to express the board's 'position'." He describes his reaction:

This was extraordinary, for more than one reason. Never in my experience has the Editorial Board desired to reach a position; it respects without effort the individuality of each member and contributor, and it expects and relishes diversity. What is even more remarkable, none of those present had given the new dictionary more than a casual glance, yet each one felt that he knew how he stood on the issue that the work presented to the public.

That astonishing and possibly premature concurrence within a group of writers whose work almost invariably exhibits judicial tolerance and the scholarly temper defines the nature and character of the new Webster: it is undoubtedly the longest political pamphlet ever put together by a party. . . . I have called it a political dogma because it makes assumptions about the people and because it implies a particular view of social intercourse. . . . No one who thinks at all can keep from being a partisan.[10]

In Barzun's critique, as in Follett's and those of *Life* and *The New York Times,* the fundamental principle of lexicography—that a dictionary's essential function is to record linguistic practice—bore the brunt of the attack. The premises of a doctrine of usage, outlined in America by Whitney in the nineteenth century and amplified in the twentieth, were scuffed as detractors berated Gove and lambasted descriptive linguistics for its degrading influence on the dictionary. Just how ineffective had been attempts to dent popular credence in an absolutist view of linguistic correctness was apparent; nearly everywhere the authority of usage in determining correctness was vigorously and rancorously challenged. If NCTE efforts had accomplished little in classrooms, they had even less effect persuading the media. Commentators still believed certain words, meanings, and uses to be right and others wrong—no matter who employs them or refuses to employ them; they wanted "wrong" usages eliminated from the dictionary altogether or, if they must be entered, then boldly blacklisted. The editors of *The New Republic* (April 23, 1962) complained that in basing its definitions "simply on current usage" the *Third* was "refusing to distinguish good from bad."

Three themes recur in the antagonistic notices of the *Third,* all accusing it of real or supposed characteristics of descriptive linguistics: it was scientific; it was permissive; it was democratic.

Perhaps the critics' chief objection to linguistics was embodied in the word "scientific." There had been opposition to *The English Language Arts* because it stressed the value of a scientific view of language, and even stronger resistance met the *Third's* bruited scientific approach. The basis for the revolt against science was complex; the traditionalists were resisting an amoral, unesthetic, nonjudgmental, statistical approach to language study.

Many scholars, teachers, and journalists who opposed the doctrine of usage in schools and lexicography saw the science of linguistics as mere objective quantitative analysis: "nose-counting." There were exasperated questions about how a linguistic "geiger counter" could detect education and culture and how an "adding machine" would measure them. A microbiologist with traditional views of usage said this: " . . . weighing the speech of casual speakers with no pretense of expertness on the same IBM card as usages of topnotch writers of past and present is an example of what the modern linguist calls 'science'."[11] Dwight Macdonald: "As a scientific discipline, Structural Linguistics can have no truck with values or standards. Its job is to deal only with The Facts. But in matters of usage, the evaluation of The Facts is important, too, and this requires a certain amount of general culture, not to mention common sense—commodities that many scientists have done brilliantly without but that teachers and lexicographers need in their work."[12] Most tellingly, English professor A. M. Tibbetts claimed that "After a time, the objective, 'scientific' study of language subtly corrupts a man. He becomes less a moralist . . . and more a pedant . . . playing with tape recorders and other gimcrackery . . . ."[13] In 1952 in another context a professor of modern languages had thought it "as unsatisfactory to divorce style and taste from linguistic arguments . . . as it is to restrict oneself to describing the chemical composition of the colors used by Michelangelo without reference to their effect."[14] These last two views mirror a sentiment still common among composition and literature teachers.

A critical stratagem was to denigrate Gove and his doctrine by association with the alleged mechanical approach of natural and social scientists: "The lexicographer is part Gallup, part IBM machine, part voting booth," wrote Garry Wills. "He does not need to think and choose. The future is shaping itself."[15] Professor Tibbetts caught the spirit exactly when he noted of himself and other traditionalists that "the average professor of literature has about as much use for science as a convinced Marxist has for *laissez-faire* capitalism."[16]

The second charge leveled regularly against descriptive linguistics and the dictionary was "permissiveness." Detractors by the dozen reasoned that by the mere inclusion of certain usages Gove approved them, thereby relinquishing his mantle of authority. By refusing to decide right and wrong, by failing to legislate correct usage, *Webster's* had yielded to the same permissiveness that was injuring art, music, literature, and morals. "This scientific revolution," said Dwight Macdonald, "has meshed gears with a trend toward permissiveness, in the name of democracy, that is debasing our language by rendering it less precise and thus less effective as literature and less efficient as communication."[17] And the *American Bar Association Journal* (January, 1962) drew an economic parallel: "Surely opening the floodgates to every word that is used, no matter how or by whom, and regardless of its propriety, is like the printing of paper money backed by no sound value. This is verbal inflation, which has the inevitable effect of debasing the currency of words." Finally, Follett read the dictionary as an attack designed to destroy "every obstinate vestige of linguistic punctilio, every surviving influence that makes for the upholding of standards, every criterion for distinguishing between better usages and worse. . . . it has gone over bodily to the school that construes traditions as enslaving, the rudimentary principles of syntax as crippling, and taste as irrelevant."[18]

In the view of these well-known and respected critics, modern linguistics and Philip Gove's lexicography patently refused to distinguish between the careful, discriminating writer and the unlettered masses.

Alongside Edith Sitwell, T. S. Eliot, Pearl Buck, and Winston Churchill, the dictionary cited Polly Adler, Art Linkletter, Mickey Spillane, and Elizabeth Taylor. "By abdicating their high office," wrote someone in the Richmond *News Leader* (January 3, 1962), "the Merriam editors have precipitated a war that will be waged wherever men who believe in excellence find themselves in conflict with men who prefer an easy mediocrity. We enlist willingly on the side of those who believe in high standards of English usage, and we feel certain that the defenders of linguistic purity will win this war in the end" (p. 122).

Many critics saw permissiveness related to "democratic" (egalitarian) imperatives—and of course to a great variety of other parameters of conflict. Some, like Pei, associated it with a "relativistic philosophy, fully divorced from both ethics and esthetics," a philosophy which concludes that "the native speaker can do no wrong." Many hated the supposed tenet of linguistics that good English is whatever is popular. Some inferred such a lessening of standards from the dropping of the label "colloquial," which seemed to eliminate distinctions between the language of careful and slipshod writers. For these critics the careful writer earned, as credit for his care, the sanction of the dictionary, while the careless one deserved the stigma of its disapprobation.

A few detractors betrayed a conviction that distinctions between "better" and "worse" English usage, between careful and slipshod writing and speaking, are important for maintaining class differences. Macdonald wrote in 1962 that "The reason most people value 'good English' . . . is that ours is a class society in which one of the chief differentiations between the top dogs and the bottom dogs is in the use of language." Years later, having first denied that he knew anything about linguistics, he said (on a tape aired on radio) that in English teaching and dictionary making the scholarship of linguists is not as important as what "the elite" think the language is.[19] Professor Sheridan Baker, whose writing handbooks had considerable currency in American universities in the '60s, lamented the *Third*'s "depressingly low intellectual and social horizon" and proclaimed that "Good English has to do with the upper classes—and there's the rub—with the cultural and intellectual leaders, with the life of the mind in its struggle to express itself at its intellectual best. Linguistic relativism has a fervently democratic base. 'Science' is only an antiseptic label for the deep social belief that we ought not to have classes at all, even among our words."[20] Pei's statement to the same effect is transparent in its implications: "There was far more to the controversy than met the eye, for the battle was not merely over language. It was over a whole philosophy of life. Should there be unbridled democracy, with a nose-counting process to determine what was good and what was bad?"[21]

Suspecting an egalitarian imperative in the work of Gove and the linguists, Pei castigated this intrusion of politics into art. Hints of similar aristocratic attitudes pepper many of the negative verdicts; Sherwood's judgment that the two views of grammar reflect two ways of life was far from idiosyncratic—and far from wrong.

Except for the novel prominence of antagonism toward "science," the twentieth-century American objections to a doctrine of usage—reflected so clearly in objections to the *Third*—resemble those of George Perkins Marsh, Richard Grant White, and William Mathews. Marsh and White had seen linguistic change as corruption and extracted correlations between language and ethics. Especially for Marsh, correctness in language was a moral question, and the language of the lower classes and immigrants mirrored their moral turpitude. The distaste of all three for foreign expressions stemmed partially from a distrust of recent immigrants often forced to occupy the lowest social positions; a general xenophobia and aristocratic aloofness operated in them as well. They denied the conventionality and intrinsic arbitrariness of language forms. For the twentieth-century critics, moral turpitude had become permissiveness, and national chauvinism yielded to disdain of American social inferiors. In short, notions of moral or social superiority persisted.

While comparison of nineteenth- and twentieth-century antagonists of a doctrine of usage exposes striking attitudinal similarities, analysis of particular items reveals two notable differences.

First, we find more wrangling over individual items in the second half of the nineteenth century than in the discord over the *Third*. Popular nineteenth-century debaters of linguistic propriety cataloged "infelicitous slips" and "egregious errors" by the hundreds. In Alfred Ayres' revered manual (1881) devoted to discussions of "the right and wrong use of words," more than fifty entries appear under the letter *A* alone. Quite a few detractors in 1961, on the other hand, perhaps wary of being proven wrong by the evidence, belittled the *Third* without reference to a single entry. Among the many others who specified objectionable usages that the dictionary neglected to stigmatize, the same few cropped up in review after review, along with an occasional idiosyncratic demurral.

Second, except for a handful of perennial favorites, the list of pests that troubled White and Marsh differs in interesting particulars from the list generated by the contemporaries of Macdonald and Follett. In 1870, as we have noted, White condemned locutions like *donate* and *jeopardize, photographer* and *pants, presidential* and *reliable.* Ayres, for one, objected to *editorial, ice-cream,* and *section* as in ("this section of the country").

The critiques of *Webster's Third* resurrected only a handful of the nineteenth-century *bêtes noires.* Commentators still disliked the adjective *enthused* and the suffix *-ize* (as in *finalize*), and damned the *Third* for entering them. But most of the expressions found objectionable by them had not been debated in the nineteenth century. Critics of the *Third,* ignoring hindsight, overlooked the locutions that had nettled their forebears; in fact they often boldly employed them. An aversion to the use of *lay* for *lie* and *like* for *as* linked the 1961 critics with their predecessors; but the differences between their respective catalogs of forbidden words and usages are more striking than the similarities. Follett objected to the new semantic content of *cohort* and *ambivalence,* censured *different than,* found *center around* an abuse of the "more correct" *center in* or *on* or *at,* and reproached the *Third* for not excluding the conjunction *like;* among newcomers to the lexicon he denounced *get hep, passel, anyplace, someplace,* and *one for the book.* Usages exercising the editors at *The New York Times* included *double-dome, yak* (as a verb), *finalize,* and *swell* (as an adjective). *Life's* editors, unaware apparently that the *Third* labeled *irregardless* "nonstandard," bristled at the inclusion of this "most monstrous of all non-words," and ridiculed *enormity* (as a synonym of *enormousness*), *-wise* in *wisdomwise* and *governmentwise* (neither of which is listed!), and *-ize* in *concretize* and *finalize* (both of which are given). Others deplored the unstigmatized listing of *complected* and lamented the blurring of *subconscious* and *unconscious, nauseous* and *nauseated, deprecate* and *depreciate, disinterested* and *uninterested.* The reviewer for *Science* magazine (November 10, 1961) rebuked Gove for failing to note that careful writers do not "mistake" *infer* for *imply,* though he himself had long since made peace with *Pleistocene* and *speedometer,* "bad formations" that chafed him personally.

Traditionalists reproved Merriam for a varied assortment of other entries: *shambles, contact* (as a verb), *tacky, snooty, schmaltz, to goof,* plural *each* ("Each of them are to pay their fine"), adverbial *due to* ("The game was canceled due to inclement weather"), *transpire* ("happen") *bimonthly* ("twice a month") and *ain't*—to mention just a few.

The *Third* was scolded by some reviewers for including certain four-letter words; others knocked it for excluding certain others.

Everyone seemed to have a private list of *faux pas* by which to judge the entire tome; and several influential publications measured its overall worth by how its editors treated a handful of shibboleths. Such circumstances rendered it impossible to satisfy anyone who contested the view that a lexicographer should record usages as they are found.

Most reviewers did not explicitly deny validity to the principles of a doctrine of usage. They acknowledged that language changes and that correctness rests upon usage and is therefore relative. If critics concurred with White's pronouncement that "There is a misuse of words which can be justified by no authority, however great, by no usage, however general," they did not publicly say so. But in practice White's conviction persisted among many who denigrated the dictionary. It is evident that not a few reviewers regarded any dictionary, especially any "Webster's" dictionary, as an official arbiter of just which word usages could be justified by "great authority" and "general usage." *The New Republic* (April 23, 1962) claimed that the new dictionary's compilers had "abandoned a function indispensable in any advanced society, that of maintaining the quality of its language."

Even Dean Henry Alford's belief—that "of two modes of expression, if one be shown to be right, the other must necessarily be wrong"—was persisting through the twentieth century. In 1961 no one disputed the status of *regardless* or *isn't* or the conjunction *as,* or the treatment of *imply* or *uninterested* or *different from* or *equally good.* Everyone accepted their widespread use in standard English. But most critics agreed that if *different from* is acceptable, *different than* should not be; if *uninterested* means "not interested," then *disinterested* cannot; and so on.

Having noted that approved handbooks frowned on such popular but disputed usages, some writers have deliberately avoided them. Even though, as the record in the *Third* indicates, no real social stigma attaches to the use of *different than* or plural *none* ("None of them brought their books"), nevertheless the use of *different from* and singular *none* carries a certain prestige, at least for those who recognize the distinctions. With this fact no one can quarrel; but the rub comes when a personally preferred locution, chosen deliberately or acquired naturally, finds itself competing for acceptance with "approved" usage. If the approved form begins to lose ground, the situation is aggravated. Under such circumstances, linguists and traditional grammarians disagree about what dictionary makers, writers of grammars, and teachers of English ought to do. Linguists insist that when cultured speakers use alternate forms (as they do in the case of "Who/Whom are you looking for?"), dictionaries and grammars should record both usages without stigmatizing either.

Leonard, Fries, and Marckwardt wanted to convince teachers that, granted liberty to use whatever forms they prefer, they must not teach as the sole acceptable usage what research indicates is but one of several forms used by educated speakers or writers of English. Teachers' personal opinions about "better" usages are one thing; their valuations of the forms other educated people actually employ and what they accept from students may have to be altogether different. They should be solidly informed about and scrupulously accurate in their descriptions of cultural levels and functional varieties of English usage.

People are always uneasy with social change; and nowhere does this fact appear more strikingly than in disputes about language. Less opposition was voiced by the bishops of the Roman Church to the acceptance of a thousand vernaculars in place of a single "hard-learned" Latin than greeted the *Third*'s claim that many educated persons use *ain't* seriously. If formerly nothing was thought more linguistically conservative than Rome, opinion about a certain few items of English usage now vigorously competes for that distinction.

Notes for Chapter VI

[1]Warfel (1899–1971) was a student of Fries at Bucknell College early in Fries's career. In fairness to the record it should be noted that Warfel later collaborated in the writing of a college English textbook that was one of the most "liberal" of its time with respect to the authority of usage. See Donald J. Lloyd and Harry R. Warfel, *American English in Its Cultural Setting* (1956).

[2]*The House of Intellect* (1959), p. 243.

[3]"Dr. Kinsey and Professor Fries" (1960), pp. 276–277.

[4]*Classical Rhetoric for the Modern Student* (1965), p. 387.

[5]In a broader sense, a linguist is a student of the structure or history of any language or a theoretician seeking to discover language universals and the nature of grammar as it exists in the minds of speakers and of language as it functions in society.

[6]"Linguistic Advances and Lexicography" (1961).

[7]"Sabotage in Springfield," *The Atlantic* (January 1962); cited from James Sledd and Wilma R. Ebbitt, eds., *Dictionaries and THAT Dictionary* (1962), pp. 111–115. Where not otherwise noted, citations of reviews of the *Third* are from this casebook if the reviews were first published prior to June, 1962.

[8]"The Dictionary as a Battlefront" (1962), pp. 45–46.

[9]See e.g., W. Nelson Francis, "Language and Linguistics in the English Program" (1964).

[10]Jacques Barzun, "What Is a Dictionary?" (1963), p. 176.

[11]Max S. Marshall in *Science* (March 2, 1962); cited from Pei, "The Dictionary as a Battlefront," p. 55.

[12]"The String Untuned," *The New Yorker* (March 10, 1962); cited from Sledd and Ebbitt, p. 185.

[13]"The Real Issues in the Great Language Controversy" (1966), p. 37.

[14]Ernst Pulgram, "Don't Leave Your Language Alone" (1952), p. 425.

[15]"Madness in Their Method" (1962), p. 99; also in Sledd and Ebbitt.

[16]"The Real Issues in the Great Language Controversy," p. 29.

[17]"The String Untuned"; cited from Sledd and Ebbitt, p. 166.

[18]"Sabotage in Springfield"; cited from Sledd and Ebbitt, pp. 112–113.

[19]The first Macdonald quote is from "Three Questions for Structural Linguists; or, Webster 3 Revisited"—Postscript to Sledd and Ebbitt, p. 257 fn.

[20]"The Art and Science of Letters" (1965), pp. 530, 525.

[21]"A Loss for Words" (1964), p. 82; see also "The Dictionary as a Battlefront."

CHAPTER VII

Different Dictionaries, Different Linguists: A Rival Lexicon and a New Linguistics

"The descriptive or structural linguists . . . would no more criticize a locution than a physicist would criticize an atom or an entomologist a cockroach." —MORRIS BISHOP, 1969

"Every other authour may aspire to praise; the lexicographer can only hope to escape reproach, and even this negative recompense has been yet granted to very few." —SAMUEL JOHNSON, 1755

THE HYSTERICAL ALARM occasioned in certain quarters by the appearance of *Webster's Third* was matched by the exuberant adulation expressed by some linguists. But in general, linguistic scientists were not as lavish in their praise as traditional grammarians were unrestrained in their maledictions. "We now know far more of the truth about language than backward-looking purists are willing to admit," wrote one linguist; "*Webster's Third International* is a praiseworthy step along the road to spreading the knowledge of this truth."[1] Another averred that the *Third* "far excels its forbears in both the quantity of the information and the accuracy of its judgments."[2] The author of a popular dictionary of contemporary usage lauded the Merriam venture as "the greatest contribution since the publication of the *Oxford English Dictionary*."[3] A respected dialect geographer heralded the work as "a monumental achievement of exhaustive and highly competent research."[4]

As traditionalists had sniped at the science of linguistics in their commentaries, so linguists fired pot shots of their own; and the name-calling by the dictionary's defenders rivaled the epithets aimed by its censors. Linguists dubbed the detractors or their views unrealistic and illiberal; "medieval, rigid, uninformed, Philistine"; "dogmatic and authoritarian"; crippling and enslaving; and "uniformly obscurantist, uniformly uninformed."[5] One christened the grammarians' approach to dictionaries "lexicolatry"[6] and called the defamers "spokesmen for literary man-

130

darinism and soft-headed gentility."[7] Another called them ignorant, sadistic, masochistic, and superstitious.[8] Plainly, Gove's liberal view of usage, his special attention to spoken English and regional dialects, and his cool disregard of rhetorical nicety represented a political triumph for those whose iconoclastic creed had won out in the sacred shrine: "Webster's Unabridged." There was such gloating as might follow a successful coup against a malevolent dictatorial state.

The Third *as Dictionary: Pros and Cons*

There was also extensive sober appraisal, both pro and con. The intemperate denunciations in newspapers, popular magazines, and a few scholarly journals were not mirrored in most publications whose editors invited professional students of language to appraise the dictionary. From *Consumer Reports* to the *Bulletin* of the American Association of University Professors,[9] and in a fair spectrum of forums between these readership extremes, there appeared more considered judgments of faults and virtues.

Since of course the *Third* did not lack flaws, it will be instructive to review those that even its admirers felt obliged to note.[10]

In passing we may cite several reservations not associated with the usage fracas. Commentators complained about the unesthetic typographical layout and the smallness of type and sparseness of spacing that made reading burdensome. There was justifiable regret that the pronunciation guide, crucial in the decipherment of the new phonetic notation, appeared only in the front matter and on back and front inside covers, and not across the bottom of each two-page spread. With so large a tome there is no easy access to inside covers, and this disregard of convenience for readers unfamiliar with phonetic notation contributed to the designed-for-linguists hue of the volume. Literary persons missed the listing of words that were obsolete before 1755, the date of Dr. Johnson's dictionary.[11] Critics voiced reservations about the complex syntax of some definitions, the infrequency of subject labels like "archaeology" and "physics," and the absence of biographical and geographical names in what had traditionally been an encyclopedic dictionary. And Gove's decision not to repeat the entry word in the examples of its use, but instead to use "~" as a substitute, also agitated some people of letters, one censor even fearing this practice was a scientist's "subtle attack on The Word."[12]

An irritant somewhat more germane to the usage battle was Gove's capitalization policy. The *Third's* entry words are printed in lower-case letters only (except for the *G* in *God*), thus saving space but lending a strange, even careless, cast to words like *christmas* and *french* and avoiding what one sympathetic critic thought a "thorny style problem." Even the admiring reviewer in *Consumer Reports* judged this practice "a willful flouting of normal expectation . . . a case of system carried to an absurd extreme."[13]

More serious was the offering of as many variant pronunciations as the editors could discern; e.g., 8 for *flightily* and 132 for *a fortiori* were deemed quite superfluous![14] While a few dialect scholars valued the *Third*'s gathering and augmenting of the scattered research on regional and social varieties of pronunciation which the *Linguistic Atlas of the United States* had generated, others found the cataloging of such phonetic alternatives a questionable if not outright useless expenditure of space. Moreover, the technical devices used to notate these variants and the inaccessibility of the pronunciation guide were aggravating. One of *Consumer Reports*' evaluators suggested that a good desk dictionary would serve the pronunciation needs of average consulters better than the excessive riches of the *Third,* whose wealth of information yields little guidance toward a recommended pronunciation. Not a few appraisers were annoyed at the high premium the myriad variations set on spoken English: merely because a small percentage of people in a particular region employ a pronunciation is insufficient reason, they thought, to enter it alongside the standard ones. Coupled with the practice of providing "variant" spellings (*momento* for *memento; hep* and *hip; thru* for *through; tho* for *though),* this openness to localisms and shortcuts and "mistakes" distressed even admirers of the new unabridged. One neutral reviewer suggested that the editors' practice nearly denies the possibility of spelling errors.[15]

The chief cause of consternation in all but the most worshipful reviews (and in one which objected to the *Third*'s impoverished semantic theory[16]) was the underemployment of status labels—the very heart of our subject. We have already noted the objection to the scarcity of subject labeling; more distressing was the paucity of status labels. Indeed, "colloquial," the most popular, and most widely misunderstood, label was discarded entirely. Gove and his associate editors used temporal, regional, and stylistic status labels. Leaving aside the temporal ("obsolete" and "archaic") and the regional ("dialectal," "British dialectal," "Southern," etc.), which did not chafe critics, the stylistic labels warrant scrutiny, for they caused *Webster's* readers—and hence Gove himself—considerable grief.

Apart from branding a number of words "vulgar" and an occasional one "obscene,"[17] the editors employed only "slang," "nonstandard," and "substandard" as status labels. Accepting Kenyon's distinction between *levels* and *varieties,* they identified two levels of unacceptability (nonstandard and substandard), leaving acceptable words and uses unmarked. With the sole exception that "slang" was used to characterize a usage limited to circumstances of "extreme informality," appropriate contexts for acceptable uses were suggested solely by the character of the illustrative citations.

In at least one sense or one usage the editors found the following sufficiently informal to be "slang": the nouns *boondocks, broad, bust, cat, clip joint, cornball, fuzz, happy dust, lulu, pig, prof, puss;* the adjectives *cool, fruity, pickled, pissed, pissed off;* and the verbs *knock-up* and *screw-up.* But it was unbranded entries like the following that really raised eyebrows by their bold, unlabeled presence: the nouns *boozer, flick, slut, prick* (a disagreeable person), and *passel;* the adjectives *groovy, pie-eyed, hell-bent, screwy,* and *swell;* the verbs *busted, concretize, enthuse,* and *juice up;* and, of course, the infamous conjunction *like.*

The "nonstandard" status label was applied to "a very small number of words [e.g., *irregardless, lay* (for lie)] that can hardly stand without some status label but are too widely current in reputable context to be labeled *substand.*" The stronger label "substandard" was applied to entries used "throughout the American language community" but differing "in choice of word or form from that of the prestige group in that community" (e.g., *ain't* for "have/has not," *drownded, learn* for "teach," *hisself, them* for "those," *youse* or *yous* for plural "you") Thus substandard usages are lower in status than nonstandard, though not essentially different in kind.

The editors acknowledged their inability to devise a "completely satisfactory objective test for slang, especially in application to a word out of context," noting that "No word is invariably slang, and many standard words can be given slang connotations or used so inappropriately as to become slang." Nor could they devise suitable objective measures for nonstandard and substandard usages, so they were forced to interpret the character of their citations subjectively.

Obscene, vulgar, slang, substandard, and nonstandard—these five were the only status labels the *Third* employed, and they were contested on two counts: that the descriptors were too few and, more serious, that they were too seldom applied. Those arguing they were numerically insufficient claimed that in dropping "colloquial" Gove had overreacted to its misuse. Several acknowledged that the term had been commonly misinterpreted as a negative description of level rather than a neutral description of function. Instead of identifying an acceptable functional *variety* of English, as was intended, it had come to designate an unacceptable *level*. In wanting to combat this misuse of "colloquial" as a label Gove was correct; but in scuttling it he disregarded what teachers, editors, journalists, and traditionalists recognized as an important distinction between the written and spoken word. And in so doing he reinforced the negative association between his dictionary and the structural linguists for whom spoken language is paramount and writing only a secondary phenomenon. As it was no secret that structural linguists had paid little or no attention to the printed word, Gove's decision not to distinguish speech from writing smacked of the same negligence. The significance of this oversight for a broad spectrum of educated and intelligent dictionary users cannot be overstated. If writers and editors consult an unabridged dictionary more often than nonwriters, this policy slighted the most frequent and responsible readers. This disregard is especially perplexing because *Webster's* citations come from written, not spoken, sources.

In their rage at this failure to distinguish between formal writing and informal conversation, deprecators unwittingly gave credence to an early but false accusation that the *Third* had repudiated *all* usage labels. This allegation undermined what discrimination the *Third*'s five labels did exercise. It also revealed that several of the *Third*'s detractors had not read its introduction or studied its contents responsibly; some of those who made invidious comparisons between the *Third* and its predecessor neglected the preface to the 1934 work and failed to verify what they surmised it had handled conservatively. For example, Bergen Evans calculated (while convalescing in a hospital) that in the very issue in which *The New York Times* editorially condemned the *Third* and praised the Second, 153 "separate words, phrases, and constructions" occur which the *Third* lists but not the Second; and nineteen other usages appear which the Second condemns! Evans adds: "Many of them are used many times, more than three hundred such uses in all." And he provides statistics for the *Life* number that said it was sticking with the Second Edition: that issue contained over forty usages not appearing in the Second![18] Such disregard of history, such unwillingness to compare, stems from an unexamined assumption that one's convictions are correct and reveals popular and very influential attitudes about linguistic correctness and the role of a dictionary to be related in kind to political or religious creeds.

Linguists should not have been surprised at the crusading fervor of the *Third*'s disparagers. What is jolting is that Gove and his publisher were naive enough to allow the book's advertising to be colored in incendiary shades. Leonard Bloomfield, a revered founder of structural linguistics, had warned in 1944 of the danger that statements about the relation of standard and nonstandard forms are likely to be interpreted as advocacy of the latter.[19] Resistance to the linguistics content of *The English Language Arts* in 1952 underscored the validity of this observation. If we assume the Merriam officers were not deliberately provocative, they seem to have been insufficiently cognizant that theirs was not the only view of usage.

A number of linguists, recognizing distinctions of appropriate usage to be so fine that any discontinuous labeling system could slight significant subtleties, approved the absence of the label "colloquial." They maintained that the quoted usage examples could indicate distinctions better than a complex status scheme. Harold B. Allen praised the *Third*'s "attempt to provide more precise indications of usage status than were given by such a label as 'colloq.' "; and Robert A. Hall, Jr., thought the editors "wisely recognized a far greater gradation in levels of usage than has heretofore been customary."[20] But other linguists, James Sledd and Allen Walker Read among them, reproached Gove for erring on the side of too little application.[21] Sledd asked how the 200,000 citations in the *Third* "will enable the inexpert reader to do what 10,000,000 quotations did not make possible for the expert lexicographer"![22]

All in all, a wide band of readers found *Webster's* too lenient in its labeling of disputed items of usage, and common judgment found the book indulgent. The editors of *Consumer Reports,* having published Read's balanced review, were inundated with the complaints of irate readers who accused the reviewer of forgetting why people buy dictionaries: "They do not buy them to obtain 'a descriptive record of the language.' They buy them precisely to find out how the language is used by people who know and care."[23]

The American Heritage Dictionary

One sensational outcome of the *Third*'s alleged corrupting permissiveness was that an affluent publisher sought to buy out G. & C. Merriam, intending to suppress the *Third New International.* "We'd take the Third out of print!" *Newsweek* quoted the president of the American Heritage Publishing Company as saying. "We'd go back to the Second International and speed ahead on the Fourth."[24] But losing its bid to the supportive Encyclopedia Britannica, American Heritage resolved instead to design its own lexicon, and it undertook, "at a time when the language, already a historical melting pot, is under constant challenge—from the scientist, the bureaucrat, the broadcaster, the innovator of every stripe, even the voyager in space," to produce a new wordbook that would not merely record actual usage but would also "add the essential dimension of guidance . . . toward grace and precision which intelligent people seek in a dictionary."[25] When in 1969 *The American Heritage Dictionary of the English Language* appeared, its dust jacket advertised "a completely new dictionary—new in content, new in format, new in the wealth of information it offers," but, most significantly, presenting "extensive notes on how to use the language," along with words and their meanings.

Although *The American Heritage Dictionary* apparently proved to be a successful business venture, the publishers were motivated by a conviction that the English language was sliding downhill, abetted above all by the latest Merriam-Webster unabridged. Foremost among the editorial policies established at an executive level was that the proposed dictionary should reflect its publishers' "deep sense of responsibility as custodians of the American tradition in language as well as history." William Morris, the editor selected for the project, reports that from their first discussion in 1963 he and the executives "shared a feeling then widely voiced in such media as the New York *Times, The New Yorker, The Atlantic Monthly,* and *The American Scholar,* that *Webster's Third New International Dictionary* had failed both press and public by eliminating virtually all usage labels and other indications of standards of usage." But "restoring such labels as 'slang,' 'vulgar,' 'informal,' 'nonstandard,' and the like—while helpful—was not enough. We felt that the dictionary user wants to be given sensible guidance in how to use the language." To this end, Morris proposed organizing a panel of judges, more than a hundred writers, editors, and public figures "who have demonstrated their ability to use the language with felicity, facility, grace, and power."[26]

The publishers agreed to empanel such a jury, whose personal opinions on suspect locutions would be solicited. On the ultimate panel sat distinguished writers, critics, historians, editors and journalists, poets, anthropologists, professors of English and journalism, even several United States senators. Jurists familiar to followers of the dictionary debate were John Ciardi, Dwight Macdonald, Wilson Follett, Sheridan Baker, Mario Pei, and Jacques Barzun—not an altogether neutral sampling. Of those panel members who had publicly taken a stand on usage and the *Third,* I believe it is fair to say they represented the orthodox, if not hostile, side of the debate. One reviewer of the *AHD* discovered that of the 95 panelists whose ages he was able to determine, only six were under 50 years old, and 28 had been born in the nineteenth century.[27]

The digested opinions of this august court were presented in over 200 "usage notes" appended to some 500 entries in the dictionary.

Predictably, one finds a generally conservative evaluation of the disputed items. More than that, certain attitudes toward usage expressed in the book's front matter and in the usage articles themselves seem idiosyncratic and eccentric, even at times quirky. Morris Bishop, author of the dictionary's general essay on usage, admits that "The panelists have in common only a recognized ability to speak and write good English. They accepted their task and turned to it with gusto. They revealed, often with passion, their likes and dislikes, their principles, and also their whims and crotchets. . . . they tend to feel that the English language is going to hell if 'we' don't do something to stop it, and they tend to feel their own usage preferences are clearly *right*."[28]

Still more interesting, however, is the extent to which the jury's verdicts reveal disagreement even among conservers of the language. On specific items they disagreed more than they agreed. In fact, they agreed unanimously on only a single usage: guilty for *simultaneous* as an adverb ("the referendum was conducted simultaneous with the election"). On a few other usages there was near unanimity: *ain't I* and *between you and I,* disapproved for use in writing by 99 percent; *dropout* as a noun, approved by 97 percent; *thusly,* disapproved by 97 percent; *slow* as an adverb, approved by 96 percent; *anxious* in the sense of "eager," approved by 94 percent. Of "fina*lize* plans for a college reunion" 90 percent expressed disapproval; *rather unique* and *most unique* were disapproved by 94 percent. But more typical were opinions more evenly divided: "*Who* did you meet?" was acceptable in speech to 66 percent and in writing to 13 percent of the panel; "He wants to know *who* he should speak to," acceptable in speech to 59 percent.

Here is *AHD*'s complete usage note for *enthuse* (a back-formation from *enthusiasm*):

> *Enthuse* is not well established in writing on a serious level. The following typical examples are termed unacceptable by substantial majorities of the Usage Panal. *The majority leader enthused over his party's gains* is disapproved by 76 per cent. *He was considerably less enthused by signs of factionalism* is disapproved by 72 per cent. Alternative phrasing might be *became* (or *waxed*) *enthusiastic* or *was less enthusiastic over.*

A check of other dictionaries on this same item shows that the *Third* enters it without label or comment; *Webster's New World Dictionary* labels it "colloquial"; *The Random House Dictionary* says: "Although it is too widely encountered in the speech and writing of reputable teachers and authors to be listed as anything short of standard, ENTHUSE is nonetheless felt by many to be poor style, and in formal writing it would be best to paraphrase it." Especially in light of the rather temperate judgments of these other dictionaries, it is valuable to note that the *AHD* disapprovers of *enthuse* include Dwight Macdonald, who is quoted in the front matter of the dictionary as crying, "By God, let's hold the line on this one!"

Despite perennial proposals for establishment of an "academy" of English usage, the founding of one had not been managed in England or America until the publishers of *The American Heritage Dictionary* established their own and promulgated its views. The employment of a usage panel was intended to prescribe what people should say by revealing what an elite group would expect of a cultured person. Regrettably, in the words of the scholar who has given the *AHD*'s treatment of usage its most thorough and objective analysis, the *AHD* was "recondite in its method of selection of items to be evaluated, incautious in its method of presenting them for assessment, probably biased in its selection of 'experts,' and erratic in its editorial handling of the opinions of those experts."[29] Able only to persuade, these arbiters fortunately exercised no *de jure* power. But the kind of forum they had for broadcasting their views was sacrosanct in America, where the kind of allegiance the Earl of Chesterfield had given to Dr. Johnson was pledged instead, by the people, simply to "the dictionary"—meaning first Noah Webster's, then *any* "dictionary."

AHD's panel reflected a harking back to the functions of wordbooks in eighteenth-century England when for eighteenth-century reasons the language was in need of ascertainment and codification. Large numbers of Americans in the latter part of the twentieth century feel a need to employ only usages whose standing is *de rigueur,* whose social acceptability is upper middle class or better; and they seek authoritative dicta from "the dictionary." Such a katzenjammer resulted from the *Third*'s ignoring of these needs that the sensible tack for the forthrightly reactionary *AHD* was to court favor among the conservers of language orthodoxy. Advice seekers may choose their counsel, and *AHD*'s editors surely did not want liberal guidance on usage; that was already assembled in the *Third*. Rather, they sought a conservative view and selected arbiters accordingly. Empaneling a significant or vociferous sample of descriptivists would not help give expression to an orthodox view of good grammar, nor would it supply guidance to those wishing to speak and write "correctly."

It is an ostrich-like conviction of linguists that without continual coaching from editors and teachers, Americans would not fret over "correctness" and that nothing valuable would be lost if their insecurities were not catered to. Others see it otherwise. A staunch prescriptivist has observed that even though most people will speak and write as they choose, "that doesn't mean that there's no demand for a priestly caste to glorify and interpret the Tables of the Law. A lot of church-goers give the Ten Commandments quite a beating at home and in the market-place, but the anti-clerical movement has never got very far in this country."[30]

Given current sentiment about "correct" English in the United States, one fact about disputed usages is that many highly respected persons frown on them. "Such people are to be heeded," say Lloyd and Warfel, sensibly advising college freshmen, "for they often have a keen sense of the niceties of writing and of formal speech; they represent, furthermore, a kind of taboo-tradition in our society which is very influential among people who teach and write."[31]

Just as a dictionary does not condone a usage by including it among its entries, so it would not endorse an opinion or attitude by reporting or describing it—as *Webster's* editors doubtless knew. Information about status is part of the description of a word. The decision of the editors of the *Third* to ignore the yearning of the editors, writers, and laity who seek out "authority" may reflect courageous wisdom or foolhardiness. Had they chosen to incorporate opinion about usage as part of an entry's description, by whatever means, they would have pleased readers concerned about the social meaning as well as the strictly linguistic aspects of disputed usages. But it is doubtful that the *Third* could have been a better dictionary for such inclusions. The methods of gathering and reporting their sociolinguistic facts would have been the crucial test of the dictionary's handling of such a sensitive issue; and techniques available in 1961 were inadequate to match the standards the *Third's* editors established for gathering and reporting facts about the actual usage of the English lexicon, opinion aside.

The publishers of *AHD* might well have been tempted to ignore the community of linguistic scholars, given their alleged lamentable influence on the *Third*. But good business sense persuaded them to consult linguists, since without them they could not have produced an adequate dictionary. Since structuralists were taking a back seat to transformational-generative linguists during the time the conservative *AHD* was being designed, the newer linguists were given a major role in decisions about all but one lexicographic aspect of the dictionary: that exception, of course, was in the matter of deciding good usage.

Involved in the *AHD* were several transformational-generative linguists and—as is necessary for etymology—some traditional historical-comparative linguists, as well as one or two descriptive-structural linguists. *AHD's* front matter includes an article on the history of English by the noted author of a transformational-generative approach to the subject; an article on the phonological dialects of English by a

prominent structuralist; an article on the relationship between grammar
and meaning from a transformational-generative viewpoint; an article on
English spelling and pronunciation from the vantage of Chomsky and
Halle, founders of the new school; and an article on computers in
language analysis and lexicography, again by a linguist.[32] The
dictionary's introductory essay on "Good Usage, Bad Usage, and
Usage," however, was written by Morris Bishop, professor of French
literature at Cornell, past president of the conservative Modern
Language Association, and a poet. Previously such usage analyses were
provided by linguists like Charles Fries *(American College Dictionary)*
and Raven I. McDavid, Jr. *(Random House Dictionary)* or by
anonymous staffs thoroughly imbued with scientific views. The selection
of Bishop signaled a literary bias in the matter of language correctness.
The incidence of rapprochement in *AHD* between transformational
linguists and traditional grammarians should not suggest a general recon-
ciliation between linguists and traditionalists; but it is noteworthy in a
dictionary whose publishers had sought to scuttle the *Third* because of its
scientific and linguistic bias.

The Transformational-Generative Linguists

One of the three new schools of linguists arising since the 1950s,[33]
transformational-generative linguists, led by Noam Chomsky of M.I.T.,
came into prominence during the early 1960s having rejected certain ax-
ioms of the structural-descriptive school with which the 1961 *Webster's*
and the relativity of correctness were associated. Not that the descrip-
tivist principles to which the dictionary subscribed were challenged;
rather, Chomsky's approach represented profound differences in his
understanding of the psychological nature of language. Sharply disagreeing with B. F. Skinner's behaviorist tenet that operant conditioning is the
foundation of verbal learning and verbal behavior, he substituted a
nativistic view of language. It is not within our scope to outline the
theory of transformational-generative grammar.[34] But we can point to
several elements of Chomsky's theory that may favor a more hospitable
relationship between transformationalists and traditionalists than traditional grammarians and descriptive linguists afforded one another.

For one thing, there is at the heart of Chomsky's approach a distinction between "linguistic performance" and "linguistic competence." The
object of Chomsky's studies is linguistic competence, the grammar of
their language that native speakers have internalized; it is a
psychologically real grammar underlying language use. Performance,

possibly influenced by the linguistic accidents of fatigue or inadvertence, is the manifestation of this competence in actual speech. Chomsky's focus is thus on grammar as it is presumed to exist in the mind of an "ideal speaker-hearer." Implicit in the performance-competence distinction is a somewhat distant parallel to the traditionalist's contrast between what people actually say or write and what the rules of English grammar indicate they might ideally have done. "It cannot be too strongly emphasized," writes a leading generative linguist, "that grammar is a description of what people *know*, not of what they do!"[35] Further, Chomsky asserts that the "meager and degenerate" character of the data from which children construct their internalized grammars supports the nativist position that some grammatical structuring is innate, a view that suggests the possibility of an inherent logic, naturalness, or rightness at least at the deepest psychological levels of language.[36] This does not mean that the use of split infinitives, for example, or *like* as a conjunction can be written off to performance errors. The linguistic competence of a person who regularly employs these constructions would contain rules requiring them. But the distinction does allow for speech "mistakes" such as false starts and "slips of the tongue," phenomena many thought not possible in the descriptivists' analysis.

In phonology, some of the generative linguists posit at a more abstract level than actual speech a psychologically real set of sound features or elements whose character, it turns out, is well represented by conventional spellings, which capture it better than a phonetic transcription of the spoken word. Whereas the descriptivists faulted English spelling for failing to harmonize with pronunciation, these linguists discern a connection between the underlying basis for pronunciation and the standard orthography. As one of them wrote, "English orthography is nearly optimal, not at the level of phonetic or actual pronunciation, but at an abstract level, a psychologically significant level from which pronunciations can be predicted and to which they can be referred. Moreover, . . . this orthography preserves information about the history and the meaning of words that is of great value in human communication."[37] Thus, for some generative linguists spoken language is not the only language, and for even this limited interest in written forms they will find traditionalists receptive.

Thirdly, the prominence the new linguists give to syntax will help to set right for traditional grammarians the disproportionately heavy emphasis on sound systems that characterizes structuralist grammars and, to a lesser extent, the *Third*. English teachers, concerned with written composition and literature, devote only slight attention to pronunciation and none to phonological systems. They are chiefly, if not exclusively, concerned with syntax and semantics and are perplexed or annoyed by phonetic symbols. Fundamental to early generative grammar is the importance of syntax in grammatical analysis. More significantly, the central role of semantics in language analysis has been argued by a faction of Chomsky's disciples.[38] Transformational-generative linguists have grappled insightfully with ambiguity, synonymy, grammaticality, degrees of acceptability, paraphrase, and language creativity—topics of interest and importance for traditionalists and literary specialists. Fruitful concern with these phenomena may win attention from English teachers and invite their scrutiny of linguistic analyses in other matters.

What has been said above should not be taken as suggesting sympathy among any faction of the transformational-generative linguists for the traditional grammarian's notion of linguistic correctness. On this question the new linguists are at one with the descriptivists. They take the speech of native speakers to be definitive, and endeavor to specify explicitly the elements and rules that generate all the sentences of a speaker. Though they have been unsuccessful to date in providing more than a fragmentary picture of English (or any other language), they attempt to formulate a model of the internalized grammar of "an idealized speaker-hearer." Of course, only insofar as one speaker's internalized grammar corresponds to another's can communication occur. But most of the transformationalists are perhaps even less interested in what we might call community grammars than structuralists were, and they have been criticized for slighting the basic fact that language is an instrument of communication in a society. Exploiting a distinction drawn by Ferdinand de Saussure earlier in the century between *langue* (the code) and *parole* (the individual's use of that code), transformational work has been excessively code-focused.

Structuralists too have concentrated on the linguistic code and the internal relationships of its components, excluding the communicative functioning of language from their purview. But other linguists have recently stepped up inquiry into pragmatic aspects of language use, which structuralists had thought inaccessible. Building on the speech act theories of language philosophers, especially J. L. Austin and John Searle,[39] this pursuit has added a crucial dimension to the space of linguistics, one very much allied with more traditional and rhetorical interests in language functioning and its felicitous use. Linguists of late are studying speech acts, conversational postulates, and the structure of discourse. Again, these concerns with the more concrete aspects of language may attract linguists and traditional grammarians to the same conferences and possibly to sober dialogue!

One aspect of generative grammar bearing on the validity of the traditionalists' view of language is the relationship between the underlying structure of a sentence and its surface structure. For the transformational-generative linguists, especially the so-called generative-semanticists among them, the structure underlying a sentence is a highly abstract entity only indirectly associated with the structure of the realized sentence in spoken or written form. A set of transformations relates the underlying form of a sentence, which according to some linguists specifies its semantic content, to the surface form, which has been shaped by the syntactic and phonological rules of the language and is the vehicle for transmitting the meaning. Though generative linguists emphatically deny any necessary connection between their explicit model for sentence-structure characterization and the processes of encoding or decoding language, they have contributed to our understanding of ambiguity and synonymy, two important points of language usage and of literary and stylistic analysis.

The notion of ambiguity can be elaborated by relating a number of distinct underlying or semantic structures to a single surface structure. Conversely, some synonymy derives from a correspondence between multiple surface structures representing a single underlying semantic configuration. To use Chomsky's chestnut, "Flying planes can be dangerous" is ambiguous precisely because two underlying structures, one relating to planes that are flying, the other to someone's flying of planes, are realized in the "same" surface form; this is, for the linguists, classical ambiguity. Sentences like "It's surprising that they lost to Alabama" and "That they lost to Alabama is surprising" have identical propositional content and are surface variations of a single underlying semantic structure; they are synonymous. Transformational-generative linguists have shown that the generation of a surface form from an underlying structure is wondrously complex; the relationship between meaning and surface structure is oblique and indirect. The surface form of a sentence is an iceberg tip compared to the great bulk of complexity that underlies and supports it.

Without prejudging the case, it would seem that the traditional grammarian's obsession with surface nuances may be less important than previously thought. Traditionalists have argued that loss of distinctions will impoverish the language (for example, if *infer* comes to be synonymous with *imply*). But English could skirt a semantic merger by exploiting one of the alternative routes that can be imagined from the base of the iceberg to its tip. If the ability to convey a difference between *imply* and *infer* or *disinterested* and *uninterested* via these lexical items is lost, English would not thereby be compelled to yield the distinction altogether. A multiplicity of surface forms can convey identical semantic content. For two words to converge semantically is only to lose one mode of conveying the distinction. As transformational-generative linguists probe into the relationships between semantic content and surface forms, emphasis on preserving lexical distinctions may abate somewhat.

Finally, a historical accident may also help linguists recoup some of the respect which the brouhaha over the *Third* dissipated. Chomsky's rationalism is grounded in seventeenth- and eighteenth-century philosophical notions, including universal grammar. While this new interest in classical rationalism has caught the attention of philosophers, the implications of a rationalist theory of language acquisition for the field of psychology are potentially revolutionary. Chomsky has revitalized the rationalist vs. empiricist debate among learning theorists and has marshaled linguistic evidence for the moribund nativist position. This linguistic work has occasioned dialogue among philosophers, psychologists, and linguists. The attention given to their linguistic colleagues, who had become virtual pariahs in some English and foreign language departments, has in some quarters prompted a fresh look by literary scholars whose own work also draws them to the philosophical and social background of seventeenth- and eighteenth-century rationalism.

Notes

[1] Robert A. Hall, Jr., review in "Webster's Third New International Dictionary: A Symposium," ed. Robert G. Gunderson, *Quarterly Journal of Speech,* XLVIII (1962), 435. This issue of *QJS,* containing seven reviews of the *Third,* will be cited in notes hereafter as "Symposium."

[2] Raven I. McDavid, Jr., in "Symposium," p. 437.

[3] Bergen Evans, "Let's Stop Maligning the Dictionary," *Chicago Tribune Magazine* (August 25, 1963); cited from Philip B. Gove, ed., *The Role of the Dictionary* (1967), p. 42.

[4] Harold B. Allen, in "Symposium," p. 432.

[5] The phrase "medieval, rigid, uninformed, Philistine" comes from Karl W. Dykema, "Cultural Lag and Reviewers of *Webster III*" (1963), p. 369; "uniformly obscurantist, uniformly uninformed" is from Allen, in "Symposium," p. 431. Francis Christensen, in "A Case for *Webster's Third,*" calls the school tradition "dogmatic and authoritarian [and] so unrealistic that the effect is to cripple and enslave. . . . In short it is profoundly inimical to the aims of liberal education . . ."; cited from Gove (1967), p. 24.

[6] McDavid, in "Symposium," p. 435.

[7] McDavid, in his edition of H. L. Mencken, *The American Language,* 4th ed., rev. and abr. (1963), p. 483 fn.

[8] Robert A. Hall, Jr., *Introductory Linguistics* (1964), pp. 368–369; see also his review in "Symposium," pp. 434–435.

[9] Allen Walker Read, "*That* Dictionary or *The* Dictionary?" (1963), pp. 488–492; Dykema, "Cultural Lag and Reviewers of *Webster III,*" pp. 364–369.

[10]For a scholarly appraisal of the dictionary by a lexicographer, see Robert L. Chapman, "A Working Lexicographer Appraises *Webster's Third New International Dictionary*" (1967). Chapman says his critique "represents the judgment of about ten lexicographers."

[11]In the Second Edition (1934) of the dictionary, words used by Chaucer had been included, though a later cut-off date for other obsolete entries was employed.

[12]Jacques Barzun, "What Is a Dictionary?" (1963), p. 177.

[13]Read, "*That* Dictionary or *The* Dictionary?" p. 492; see also "Symposium," pp. 438–439.

[14]Chapman, p. 207 *(flightily)*; Robert Sonkin, in "Symposium," p. 440 *(a fortiori)*.

[15]Chapman, p. 205; other reviewers objected to *torturous* alongside *tortuous,* and *admissable* and *feasable* with their *-ible* counterparts.

[16]Uriel Weinreich, "*Webster's Third:* A Critique of Its Semantics" (1964).

[17]The "four-letter words," though not *damn* or *hell,* are "usually" or "sometimes" or "often" "considered vulgar," along with nouns like *pussy* and verbs like *screw.*

[18]"But What's a Dictionary For?" (1962), p. 58. The editorials in the *Times* and *Life* are reprinted in James Sledd and Wilma R. Ebbitt, eds., *Dictionaries and THAT Dictionary* (1962), along with the directive issued to the staff of the *Times* informing them that "Editors representing the news, Sunday and editorial departments have decided without a dissent to continue to follow Webster's Second Edition for spelling and usage. Webster III will be the authority only for new, principally scientific words" (pp. 122–123).

[19]"Secondary and Tertiary Responses to Language" (1944).

[20]"Symposium," pp. 432, 434.

[21]Read, "*That* Dictionary or *The* Dictionary?" and Sledd, " 'Standard' Is a Trademark" (1963).

[22]"The Lexicographer's Uneasy Chair" (1962), pp. 684–685.

[23]For the editors' comment, see *Consumer Reports,* XXVIII (1963), 510; for the letter quoted and additional editorial remarks, see *Consumer Reports,* XXIX (1964), 2.

[24]William Morris, ed., *The American Heritage Dictionary of the English Language* (1969), p. vi.

[26]William Morris, "The Making of a Dictionary—1969," *College Composition and Communication* (October 1969); cited from Herman A. Estrin and Donald V. Mehus, eds., *The American Language in the 1970s* (1974), pp. 52–53.

[27]Patrick E. Kilburn, "The Gentlemen's Guide to Linguistic Etiquette" (1970), p. 5. Included on the Panel were writers Katherine Anne Porter, Isaac Asimov, and Langston Hughes; critics Walter Kerr and Brendan Gill; historians Bruce Catton, Eric F. Goldman, and Barbara Tuchman; editors Erwin D. Canham, J. Donald Adams, Theodore M. Bernstein, and Vermont Royster; U.S. Senators Eugene McCarthy and Mark Hatfield; poets Marianne Moore, Donald Davidson, and Allen Tate; anthropologist Margaret Mead; professors of English George R. Stewart, Wallace Stegner, Morton W. Bloomfield, and Mark Van Doren.

[28]"Good Usage, Bad Usage, and Usage," *AHD,* p. xxiii.

[29]Thomas J. Creswell, *Usage in Dictionaries and Dictionaries of Usage* (1975).

[30]Louis B. Salomon, "*Whose* Good English?" (1952), p. 444.

[31]*American English in Its Cultural Setting* (1956), p. 447.

[32]Morton W. Bloomfield, "A Brief History of the English Language"; Henry Lee Smith Jr., "Dialects of English"; Richard Ohmann, "Grammar and Meaning"; Wayne O'Neil, "The Spelling and Pronunciation of English"; Henry Kucera, "Computers in Language Analysis and in Lexicography."

[33]For introductions to the other approaches, which have not received as much scholarly attention as generative-transformational grammar, see Walter A. Cook, S.J., *Introduc-*

tion to Tagmemic Analysis (1969); Sydney M. Lamb, *Outline of Stratificational Grammar* (1966); David G. Lockwood, *Introduction to Stratificational Linguistics* (1972).

[34]Introductory discussions of transformational-generative grammar may be found in Ronald Langacker, *Language and Its Structure,* 2nd ed. (1973); John Lyons, *Noam Chomsky* (1970); Victoria Fromkin and Robert Rodman, *An Introduction to Language,* 2nd ed. (1978).

[35]Paul M. Postal, Epilogue, in *English Transformational Grammar* by Roderick A. Jacobs and Peter S. Rosenbaum (1968), p. 272.

[36]*Aspects of the Theory of Syntax* (1965), p. 58; see also *Language and Mind,* Enl. ed. (1972), p. 78.

[37]O'Neil, "The Spelling and Pronunciation of English," *AHD,* p. xxxv.

[38]For a somewhat technical overview of the issues between the "interpretive semanticists" and the "generative semanticists," see Barbara Hall Partee, "On the Requirement that Transformations Preserve Meaning," in Charles J. Fillmore and D. Terence Langendoen, eds., *Studies in Linguistic Semantics* (1971), pp. 1–21, or the same author's less technical "Linguistic Metatheory," in William Orr Dingwall, ed., *A Survey of Linguistic Science* (1971), pp. 650–680.

[39]J. L. Austin, *How to Do Things with Words* (1962); John R. Searle, *Speech Acts* (1969).

CHAPTER VIII

The Empirical Study of Attitudes toward Language and Correctness

"A speech community cannot be conceived as a group of speakers who all use the same forms; it is best defined as a group who share the same norms in regard to language." —WILLIAM LABOV, 1972

"Grammar indeed originated as a pedagogical and literary genre, and has been revitalized as a logical one; neither its traditional nor its mathematical pedigree is much warrant for taking it for granted that it is the form in which speech comes organized for use. . . . Classical antiquity did not stop with grammar, but went on to rhetoric . . . . So should we, but without the normative, exclusionary bias that has dogged the genre of grammar throughout its history . . . ."

—DELL HYMES, 1974

IN THE 1960s, Noam Chomsky's probing of the psychological representation of grammar was only one of several lively developments in linguistics. Chomsky's concern was with "an ideal speaker-listener, in a completely homogeneous speech-community."[1] But anthropologists and linguists knew of no homogeneous speech community; and some scholars sharing Chomsky's interest in the underlying patterns of language broke free of his idealization in order to seek an understanding less isolated from the social and cultural functioning of language.

William Labov proposed a linguistics that was socially more realistic, while Dell Hymes went further in urging a socially constituted linguistics.[2] Noting the fruitful research activities coupling linguistic and social parameters, both Hymes and Labov advocated revamping the narrow study of grammatical codes that had occupied both structuralists and transformationalists. The term *sociolinguistics* emerged as a name for this new area of study.

Thus, alongside the linguistic systems Chomsky and his followers were developing, there was a movement among other scholars from strictly

147

grammatical approaches to social and functional ones. From a focus on the code itself, sociolinguists turned to the situations in which the varieties of the code were used. They shifted attention from the cognitive functions of language to its social meaning and its social use. The important structuralist distinction between "sames" and "differents" in a language system took on added significance as sociolinguists discovered that expressions having the same reference were socially different, while certain referentially different expressions were systematically alike in their social and interactional valuation.

Linguists knew that language varies with place and time, as with the offshoots of Indo-European. They had also noted that the speech of an individual changed with shifting topics and circumstances. (Even Bishop Lowth observed that relaxed speech differed from platform speech.) But many differences within a speech community had frequently been charged to "free variation" or to other dimly understood factors. That the variation might be highly systematic or functional was not perceived.

In time linguists came to recognize systematic differences not only between the varieties of standard English spoken in Boston and Los Angeles, but also between those spoken by educated New Yorkers in relaxed circumstances and more formal ones and between those spoken by middle-class Blacks in Detroit and fishermen in New England. They began to grapple with the difficulties of describing differences between the variety written by scientists for publication in learned journals and that used in news reports by journalists. Partial descriptions were produced of the varieties of English in the United States and England, especially the so-called social, as distinct from regional, varieties or "dialects." *Variety* includes the notion of dialect, but because popular usage tends to limit *dialect* to regional varieties, linguists now prefer the broader, more neutral, term *variety*.

In multilingual communities each language in the linguistic repertoire is assigned to a particular domain. In the Mexican-American community in Los Angeles, for example, Spanish is spoken at home and in church, while English is the language of government generally and of education beyond a certain level. In countries like Belgium, Indonesia, India, and Iran, the complexity of such linguistic interrelationships is extraordinary. Individuals control several languages, and their functional allocation over the communicative tasks of daily life is intricate. In Tehran, the capital city of Iran, Christian families may speak Armenian or Assyrian at home and in church, Persian at school, all three playing in the streets, and Azerbaijani Turkish at shops in the bazaar. Moslem men from the northwest working as laborers in the capital may speak an informal variety of Persian with their supervisors at construction sites, a variety of

Turkish with their fellow laborers, a local Iranian dialect when they visit their village home for the New Year holidays; and they may listen daily to radio news broadcasts in standard Persian and to passages from the Koran in Arabic. In this country of about 35 million people, languages of five separate families are spoken natively, and many individuals command four or five languages or mutually unintelligible varieties. The situation is still more complex in India, with over a dozen major languages and more than eight hundred dialects.

In such multilingual speech communities, the languages and their functional allocation must be mastered, and every person must learn to switch entire linguistic codes as naturally and unobtrusively as he uses the names of the different people at the family meal. The codes of a multilingual speaker can usually express the same referential meanings. But the social meanings assigned by the community to the *use* of various codes will differ.[3] Similarly, in a monolingual community the varieties of a single language may have equivalent referential or denotative significance, but social valuation is not indifferent to the selection. The intimate variety spoken between husband and wife in private differs from that spoken by the same man to his misbehaving son and from those he would address to a lax employee and to business associates on the golf course and to his representative in Congress in a discussion of pending legislation. In each case the speech variety is systematically tailored to the occasion. Imagine the variety used with the errant son employed instead to enlist the support of the member of Congress, or vice versa. While the denotations of the words could be identical, the connotations would undermine the effectiveness of the communication. It strikes us as ludicrous to imagine the use of any one variety on the other occasions. From the linguistic repertoire speakers must be able to select a suitable variety for each speech situation and shift to other varieties as situations change. If there is a change in the setting, the topic, or the person or persons addressed, custom may mandate a shifting of the speech variety; even a shift in the relationship between speaker and addressee may require a different variety.

Just as bilinguals and multilinguals switch linguistic codes with culturally defined shifts of speech situations. so monolinguals switch varieties of a single language. Alternation between varieties demands the concomitant selection of all characteristic phonological, syntactic, lexical, and semantic features. Settling on a variety commits one to all the features at every level of grammar that co-occur within that variety. Features characteristic of different varieties can be mixed only for specific exploitative purposes, as when a Californian might for humorous effect quote a senator using a Boston "accent." The selection of a particular variety restricts one to the systematic characteristics of that variety just as one is normally restricted to the features of one language at a time in a multilingual community.[4] Though we can assume a speaker's internalized repertoire is psychologically unified in a fashion still little understood, each variety of a language can be described in a distinct grammar. Every monolingual speaker, besides acquiring the grammars for these varieties, must learn their appropriate allocation.[5]

Noting that investigators had reported great variance in the speech of New Yorkers and that this variation seemed disordered and unaccountable, William Labov, then a graduate student at Columbia University, carried out a preliminary survey which led to his hypothesizing that the occurrence of *r* in words like *car* and *beard* was socially distributed in systematic ways. New Yorkers only sometimes pronounce the *r* in such words, and Labov set out to discover the pattern. He postulated that if groups of New Yorkers were socially ranked, their use of *r* would be differential according to rank, with more *r* in the higher social classes than in the lower.

Labov designed a pilot study in which employees of three socially stratified New York department stores—Saks, Macy's, and S. Klein—were asked the whereabouts of particular merchandise whose location he knew to be on the fourth floor. He simply inquired in each case where he might find, say, lamps or luggage. Then he pretended not to have heard the response and elicited a second, presumably more careful, pronunciation of "fourth floor." He thus had two occurrences of the variable (r) in each of two stylistically different responses, one quite casual, the other more deliberate, for each respondent. Having moved on out of sight, he noted which of the possible four occurrences of *r* had been realized, as well as some data about the sex, race, approximate age, job, and location in the store for the respondent.

The distribution was as predicted, with most *r* in Saks, the highest-ranked store, and fewest in S. Klein, the lowest-ranked. The technique also revealed differential use of (r) between the first and second utterances of "fourth floor." In each store there tended to be more occurrences of *r* in the emphatic pronunciation than in the casual first one. What earlier analysts had assumed to be free variation was not random at all. Greater occurrence of *r* characterized higher socioeconomic status and more careful speech. Correlations were also established for sex, race, and job. The department store study gave preliminary confirmation to Labov's hypothesis and paved the way for a more systematic investigation of phonological variables.[6]

Labov subsequently surveyed Lower East Side residents of Manhattan. Sociologists had earlier gathered socioeconomic data about these

New Yorkers, and from a secondary stratified sampling Labov interviewed residents and gathered data about their use of phonological variables and about their conscious and unconscious attitudes toward their own speech and that of fellow New Yorkers. Again (r) was studied, along with the vowels of words like *bad* or *jazz* and words like *law, lost,* and *talk,* and the consonant sounds that initiate words like *thing* or *three* and *that* or *there.* The findings have profound implications for our understanding of the functioning of language variation.

Labov studied four socioeconomic classes in this sample: upper middle class (UMC), lower middle class (LMC), working class (WC), and lower class (LC). Each of the five phonological variables was found to be socially stratified. For each variable, each class used more of the prestige form than the immediately lower class. This was a remarkable discovery; language discrimination was more subtle across classes than anyone had previously imagined.

Even more surprising was confirmation of the stylistic differentiation *within* each class: every social class produced more stigmatized forms in successively more relaxed speech. Labov investigated four degrees of formality, from casual style through the reading of word lists, observing distinctive channel cues for each. For every socioeconomic class the percentage of stigmatized variants was highest in the most casual speech and systematically decreased as the speech style became more formal. For example, the percentage of stigmatized *d* for the initial consonant of *that* or *these* (producing the infamous "dat" and "dese") was dramatically higher in the relaxed speech of the Lower East Siders, including UMC speakers, than in their careful speech. Similarly, limiting attention only to *relaxed* pronunciations of words like *this* and *then,* the percentage of initial *d* was greater among the WC New Yorkers than among the UMC or LMC. For all classes the "dat" and "dese" pronunciations increased as formality decreased. But at each degree of formality the LC had fewer prestigious forms than the WC; the WC had fewer than the LMC; and the LMC had fewer than the UMC. Looking at another of the phonological variables, namely the initial consonant of words like *three* and *thirty,* Labov found that in casual speech the LC pronounced *th* as *t* in over 90 percent of cases, compared with 70 percent for the WC, about 30 percent for the LMC, and less than 15 percent for the UMC.[7]

Thus the pattern governing variable phonological usage interweaves degrees of formality with social levels in systematic ways. This finding undermines the widely accepted insight of John Kenyon, who in 1948 proposed that levels of acceptability and degrees of formality are different and should be distinguished. Kenyon had claimed, as we have noted, that each usage is standard formal or informal, or nonstandard formal or informal. Labov proved rather that the same linguistic usage could be standard informal for one social group and nonstandard formal for a lower social group. For example, the UMC speakers in his New York City studies "dropped" their *r*'s about 82 percent of the time in informal speech but in only about 65 percent of cases on more formal occasions, whereas the LC speakers dropped their *r*'s almost 100 percent of the time on informal occasions but approximated standard informal usage on formal occasions. Similar results were obtained for the other phonological variables. It remains to be seen whether syntactic and morphological variables, the chief concern of traditional grammarians, follow similar patterns.

Labov discovered that the greatest differentiation of speech forms between socioeconomic classes generally occurs in the most *casual* circumstances. For some features, in fact, class differences virtually vanish in the most *formal* circumstances, where the number of stigmatized variants drops dramatically for all speakers. This demonstrates that *evaluation* of phonological variation is more uniform across social classes than actual *usage* is. All social classes in New York are united in their appraisal of the prestige of variable phonological forms, though their usages differ significantly. In fact, says Labov, social stratification of variable usage *depends* on a uniform *evaluation* of the variation across classes. Such unconscious recognition of norms is so important a part of the fabric of communication that he proposes defining speech communities not by the common *usage* of linguistic forms but by the shared *norms of evaluation:* a speech community is thus "a group of speakers who share a set of social attitudes towards language."[8]

In his research in New York, as in an earlier study of Martha's Vineyard, Labov found not only that social and economic factors correlate with speech characteristics, but also that personal goals influence choice of phonological variants. In Martha's Vineyard, young men intending to study on the mainland and seek their livelihood there spoke more like mainlanders and less like Vineyarders than friends who intended to take up employment on the island. The speech of upwardly mobile New Yorkers resembled the target group's speech more than that of their own socioeconomic class; those who were downwardly mobile, having aimed higher and failed, had speech patterns resembling those of classes even lower than their own.[9] Similar findings are expected for other groups; and the motivating factors for youngsters whose aspirations differ from those of their own social group (however that is defined) may determine eventual adherence to norms of standard English. One must wonder about the implications of this finding for the teaching of standard morphological and grammatical usages to students whose prospects for socioeconomic advancement are severely limited.

Labov's investigations show that despite significant variation in their *use* of certain socially diagnostic features in the sound system, New Yorkers are united in their *attitudes* toward the correctness of phonological variables like (r) and (th). The pronunciation of *r* in *park* and *floor* is more highly valued than its absence; "den" for *then* and "tree" for *three* are uniformly stigmatized, though at different absolute values of usage. Labov's work demonstrates that a certain large English-speaking community of New York City shares a single set of norms with respect to these variable phonological usages, though each social class differentially approximates the norm in its own speech.

A regular structure of social and stylistic variation characterized the behavior of all five phonological features in Labov's work. Social classes generally remain ranked in the same order in terms of use of the prestige forms, for all degrees of formality. However, a peculiar deviation occurs with the LMC. In the most casual speech the differential use of (r) ranks the social classes in order, as expected. But, unlike the pattern for the stable variables, at the more formal end of the scale the LMC exceeds the UMC in its realization of the prestige form. *In its most formal style,* the LMC achieves a higher percentage of *r*-pronunciation in words like *car, beard,* and *fourth* than the UMC achieves in the same style.[10] This pattern may indicate that the social meaning attached to *r* by LMC speakers is greater than that attached to other phonological variables or is of sufficient weight to cause hypercorrection; there is evidence that hypercorrection is associated more with upward mobility than with LMC status per se. The social meaning of *r* is sufficiently important that the second highest ranking group compensates for its insecurity in this matter. Transfer of such patterns to morphological and grammatical usages, if that is what further research uncovers, will help explain hypercorrections like "between you and I" and "she is the person whom, I imagine, will win."

Curious about the attitudes of New Yorkers to various features of their speech, Labov employed two testing modes in order to explore subjective evaluations of the stratified variables. He designed an index of linguistic insecurity (ILI) to gauge the degree to which people perceive a gap between their actual usage and what they regard as correct. Simply by counting the number of discrepancies between what subjects identify as the correct form and what they think their normal practice is, the ILI measures insecurity. The more self-adjudged correct forms speakers think they use, the lower the ILI and the more linguistically secure they may be considered.

Labov also used a "matched-guise" technique in which five speakers were taped reading the same passage and the tapes then interlaced so that the same speaker appears at different times speaking different sentences.[11] He assembled a tape of 22 sentences spoken by an assumed 22 New Yorkers and then elicited from a group of listener-judges evaluations of each person's speech. The editing allows for several independent judgments of the same speaker by each evaluator. After the judges rated the supposed 22 speakers on a semantic differential scale for job suitability, Labov correlated the linguistic variables with the evaluations. The structuring of the taped passages provides different concentrations of particular diagnostic features and hence elicits separate judgments of a single speaker using more or fewer of certain stigmatized features. The tests showed that people in all social classes readily make judgments about job suitability solely on the basis of a person's pronunciation of everyday words and that similar rankings are assigned by all social classes.

The matched-guise technique previously used by researchers at Montreal's McGill University had revealed that for such nonlinguistic traits as height, dependability, education, intelligence, and even good looks, monolingual speakers of English consistently rated bilingual speakers higher when speaking English than when speaking French. The same person was imagined by English speakers to be handsomer, more intelligent, taller, and more ambitious and dependable if he was speaking English than if he was speaking French. Surprisingly, identical results (not the reverse!) were produced by monolingual French speakers listening to the same tapes; for them as well, English suggested better looks, more character, more intelligence, and so on. Only on "religiousness" and "kindness" did the French speakers rate the French Canadian guises more highly than the English speakers did; for all other characteristics they in fact rated them lower than the English speakers had.[12]

Matched-guise tests have been employed elsewhere, and a good deal about subjective reactions has been uncovered. In an experiment similar to that in Montreal but with quite different results, researchers in Israel found Jewish and Arab adolescents mutually antagonistic in rating bilingual speakers of Hebrew and Arabic. Both Jewish and Arab subjects rated the guises representing their own cultural group higher on traits of honesty, friendliness, good-heartedness, and acceptability as relatives by marriage.[13] In Texas, student teachers were presented with composite sets of randomly combined photographs, compositions, audio tapes, and drawings of third-grade boys and asked to form impressions of them. The experimenters concluded that, more than the compositions and drawings, the photographs and speech samples influenced judgments of personality and intelligence.[14] Again, in Montreal, speakers of standard

European French were judged more intelligent, better educated, more ambitious, and even more likeable than both upper-class and lower-class speakers of Canadian French.[15] In the Philippines, speakers of American English were more highly esteemed than speakers of either Filipino English or Tagalog.[16] Similar experiments have indicated that personality traits are inferred from different regional varieties of American English.[17]

These sociolinguistic studies demonstrate that linguistic features *do* influence the social, intellectual, and personal judgments that people make of one another. Such features include choice of regional or national dialect, linguistic hesitancy, and the concentration of stratified phonological variants like the absence of *r* in *car* and the pronunciation "tin" for *thin* or "dese" for *these*. Even linguistically naive Americans can accurately distinguish social differences across regional varieties.[18] These subjective evaluations of socially stratified usages are acquired in early adolescence and are remarkably uniform throughout a community. Since none of the valuated phonological features in New York is normally taught in the schools, there is no question here of academic influence on their valuation. They are an integral part of the unconscious processes of speech learning and valuation that go on constantly perhaps in every linguistic community. Simply put, a New York man or woman who is *not* heard saying "tree" for *three* or "wit" for *with* tends to be judged by other New Yorkers as smarter, handsomer, better educated, and more highly placed occupationally than the very same person heard *using* such forms in casual speech. It has also been learned that those New Yorkers who *do* use a stigmatized phonological feature in their own speech are most sensitive to similar pronunciations in others.[19] In other words, what Labov calls "stigmatized" or "prestige" forms are that precisely because they are perceived as class-related by the people who use them or recognize them. The judgments rendered by the monolingual French speakers in Montreal and the Arabic speakers in Israel suggest that this characteristic of linguistic judgment with respect to pronunciation may be widespread, whether or not it extends equally to grammatical features.

Labov and other sociolinguists have demonstrated that, as some traditional grammarians have claimed, an essential element in the *description* of a linguistic form is its subjective evaluation. A description that ignores subjective evaluation overlooks some of the richest information about a usage, information that is important not only in the current social fabric of a community but for the recording or implementation of historical change.

It was the position of the *Third* and of its contemporary exponents of the relativity of usage that the actual speech of people is worthy of discussion but that their judgments of linguistic correctness are not. Labov's work will doubtless affect the treatment of usage in future dictionaries. If his view prevails—that a speech community is "a group of speakers who share a set of social attitudes towards language"—then the emphasis on subjective evaluation that traditionalists had urged but structural linguists had condemned will receive greater attention from lexicographers. But it must be kept in mind that New Yorkers (at least) have proved distressingly inaccurate in their conscious reports of their own speech. Labov writes that they showed "a systematic tendency to report their own speech inaccurately. Most of the respondents seemed to perceive their own speech in terms of the norms at which they were aiming rather than the sound actually produced."[20] We may wonder whether the same systematic subjective tendency has colored the discussion of grammatical and lexical usage over the past two centuries!

The work of sociolinguists who have systematically explored language use in speech communities in the United States and elsewhere is destined to alter linguistic and lexicographic methodology. Borrowing sophisticated techniques from experimental social psychology, linguists and psychologists have joined with anthropologists to study usage and language attitudes among minority groups, dominant social classes, and people of varied socioeconomic status and mobility. These investigators have established correlations of the kind that concern traditional grammarians, English teachers, and the custodians of language. Perhaps even more important, their work has drawn to the attention of linguistic scientists the systematic nature of subjective *attitudes* and their central importance in historical language change, as well as in social and educational judgments and reports.

To determine attitudes toward usage in 1969, *The American Heritage Dictionary* polled a group of distinguished, if conservative, speakers and writers of English. We may expect that in 1990 or thereabouts, "Webster's Fourth," influenced by investigations like Labov's, will have determined from more reliable data than conscious opinion exactly what the subjective evaluations of respected Americans toward debatable usages really are.

Notes

[1]Noam Chomsky, *Aspects of the Theory of Syntax* (1965), p. 3.

[2]See Dell Hymes, *Foundations in Sociolinguistics* (1974), pp. 193–206. Two excellent introductions to aspects of sociolinguistics are Peter Trudgill, *Sociolinguistics* (1974) and William Labov, *The Study of Nonstandard English* (1970).

[3]Jan-Petter Blom and John J. Gumperz, "Social Meaning in Linguistic Structure: Code-Switching in Norway," in John J. Gumperz and Dell Hymes, eds., *Directions in Sociolinguistics* (1972), pp. 407-434.

[4]Susan Ervin-Tripp, "On Sociolinguistic Rules," in Gumperz and Hymes (1972), pp. 213-250; first published in a different form in 1969.

[5]See Joshua A. Fishman, "Domains and the Relationships between Micro- and Macro-sociolinguistics," in Gumperz and Hymes (1972), pp. 435-453, or the same author's "The Sociology of Language," in Pier Paolo Giglioli, ed., *Language and Social Context* (1972), pp. 45-58.

[6]The department store survey was first reported in chapter 3 of Labov's *Social Stratification of English in New York City* (1966); it is conveniently summarized and updated in his *Sociolinguistic Patterns* (1972), pp. 43-65.

[7]See Labov, *Social Stratification,* pp. 207-265, and *Sociolinguistic Patterns,* p. 113.

[8]*Sociolinguistic Patterns,* p. 248 fn.

[9]William Labov, "The Social Motivation of a Sound Change," chapter 1 of *Sociolinguistic Patterns;* first published in *Word,* XIX (1963), 273-309; "The Effect of Social Mobility on Linguistic Behavior," in Juanita V. Williamson and Virginia M. Burke, eds., *A Various Language* (1971), pp. 640-659; first published in *Sociological Inquiry,* XXXVI (1966), 186-203.

[10]In casual speech, in the interview situation, and even in reading passages, the stratified pattern is followed. But when word lists are read, the LMC unexpectedly pronounces more *r* than the UMC. We might mention that this kind of "hypercorrect" pattern represents a nonstable phonological variable and is important in the introduction of changes in language.

[11]See chapter 11 of *Social Stratification* and chapter 6 of *Sociolinguistic Patterns.*

[12]Wallace E. Lambert, "A Social Psychology of Bilingualism" (1967).

[13]Wallace E. Lambert, Moshe Anisfeld, and Grace Yeni-Komshian, "Evaluational Reactions of Jewish and Arab Adolescents to Dialect and Language Variations" (1965).

[14]C. R. Seligman, G. R. Tucker, and W. E. Lambert, "The Effects of Speech Style and Other Attributes on Teachers' Attitudes toward Pupils" (1972).

[15]Alison d'Anglejan and G. Richard Tucker, "Sociolinguistic Correlates of Speech Style in Quebec," in Roger W. Shuy and Ralph W. Fasold, eds., *Language Attitudes* (1973), pp. 1-27.

[16]Reported in d'Anglejan and Tucker (1973) from G. R. Tucker, "Judging Personality from Language Use: A Filipino Example," *Philippine Sociological Review,* XVI (1968), 30-39.

[17]Reported in d'Anglejan and Tucker (1973) from N. N. Markel, R. M. Eisler, and H. W. Reese, "Judging Personality from Dialect," *Journal of Verbal Learning and Verbal Behavior,* VI (1967), 33-35.

[18]Reported in d'Anglejan and Tucker (1973) from D. S. Ellis, "Speech and Social Status in America," *Social Forces,* XVL (1967), 431-437.

[19]Labov, *The Study of Nonstandard English,* p. 32.

[20]*Social Stratification,* p. 480.

Epilogue: Whose Is the Right to Say What's Right?

"But somehow the idealist in us cannot fully acquiesce in any belief that holds up no view of a goal. Much as we condemn the purist's view and point to the ignorance with which he deals with the language we cannot help feeling that there may be something entirely valid behind his protests." —CHARLES FRIES, 1927

"I am not one of those who recognize the worst usurper as legitimate as soon as he is firmly established on his throne. There is something called political morality which is greater than momentary power. So . . . I dare to declare that there is also a higher linguistic morality than that of recognizing the greatest absurdities when they once have usage on their side." —OTTO JESPERSEN, 1925

ONE MAY LOOK back now with little wonder at the discord generated by the dictionary controversy of the 1960s. For although it seemed to have some of the character of a sudden conflagration—unexpected in an arena such as lexicography—we can see now that the embers had been smoldering for generations. It was fueled by educational, philosophical, political, and moral timber. It was the Armageddon of two warring camps, each with deep-seated convictions about language and its place in life, each struggling to vanquish the other and silence its pronouncements about what is good and bad. It may be recalled that in the nineteenth century Kirkham, Marsh, Mathews, and White all associated "bad grammar" with moral decadence; and similar associations have not been absent from twentieth-century discourse. Remember Professor Sherwood's revealing comment about the two approaches to language: old grammar and new grammar represent to their proponents different ways of looking at life. Not just *language,* but *life!*

"Unless we can restore to the words in our newspapers, laws, and political acts some measure of clarity and stringency of meaning, our lives will draw yet nearer to chaos,"[1] warns George Steiner, the socioliterary critic. The editor of *The Atlantic* writes that "The debasement of language is a major malady, one of the most serious problems of our time" and asks "who knows what benign consequences might follow"

158

if "a cigar again becomes a smoke instead of a sexual experience" and "a hamburger ceases to be a Taste Treet Supreem."[2] Political corruption has been linked to language—as, for example, in the comments that ridiculed the enfeebled usage of the Watergate protagonists. NBC's house grammarian—as the dust jacket of *Strictly Speaking* calls Edwin Newman—speculates that "It is at least conceivable that our politics would be improved if our English were, and so would other parts of our national life."[3] Newman's conviction that language "sets the tone of society" reveals how entangled still are cause and effect in judgments about poor language and societal debasement. Whether redundancy, murkiness, and dense diction prompt chicanery or merely cloak it is an open question for some; but language guardians seem to suggest that *infer* for *imply, disinterested* for *uninterested,* and even *like* for *as,* to cite a few cases, can lead to ambiguity, obfuscation, and eventually to the dissipation of the language.

The existence of protective institutions like the French Academy notwithstanding, the fact is that all languages have become what they are mostly without supervision. Still, as long as writers and speakers are inventive or inattentive or overcautious, fresh language forms and fresh uses will arise and may attract the scrutiny of lexicographers, editors, teachers, linguists, and social critics. Some will accept them as an anthropologist might; some will warn like a judge; others will mimic; most will ignore. This scrutiny, however, encompasses only the tip of the iceberg, while beneath the surface of awareness lies the great bulk of language, unattended and unnoticed in its inexorable movement. Moreover, for that small part of English that is subject to scrutiny, huge expenditures of energy have generated much heat but little light, and now we want to review what has been revealed and to pass judgment where analysts have cast more shade than light.

As we scan more than two centuries of debate about English usage, we can identify three criteria commonly applied in evaluating language: intelligibility, rhetorical quality, and grammaticality.

As a form of communication language must first be intelligible—clear in its meaning. Intelligibility is the primary requisite of language. Speech, to be effective, must first be understood. On this matter there is harmony between linguists and traditional grammarians.

Beyond this, however, there is not much agreement. Linguists regard a language as a psychologically rooted and socially evolved communication system whose data are to be analyzed and described. The traditionalists say that, besides being a tool for communication, language is a crafted end that can be judged for its rhetorical character. (Linguists would concur in this view, but *as* linguists they are not sensitive to

rhetorical value.) As with any craft, better and worse are real in
language, and if to most linguists whatever is is right, traditional grammarians discern degrees of effectiveness, beauty, economy, and scale.
Further, their aims are lofty and their critiques—proffered by journalists
and editors, by political, social, and cultural critics, and by educators—attempt reformation, elevation, and refinement. Aristocratic
by preference, devoted to literature and the classics, and practiced in the
monitored phrase, they see themselves as protectors and conservers of
the durably admirable. Intelligibility is not enough; economy, exac-
titude, and grace are sought—and continuity with an illustrious past.
And the reading public seeks their guidance and honors their
judgments—at least by lip service, if not in observance. As models of
sensitivity and good taste, they are salaried to be opinionated.
(Authoritarians, as one of them noted, are not paid to ignore the use of
like as a conjunction!⁴) Above all, their function in society is widely
regarded as essential to the maintenance of high intellectual and moral
standards. Jacques Barzun expressed this view in a letter to a feuding
linguist:

> A living culture in one nation (not to speak of one world) must insist on a
> standard of usage. And usage . . . has important social implications apart
> from elegance and expressiveness in literature. The work of communication
> in law, politics and diplomacy, in medicine, technology, and moral specula-
> tion depends on the maintenance of a medium of exchange whose values
> must be kept fixed, as far as possible, like those of any other reliable cur-
> rency. To prevent debasement and fraud requires vigilance, and it implies the
> right to blame. It is not snobbery that is involved but literacy on its highest
> plane, and that literacy has to be protected from ignorance and sloth.⁵

Whereas the linguists admittedly profess no interest in conservation
and rhetorical quality, they do—like the traditional grammarians—stake
a claim on "grammar." But a lack of shared meaning for the words *grammar* and *grammatical* has plagued the discussion on both sides.

To linguists, one object of "grammar" is to understand and describe
the systematic properties of the linguistic code for the varieties of every
language. They define "a grammar" as a set of elements and rules from
which the sentences of a language can be generated. Its locus is, in the
first place, in speakers' minds and, derivatively, in a linguist's description. Linguists conceive of several grammars for each language, one for
every social or regional variety having its own set of rules.⁶ And just as
English is not a better object of study than, say, Dutch or French, so
standard English ("network standard," for instance) is not intrinsically
better than any other variety. Social and political forces in history, not

linguistic ones, determine which variety becomes the standard. Combinations of political, commercial, and geographical factors made the regional varieties of London, Paris, and Tehran standard in their cultures, but other existing varieties were linguistically as capable of comparable standardization.

The linguists hold that if a sentence conforms to the rules of any variety of English, then it is *grammatical* in English (though not necessarily intelligible or acceptable in a particular context). Grammatical sentences can, of course, be inappropriate to a situation, and they can be unesthetic or inefficient or redundant. Nor need they be true. A perfectly grammatical sentence can wander, distract, confuse, finesse, and deceive, or—ideally—communicate directly, truthfully, even elegantly. To communicate grammatically is not necessarily to communicate well. (As film critic and language guardian John Simon said of Sir Laurence Olivier's speech at the 1979 academy awards presentations, "It seemed to be very grammatical, but it made no sense!")[7]

Nor is a sentence that is grammatical in one kind of English necessarily grammatical in other varieties. "Him and me played handball together when we was in the army" is ungrammatical in standard English, but it conforms to the rules of another variety. Because it cannot be generated by the grammar of *standard English,* traditionalists call it "ungrammatical," whereas linguists prefer to designate it as "inappropriate" when used in a context calling for standard usage. According to linguists, it is inaccurate to say that "Him and her were friends" is "incorrect" or "ungrammatical." In contrast, "Him and were her friends" *is* ungrammatical because no variety of English has rules that will generate it. Similarly, both "He doesn't want any" and "He don't want none" *are* grammatical, though only the former is standard English. "He don't want none" is not ungrammatical any more than Russian or French sentences (or some of Shakespeare's, for that matter) are ungrammatical simply because they cannot be generated by the grammar of present-day standard English. But because it is *nonstandard* (ungrammatical in the variety called standard English), traditionalists call it simply "ungrammatical"; for them, "grammatical" means "standard." Linguists maintain that "ungrammatical" has been wrongly applied without distinction to sentences that are merely nonstandard, as well as to ungrammatical ones in the narrower sense.

In the next few pages I will try to summarize the major aims that modern American linguists have been concerned to accomplish in connection with attitudes toward "good usage." Each part of the discussion will be preceded by one or more quotations from the more militant anti-linguistic language guardians; these give sometimes their views of the issues and sometimes their interpretations of the linguists' views. Though I dare speak for the linguists, I cannot speak for their opponents; so I have selected from statements of their spokesmen a few I believe fairly representative. Follett's *Modern American Usage* (1966) is cited often because to some extent the quotations represent more than a single individual's views. [8]

> *"And as on other issues they [Americans] divide into two parties. The larger, which includes everybody from the proverbial plain man to the professional writer, takes it for granted that there is a right way to use words and construct sentences, and many wrong ways. The right way is believed to be clearer, simpler, more logical, and hence more likely to prevent error and confusion."*—FOLLETT, 1966

> *"The hostility to Latin among linguists and educationists is in fact perverse. Those who speak so harshly against Latin do not show much familiarity with it, whereas few of those who have even a tincture of Latin deny that it throws light on both the structural and the stylistic features of English. . . . If there exists a better pedagogic device than Latin for showing how the Western languages work, it has not yet been found."*—FOLLET, 1966

Linguists wanted to dislodge certain notions, both implicit and explicit, that traditionalists had wittingly and unwittingly broadcast among students. Prominent among the nettling myths were the following: that language is not a social compact but a natural (or even God-given) entity corruptible by man and that therefore by nature or decree *right* meanings, spellings, pronunciations, and usages do exist; that most language change is corruption and gives rise to *wrong* usages; that Latin grammar provides a suitable model for English; and that grammars and dictionaries should prescribe and delimit what is correct. Linguists flatly rejected all four claims.

In place of these notions, some prominent linguists, including Krapp, Marckwardt, and Fries, urged teachers to recognize and accept the arbitrariness of language symbols and to inculcate a *positive* sensitivity to actual language practice—to encourage observation of which forms are used, under what circumstances, and by whom. Because usage is relative and because correctness rests upon usage, they wanted students and teachers to observe actual language customs for themselves, and they held out the promise of better employment of English from such observation. Ancillary to this aim was discouragement of reliance on grammars and dictionaries as *final* arbiters. Aware that such codifications were out of date at best and needed supplementary information, linguists attempted to undermine the unquestioning allegiance that Americans vested in handbooks and "the dictionary."

As for language change being corruption, linguists felt that, call it what you may, change is inevitable and that in fact today's languages work as well as yesterday's. Since the sound-meaning correspondence is essentially arbitrary, whether a meaning is signaled by one symbol or another is not of consequence so long as the social compact holds. The linguists who played major roles in the evolution of a doctrine of usage did not address the potential difficulty of impaired communication if language were to change too quickly. But one can fairly infer from their treatments that they believed the constraints of everyday communication would adequately control the pace of change. They were also aware that no major disruption in communication has been reported as resulting from ordinary (and in some cases extraordinary) language change throughout history, and they could have pointed to the riches of the modern Romance languages (from Latin) and to those of Dutch, German, and English (from the earlier Germanic dialects) as counter evidence to the equation of change and disintegration. Further, they deplored the too prevalent blindness to the fact of past change, and they believed that any attempt to retard change would be mostly futile.

As for Latin's providing a suitable model for the study of English, linguists try to view each language in terms of its own structured patterns. Especially when certain English structures were obscured by imposed Latin ones, and certain usages were judged incorrect because they were unacceptable in Latin, the linguists were outraged. But their view of the unenlightening influence of Latin grammar on English is not new; we saw it in Priestley and Webster.

As to the claim that "the right way" to use words is "clearer," "simpler," and more "logical," the linguists wanted teachers to distinguish between clarity and simplicity on the one hand and logic on the other. They would say that what makes language clearer is surely to be preferred but that what makes language unclear is not thereby "wrong" or "ungrammatical." Moreover, "the right way"—if that means *grammatically* right—can also be muddy; witness Simon's judgment of Olivier mentioned above. And essentially the same thing may be said of simplicity; it is desirable but is not inherently related to grammaticality. When it comes to logic, however, the linguist and the traditionalist part ways.

Linguists recognize that a logic of some kind structures the underlying forms of sentences. They also know that not logical but perceptual, interactional, and stylistic strategies govern the surface structures of sentences. But they maintain that the application of logic to surface forms of sentences is inappropriate and that what passes for logic is too often little more than familiarity. The inappropriateness stems from the most straightforward reason, say the linguists: sentence structures carry their meanings solely by tacit agreement, not by virtue of inhering associations or relations. For example, the absence of the copula in the variety of American English known as Black English or Black English Vernacular ("They my books") is not illogical any more than Russian and Arabic, with similar structures, are illogical languages. The relationship between subject and complement is implicit, and knowledge of the conventions of a variety (or a language) ensures complete, unambiguous interpretation.[9] Nor is the multiple negation ("double negative") of Black English and other American varieties illogical. As is well known, Chaucer used multiple negation in an earlier stage of the language, and other languages (e.g., Russian and Finnish) likewise use it. (Why should multiple negation be judged illogical when multiple affirmation is the rule? And those who argue from analogy with algebra—two negatives make a positive—might consider that in algebra three negatives make a negative, four a positive, five a negative again, and so on. Does anyone argue for this parallel in English?) It is sufficient to recognize that each language has its own unambiguous conventions; and of course these allow for two negatives to be positive sometimes—as in "She was hardly unenthusiastic about the promotion" or "Diamonds are not inexpensive."

Agreed to by common, tacit consent, usage determines meaning, and if multiple negation comes to carry negative force, as it plainly does in English in certain contexts, then whatever logics might be invoked to the contrary notwithstanding, sentences with such multiple negation will be unambiguous. Logic as it has been commonly applied to matters of established usage is irrelevant. Follett's comment that "Language is made logical and clear by observing the norms of grammar and syntax" wins assent from linguists. For logical and clear language is language that can be unambiguously understood; that in turn is language that follows custom, or what Follett here calls "the norms of grammar and syntax." It is these norms—logical or nonlogical or illogical—that allow for accurate understanding within the conventions of a language variety. Linguists would deny that the existing norms of grammar and syntax are *inherently* more logical and clear than other conceivable norms.

"They are the professional linguists, who deny that there is such a thing as correctness. . . . they denounce all attempts at guiding choice . . . . on this conception of language as a natural growth with which it is criminal to tamper they are at one."—FOLLETT, 1966

*"In writing as in morals, negative and positive merits are
complementary; resistance to the wrong and the weak is,* ipso facto,
cultivation of the right and the strong."—FOLLETT, 1966

The notion of "strictly speaking" suggests that correct English is
English that has been adequately monitored. But, say the linguists, every
variety has its norms, and the rules for all varieties are "strict." They
aren't more lax for casual speech or lower-class speech than for formal or
middle-class speech; rather, they are different. The rules of formal written English are certainly less well known than the equally strict rules of
informal speech—not because they are more difficult but chiefly because
people have less exposure to them; written English is not "native" to
anyone. Similarly, people trying to speak the informal English of the
lower socioeconomic classes would speak it "incorrectly" if they were not
fluent in that variety. This is what Fries meant when he said that each
variety has "a correctness." But no linguist to my knowledge has denied
that there is such a thing as correctness.

Some traditionalists seemed unaware that what linguists were advocating for all teachers and students of English was not less but more
knowledge and appreciation of the "genius" of the language, through
study of its history and current spoken varieties as well as its literary products and standardized forms. A few apparently believed that the
linguists wanted school children to receive no instruction in standard
English but learn solely through independent observation and practice.
Perhaps it was some such conviction that led Jacques Barzun to charge
that linguists were combining "the affectation of science with the 'progressive' principle of learning by doing, here carried to a ludicrous extreme."[10]

But, plainly, Fries and the other linguists were not seeking to discount
the study of grammar nor the analysis and practice of good written expression. It is ludicrous to suggest that they intended to loose the
language from guidance so that they could watch it, unrestrained,
disintegrate. Linguists, too, felt a proprietary interest in language and,
finding traditional grammarians trespassing, they sought to check them.
Proud of their insights, a few linguists messianically preached that if
their learning were better disseminated prescriptivism would topple, for
even amateur observers of the development of English conceded the
basic futility of prescriptivism. Further, linguists suggested that a
linguistic approach to language would be inherently interesting and
would thus enhance the activities of English classes.[11]

Linguists like Krapp, Marckwardt, and Fries were appalled by the
perpetuation of the kind of "purism" that equated locutions like "It's me"

with expressions like "8 × 4 = 31."[12] In their campaign to legitimize diversity and lend confidence to the insecure, linguists fought to oust several dozen *bêtes noires* from the canon of shibboleths. Contending that the traditionalists' prescriptions and prohibitions were often unimportant and their claims untrue or inexact, linguists attempted to discredit them. They were incredulous at the reluctance of traditionalists to concede that meaning is not compromised when one says (or writes) *like a cigarette should,* or *less students,* or *to quickly go.* The history of English, they pointed out, testifies to its enrichment by thousands of words originally functioning as one part of speech or with one meaning or usage and subsequently used quite differently. In disgracing the pedigrees of particular prohibitions, some linguists doubtless intended to shake loose the traditionalists' stranglehold on public opinion. They proselytized actively (more actively than wisely at times) for converts to their creed that "all usage is relative and correctness rests upon usage."

"The language, they say, is what anybody and everybody speaks."
—FOLLETT, 1966

"As scientists they maintained that the speech of any group is good speech for that group . . . ."—BARZUN, 1959

Seemingly infatuated with dialect diversity, many linguists sought to generate respect for the wide variety of linguistic forms. This acceptance of multiformity underlay much of the democratic disposition their writings suggested (and vice versa), and it stimulated considerable investigation of regional dialects in the middle third of this century and of social dialects more recently. Linguists gathered regional data for a *Linguistic Atlas of the United States.* Fascinated by the myriad pronunciations and diverse forms that peppered the American language, dialect geographers also hoped historical demographers might benefit from the patterns of migration and social networks suggested by dialect systems.[13]

However arcane the linguists appeared in their knowledge of history and dialect, they were indeed democratic in their openness to everyone's usages and in their zeal to foster acceptance of linguistic pluralism. From this openness many observers wrongly inferred that linguists condoned slovenly speech and writing. In fact, of course, their own prose was orthodox and quite traditional. ("It is . . . one of the striking features of the libertarian position that it preaches an unbuttoned grammar in a prose style that is fashioned with the utmost grammatical rigor," acknowledged Follett.) Indeed, W. D. Whitney in the nineteenth century and Brander Matthews among others in the twentieth expressed frank distaste for certain locutions and neologisms.

Long before 1961 many people—linguists and grammarians—realized that certain rules of school grammar were out of harmony with educated practice. Linguists particularly felt that textbooks excessively drilled students in usages they would seldom observe or need to employ. The rigidity of these prescriptive rules was thought to hinder creativity by stirring uncertainty into students' efforts to use the English language, especially in writing. As examples of insecurity-fostering works, linguists noted titles like *Your Telltale English*, and *Get It Right*, and *Don't Say It*. "Will America Be the Death of English?"—the subtitle of Newman's *Strictly Speaking*—places it in the same genre. One linguist described the injunction to be "correct" as something that rests "like a soggy blanket on our brains and our hands whenever we try to write."[14] Another sensibly urged teachers "to turn out students who have a feeling that the English language is a medium they can control, not a Procrustean bed into which they must fit, cut, and trim whatever they have to communicate."[15] A third reported of Jamaican creole speakers that their written compositions are "dull and vapid because the children are so fearful of lapsing into their native creole that they cannot express themselves freely."[16] And a British linguist warned that "A speaker who is made ashamed of his language habits suffers a basic injury as a human being: to make anyone, especially a child, feel so ashamed is as indefensible as to make him feel ashamed of the colour of his skin."[17] Two anecdotes from my own experience support the linguists' contention. A Thai student told me that when she first arrived in the United States and would inquire about the acceptability of particular sentences, Americans often referred her to someone else, claiming ignorance of "grammar" and inability even to speak "good English." The second incident was reported by an American graduate student who had used the word *concretize* in a literary seminar: "The person I was addressing screwed up his face, and several groans echoed through the room. I felt vulgar and crude—like a schoolboy with dirty hands, surrounded by more refined men of letters."

Believing that language, regulated by the workaday constraints of communication and by social pressures (including the harsh kind meted out to my student in his literary seminar!), needs more to be observed and described than consciously molded, linguists have challenged what they regard as myths about language and grammar. Grammar should describe what is, they say, not prescribe what ought to be in terms of what might be or what used to be. Exasperated by unrealistic "standards" that reinforce old superstitions and instill new ones, they have vigorously attempted to overturn them.

"IRREGARDLESS. *No such word.*"—SHERIDAN BAKER, 1966

"Augur does not take for after it; augur cannot take for after it."
—NEWMAN, 1974

*"By shaking faith in the correctness of a few items in grammars
of the English language, these detractors have destroyed faith in
every book on the subject. . . . By focusing attention on 'it is
me,' . . . and similar instances of divided usage, these self-called
'descriptive' grammarians have hooted at 'prescriptive' grammars
and have created in educational circles a thoroughly rebellious
attitude toward all formal study of the English language."*
—WARFEL, 1952

Linguists think traditionalists should distinguish harmless usages like
"split infinitives" and the use of *like* as a conjunction from the verbal
pomposity, redundancy, and obfuscation that do really hinder communication and can dissipate the expressive potential of the English
language. The traditional grammarian who rightly lambastes inflated,
empty phrases and denatured, clichéd English too often confuses
language that is bad because it communicates poorly with language that
is simply not traditionally "correct." With laudable motives, Edwin
Newman criticizes both the harmful excesses of opaque government ver-
biage and new usages that communicate perfectly well. But his appeals to
logic, etymology, and personal standards of correctness represent either
ignorance of the history of English or unexplained disagreement with its
implications. Frustrated and perplexed by popular acceptance of the
myths propagated by such dicta, linguists have often balked at
acknowledging the value even of the legitimate critiques of the traditionalists. Instead, they have ridiculed what they saw as frettings over
neologisms, lexical mergers, and minor syntactic and morphological
variants, and as prissy niggling over spelling variants that even copy
editors fail to catch. And linguists still think that when language guardians focus on traditional shibboleths, they too often miss the forest for
the trees.

Most linguists would agree that American students could use language
more effectively than they do, but they do not concede that the triumph
of traditional judgment on variant usages would enhance communication. Attention to the well-wrought phrase is certainly legitimate; but
linguists argue that traditionalists have condemned a host of well-
wrought locutions.

Traditional grammarians deny that the changes in usage they rail against are innocuous peccadillos. They believe that some of those usages cause obscurity or ambiguity. Unfortunately, their writings too sparsely illustrate their contention. Lamenting the loss of semantic distinction in the merging of *infer* and *imply,* for example, their discussions of what an author "really meant" or "should have said" usually demonstrate that the condemned usages are neither opaque nor ambiguous in context.

> *"Present-day linguistic theory writes off the written, saying it is not language at all; only speech is language."*—FOLLETT, 1966

> *"It is useless to speculate about the motives of students whose zeal for enshrining the slip of the tongue makes them despise the richest source of fact about their subject. But it is important in the middle of the twentieth century to reassert the worth of the alphabet."*—FOLLETT, 1966

> *"This term [speechways] puts writing in its place among things artificial and unimportant, and the objectivists deride the grammar book and the schoolmarm who together tried to maintain the norms."*—FOLLETT, 1966

American descriptive linguistics springs from a combination of historical linguistics and cultural anthropology. This descriptivism flourished in the exploration of native American languages, with their sometimes rich but unwritten traditions. The investigation of cultures that lack written expression increased respect for spoken language and sharpened understanding of relationships among speech, writing, and language. For anthropological linguists, speech was primary: it preceded writing. A real and effective *language* could exist solely in spoken form, if not solely in written form. Even for historical linguists, there was a *speaker* behind every written document. Further, the Amerindian tongues, from which the founders of American descriptivism nurtured their mature views of language, differ so dramatically in structure from European tongues that a fresh look at the European languages was inevitable. Unfortunately, when those linguists wandered with their analytical tools into the garden of the philologists and traditional grammarians and transferred to English, with its rich literary history, the investigative approach developed for the unwritten Amerindian languages, they did violence to good sense and alienated almost everybody as a result.

It is certainly reasonable to claim that spoken language is primary or fundamental. But it was certainly wrong to say for English—as linguists did—that spoken language *is* the language. Linguists overreacted to the fact that laypersons, when they talk of language, employ terms that apply better to writing. Before school age, speech is acquired without much conscious instruction, so we generally lack terms we can rely on to refer to its phenomena and functioning. But in school we learn terms useful for discussing writing, and in subsequent discussion of "language" those terms are naturally transferred, even though they are often not apropos and can even be misleading. To the extent that nonlinguists talk of "language," writing is their reference point, and writing and speech are often confused, as when people talk about "sounding out all the letters" of a word. Some linguists, partly in reaction, have conveyed the impression of excluding writing from the scope of language. Given the popular equation between writing and language, this was badly miscalculated.

Cavalierly brushing aside the schools' special focus on written language (where the old-fashioned spelling bee highlights the academic emphasis on the alphabet), linguists also slighted the fact that dictionaries serve chiefly to assist in the understanding and practice of *written* communication. Those who consult dictionaries do so as reflective readers and writers more often than as speakers.

Some of the linguists' anti-grammarian zeal was doubtless sparked by the fact that so many grammarians had tumbled into the so-called classical fallacy—assuming the primacy of writing, with speech taking its cue from the written word. This became especially important once the linguists had delved into the unwritten indigenous languages of America. But traditionalists like Pei and Bishop pointed out that the linguists were themselves guilty of sometimes confusing writing and speaking, of ignoring differences between the two, and of undervaluing the place of writing.[18]

When linguists were attending to speech and when the writers of *The English Language Arts* and *Webster's Third* were announcing that spoken language *is* the language, NCTE leaders were urging "realistic" descriptions of "English." But "English" for most teachers then meant *writing*—indeed, monitored, *edited* writing! True, Marckwardt and Fries analyzed both written and spoken samples, but they did not sufficiently emphasize the cultural or linguistic differences between them.[19] In fact, linguists generally preached things appropriate mostly to spoken English and disregarded concerns with written expression.

If grammarian and linguist have both failed too often to distinguish between writing and speech, each also has refused to honor the other's interests, aspiring instead to annexation. As early as 1903, some linguists promoted *informal spoken English* as the proper basis for school programs: "The most important aim of education in the mother-tongue must . . . always be the development of power over the spoken rather than over the written language."[20] In 1940, Fries wrote that "We must agree to base our teaching upon an accurate, realistic description of the actual practices of informal Standard English . . . ."[21]

It must be granted that linguists have paid insufficient heed to the concerns of writers and readers and have certainly not provided teachers with useful statements about "edited" English. And it must be admitted also that too many literary scholars in discussing language have ignored speech.

In spurning traditional concerns with formal writing and rhetorical quality, linguists have conveyed an iconoclastic impression. *Leave Your Language Alone!* was the disconcerting title of one notorious book,[22] and it meant to many editors and teachers what they thought all linguists advocated—a hands-off, anything-goes laxity. This book was surely intended as an antidote for the many that fostered linguistic insecurity. But to the traditionalist who equated language with writing, the injunction to leave *language* alone was particularly suspect and provocative. "Leave Your *Speech* Alone" would not have antagonized teachers nearly so much. Other ill-considered titles and headlines and remarks of linguists here and there have lent credence to the suspicion that linguists share an antipathy for the study of grammar and writing. The title *Leave Your Language Alone!* fueled the already widespread fear that linguists advocated accepting whatever students write as beyond reproach.

Beyond creating an impression of iconoclasm, linguists can be faulted for discounting the importance societies attach to good language use—and not merely technologically advanced societies. As early as 1927 Bloomfield admitted surprise at finding awareness among the Menomini Indians of Wisconsin as to who the good speakers among them were. More important, he acknowledged in 1944 that besides secondary statements about language—the kind that linguists and grammarians make—there are hostile tertiary reactions that can be aroused when accepted views are challenged.[23] He recognized that tertiary reactions are not always rational, and implicitly admonished other linguists to use kid gloves in handling such matters. But many linguists ignored his advice, flouting traditional views of language and provoking the hostile reactions we have witnessed especially since 1952.

Sociologists recognize, in the words of Francis Merrill, that "As social expectations evolve through social interaction, they take on elements of right and wrong, of what ought and ought not be. In short, they become social *norms,* namely group expectations with moral overtones."[24] Merrill adds that certain norms, representing not *ideal* patterns but widely accepted ones, have strong socially imperative content and are followed out of "moral duty." Coming to this recognition slowly, linguists have alienated many of those they sought to persuade by overlooking the tacit "moral" content of linguistic correctness.

To combat certain popular views of language and language correctness, linguists became "debunkers." For certain aspects of social living, learned or scientific debunking can be initiated without challenging the powers that be. But not so in religion, for example. And not so in language either, when dictionaries and traditional grammarians are the high priests advancing the popular view.

In this context it is interesting to note that apparently it did not occur to Bloomfield that his notion of tertiary responses cut both ways. Recognizing secondary responses from both linguists and traditionalists, he appears to have thought tertiary responses were limited to laypersons whose views are challenged by the claims of professionals. But we have also seen that when the conventional wisdom of linguists is challenged—as it quite vigorously was after publication of both *The English Language Arts* in 1952 and *Webster's Third* in 1961—linguists too display hostile tertiary responses. What Bloomfield overlooked was that much of the "popular" view of language correctness is also maintained and advocated by *professional users* of the language (writers and journalists) and by one group of *professional analysts* of language (literary critics). Bloomfield's dichotomy between popular and scientific views is thus too simple in the matter of language, where several professional groups have staked a claim. The challenge by the other language professionals sufficiently threatened linguists to evoke their hostile tertiary responses.

A good deal more could be said about the aims of the linguists. I hope it is sufficiently clear that their views are not without merit. Just as clearly, the concerns of traditional grammarians warrant recognition by linguists. Both groups have a commitment to language, the linguists to understanding of its nature, the traditionalists to refinement of its use. The object, if not the focus, of the commitment is shared. Why, then, does such extraordinary dissension exist between them? How did two groups so studious of language come to regard it so differently, and to regard one another's views as wrongheaded and even perverse? The question is not easy to answer, and any generalization will have exceptions; but in this chapter I have attempted to indicate some of the areas where linguists and language guardians view their shared object of study in radically different ways. Let me now conclude.

Linguists *observe* and *analyze* facts of usage; traditional grammarians are pledged to *judging* those facts, and they fear that the academic ascendancy of linguistic science will slight appraisal and depreciate value. But both linguists and traditionalists must recognize, as one literary scholar who is also at home with linguistics has observed, that "Embedded in these disputes and complaints is a philosophic problem of the first magnitude . . . . The problem of what to teach youngsters in English is first of all a question of value, not fact. . . . we not only have to find out what are the facts of language but what are the facts of society and man, problems which are difficult and which involve from the very beginning value questions."[25]

Unfortunately, we must conclude that if assessing the value of the facts is important (as I believe it is), both descriptivists and prescriptivists have been derelict, for we find neither in the doctrine of usage nor in the doctrine of correctness a set of principles for setting value on language usages. I. A. Richards said thirty years ago about the doctrine of usage, "I believe it to be, on the whole, the most pernicious influence in current English teaching, doing more than all other removable errors together to inhibit the course of self-critical and profitable reflection against illegitimate applications of logic and philosophy to language."[26] But he was equally harsh on proponents of the doctrine of correctness—and for the very same reason. In both cases, the disputants have mostly failed to apply self-critical and profitable reflection to the complex problems and concerns underlying the dispute.

In the enduring doctrinaire antagonism, linguists lost ground to the forces that prescriptivists marshaled in the print media. Linguists got tattered as alarmed reaction to the *Third* showed their explanations unconvincing and proved that NCTE's efforts to foster a relativist view of correctness had been abortive. The Linguistic Society of America reported to the National Commission on the Humanities, in 1964, that "the impact which the recent advances in linguistics have had upon the general public [is] essentially zero." And the report added: "Largely because of the furor over the third edition of *Webster's New International Dictionary,* a fair portion of highly educated laymen see in linguistics the great enemy of all they hold dear."[27]

That "furor," then, did help persuade linguists that they had failed to communicate what seemed to them like obvious and important truths. Their frontal attacks upon the doctrine of correctness, far from eroding its support, appeared to threaten the stability of the language itself and in fact solidified resistance to a relativistic view of usage. Linguists were forced to confront the sensitivity of sentiment about usage, especially written usage. There are signs today that linguists will honor the concern for the printed word that teachers and others share. Further, reversing their earlier challenge to the legitimacy of language evaluation, linguists have launched investigations into its systematic properties. Some of them are also analyzing what distinguishes planned from unplanned discourse.[28] And in summer workshops and elsewhere, some have tried to sort out what their science can helpfully offer teachers of composition and literature.[29] The strident tones of earlier efforts to convert the traditionalists have all but vanished.[30]

The controversy surrounding the *Third* has had a mixed effect on English teachers and professors. Many, already influenced by the NCTE and sensitized to actual usage by the linguists' research, responded favorably and accepted the *Third*'s descriptions as a basis for realistic instruction. Presumably, many at least wondered about usages they had always frowned on—or insisted on. Others, of course, sympathetic to the alarms of extremist reviewers, inferred that linguists, not nearly so descriptive as they claimed, had tried to foist mere wishful thinking on the public. A sprinkling of arch-conservative prescriptivists attempted to prove certain of the dictionary's descriptions biased or even fraudulent. Sheridan Baker, author of several orthodox style manuals, claimed that the entry on *ain't* was a product of "the linguist's long-standing hope that he will see *ain't* move up to 'cultivated' usage." Uncovering a questionable statistic in an interpretation of the data of linguistic geographers, he construed the error as typical of "a linguistic movement, a group point of view, that has slowly substituted itself for the facts."[31]

Language guardians like Baker and Dwight Macdonald, finding certain locutions distasteful, refuse to accept them no matter who uses them or how often because, in Baker's words, they are persuaded that "Good English has to do with the upper classes . . . with the cultural and intellectual leaders . . . ."[32] Such people seem determined to designate the cultural and intellectual leaders, if not by making the rules, then by refereeing the game. To these, no doubt, Macdonald appealed when he said, "If nine-tenths of the citizens of the United States, including a recent President, were to use *inviduous,* the one-tenth who clung to *invidious* would still be right, and they would be doing a favor to the majority if they continued to maintain the point."[33]

It seems sensible to respect linguists in their self-restricted task of examining the basic structures and varieties of language, and to respect the masters of rhetoric in legitimate aims to improve the quality of verbal discourse, especially as formal spoken and written crafts. To wage quixotic battle against *ain't, irregardless, finalize,* and other debatable usages, however, seems wasteful, given the need for better communication on a more fundamental level; so say many linguists. To stand on the sidelines mechanically recording what people say, and to dignify relaxed and untutored language with analysis and description in dictionaries, approaches the perverse; so say some other writers.

We have had here a classic conflict—between two groups struggling for the right to speak definitively about language, especially language correctness. To such conflict we might find it interesting to apply Michel Foucault's thoughtful analysis of discourse on medicine. Foucault asks: "Who, among the totality of speaking individuals, is accorded the right to use [the language of medicine]? Who is qualified to do so? Who derives from it his own special quality, his prestige, and from whom, in return, does he receive . . . at least the presumption that what he says is true?"[34]

But we might do even better to reflect on the sober conclusions of I. A. Richards, noting that the overall study of language "is concerned . . . with the maintenance and improvement of the use of language"—that it is, in other words, inescapably normative. We have seen this normative approach to language in the writings of the best of the linguists and in the best of the traditional grammarians. "No doubt," Richards acknowledges, "the job of 'collecting and arranging the facts of speech' has been much interfered with by silly normative prejudices in the past. Linguistics and medicine may be expected to develop analogous fads and quackeries. But that does not excuse retaliatory aggression."[35]

Of course, there have been in America—both before and after the publication of *Webster's Third*—many linguists (even descriptive linguists) and many professors of English who have resisted any temptation to become professional antagonists. There have been linguists who always understood the need of most Americans to learn to use standard written English more or less as a second language—and the need of all Americans to understand it. There have been traditional rhetoricians who always insisted on the importance for teachers of understanding and emphasizing basic language structures and who decried undue stress on the "marking of errors."

Writing in 1951 (ten years before *Webster's Third*), Harold Whitehall, chairman of Indiana University's linguistics department, said this:

Because an American can understand other Americans no matter what regional or social class they come from, he is apt to underestimate the necessity for a generalized and abstract written American English. Because he finds no pressing reason for standardizing his speech, he is likely to misunderstand the necessity for standardizing his writing. . . . to speak with a local accent is not disadvantageous; to write serious prose with a local accent definitely is. . . . To gain command of serious written English is to acquire, quite deliberately, an abstract and generalized variety of the language differing by nature and purpose from any social or regional variety whatsoever. It is to sacrifice the local for the general, the spontaneous for the permanent. It is to bring to the study of written American English something of the perspective we normally reserve for the study of foreign languages. [36]

And he also said this:

> . . . the linguists themselves have, for the most part, shown little interest in the application of their methods and results to that most important area of language pedagogy—the course in English composition. . . . The task of educational adaptation, however, is not an easy one. A bridge of explanation between the old and the new, between the traditional and linguistic approaches to composition teaching, must be erected very cautiously and carefully. (p. vi)

In 1965, Edward Corbett, distinguished author of several textbooks on rhetoric, expressed a view that almost no one (and certainly no descriptive linguist) would disagree with:

> If American schools had been as much concerned with grammar, logic, and rhetoric, as they have been with "good usage," the quality of student writing today might be better than it generally is. [37]

In 1975, Kenneth Oliver, professor of English and comparative literature, with credentials quite acceptable to traditionalists, outlined a curriculum in English grammar for grades one through ten. This is his first paragraph:

> By the age of three most children are not only speaking in sentence patterns, but are creating sentences which they have never heard before. Long before they know what grammar is, they are saying whatever they want to say—or at least they think they are—and they are using every, or nearly every, basic sentence pattern that exists. Should we then use valuable school time to teach grammar? [38]

His answer, of course, is yes; and his reasons are altogether similar to those of the linguist quoted above. And in his curriculum, students would "learn something about the origins and development of the English language" and "about dialects, slang, and the melting-pot nature of American English" (p. 41). In his summing up he says:

> The curriculum proposed here has put emphasis on mastery of language; it has not stressed the marking of errors. These should be corrected, but they should not be allowed to dominate the instruction or the students' attention. Students should learn that errors are distractions to the reader . . . but not that they are sure signs of failure. (p. 42)

In short, there seems good reason to hope that the apparent dichotomy of views that I have traced in this book will increasingly give way to the clearer defining of real issues and the working out of solutions to important problems both factual and evaluative: that accommodation and cooperation among linguists and other scholars will increasingly help educators turn out students who *can* read and write effectively—and will thus increasingly foster respect among all concerned.

It is past time for linguists and traditional grammarians to put aside their suspicions and antagonisms and recognize that enough remains to be discovered in both the factual and the evaluative aspects of language to occupy all who will investigate. Indeed, the hard line between "English" and "language" may dissolve entirely. And that is just as it should be.

Notes

[1]Quoted by Robert Manning in *The Atlantic* (May 1971), p. 4.

[2]Manning, *ibid.*

[3]*Strictly Speaking* (1974), p. 5.

[4]A. M. Tibbetts, "Two Cheers for the Authoritarian" (1964).

[5]See Donald J. Lloyd, "Snobs, Slobs and the English Language" (1951), p. 282.

[6]The psychological interrelationships of grammars for speakers fluent in several varieties is not yet well understood.

[7]On NBC's "Today" show in April, 1979.

[8]Follett died before the manuscript was completed, and it was given over to Jacques Barzun, who edited and completed it with the collaboration of six colleagues: Carlos Baker, Frederick W. Dupee, Dudley Fitts, James D. Hart, Phyllis McGinley, and Lionel Trilling. It seems fair in general to assume that the views expressed in this guidebook were shared by Barzun and his collaborators even if the tone and style are chiefly Follett's.

[9]See William Labov, "The Logic of Nonstandard English," in James E. Alatis, ed., *Report of the Twentieth Annual Round Table Meeting on Linguistics and Language Studies* (1970), pp. 1–43; conveniently excerpted in Pier Paolo Giglioli, ed., *Language and Social Context* (1972), pp. 179–215.

[10]*The House of Intellect* (1959), p. 241.

[11]Paul Roberts, "The Relation of Linguistics to the Teaching of English" (1960); cited from Harold B. Allen, ed., *Readings in Applied English Linguistics,* 2nd ed. (1964), p. 404.

[12]Leila Sprague Learned, "A Defense of Purism in Speech" (1913), p. 683.

[13]See Hans Kurath, *Handbook of the Linguistic Geography of New England* (1939) and *A Word Geography of the Eastern United States* (1949).

[14]Donald Lloyd, "Our National Mania for Correctness" (1952), p. 285.

[15]Albert H. Marckwardt, *Linguistics and the Teaching of English* (1966), pp. 74–75.

[16]David DeCamp, "Introduction: The Study of Pidgin and Creole Languages," in Dell Hymes, ed., *Pidginization and Creolization of Languages* (1971), p. 26.

[17]M. A. K. Halliday, "The Users and Uses of Language," in Joshua A. Fishman, ed., *Readings in the Sociology of Language* (1968), p. 165.

[18]Pei, "A Loss for Words" (1964) and "The Dictionary as a Battlefront" (1962); Morris Bishop, "Good Usage, Bad Usage, and Usage," *American Heritage Dictionary* (1969), pp. xxi-xxiv.

[19]Marckwardt's *Linguistics and the Teaching of English* fully recognizes the importance of the differences between written and spoken English for the classroom teacher.

[20]George R. Carpenter, Franklin T. Baker, and Fred N. Scott, *The Teaching of English in the Elementary and the Secondary School* (1903), p. 58.

[21]*American English Grammar* (1940), p. 290.

[22]Robert A. Hall, *Leave Your Language Alone!* (1950). Though fewer than 9,000 copies were sold under this title, this first edition was reviewed in about thirty publications and more widely discussed and damned. When the paperback publisher requested it, the title was changed to *Linguistics and Your Language* (1960), and the book sold well: by late 1966 about 90,000 copies had been purchased. Hall had published the 9,000 "hard" copies without the backing of a commercial or university press.

[23]"Literate and Illiterate Speech" (1927), repr. in Francis Hockett, ed., *A Bloomfield Anthology* (1970); "Secondary and Tertiary Responses to Language" (1944), also repr. in Hockett.

[24]*Society and Culture,* 3rd ed. (1965), p. 109.

[25]Morton Bloomfield, "The Problem of Fact and Value in the Teaching of English," *College English,* XIV (1953); cited from John A. Rycenga and Joseph Schwartz, eds., *Perspectives on Language* (1963), p. 277.

[26]*Interpretation in Teaching* (1938), pp. 174-175.

[27]The LSA appointed a distinguished committee (Charles Ferguson, Morris Halle, Eric Hamp, Archibald Hill, Thomas Sebeok, William Moulton), whose findings appear in the *Report of the Commission on the Humanities,* published by the American Council of Learned Societies (1964), pp. 152-158.

[28]See, e.g., Elinor Ochs Keenan and Tina L. Bennett, eds., *Discourse Across Time and Space* (1977).

[29]See, e.g., D. Terence Langendoen's *Essentials of English Grammar* (1970), the fruit of his working with English teachers at Ohio State University in summer classes; see also Richard E. Young, Alton L. Becker, and Kenneth L. Pike, *Rhetoric: Discovery and Change* (1970).

[30]Marckwardt's *Linguistics and the Teaching of English* could serve as a model of the linguist's dispassionate interest in solving the problems of teachers without inflating the potential role of linguistic science.

[31]"The Error of *Ain't*" (1964), p. 91.

[32]Sheridan Baker, in his presidential address to the Michigan Academy of Science, Arts, and Letters; see "The Art and Science of Letters" (1965), p. 525.

[33]"The String Untuned," *The New Yorker* (March 10, 1962); cited from James Sledd and Wilma R. Ebbitt, eds., *Dictionaries and THAT Dictionary* (1962), p. 187.

[34]Michel Foucault, *The Archaeology of Knowledge,* trans, A. M. Sheridan Smith (1972), p. 50.

[35]*Speculative Instruments* (1955), p. 54.

[36]*Structural Essentials of English* (1956), pp. 4-5.

[37]*Classical Rhetoric for the Modern Student* (1965), p. 396. Corbett urges teachers to warn students "not to develop a neurotic concern about usage."

[38]*A Sound Curriculum in English Grammar* (1975), p. 1.

Bibliography

REFERENCES CITED

(See also, at the end of this listing, a list of Suggested Readings.)

Alatis, James E., ed. *Report of the Twentieth Annual Round Table Meeting on Linguistics and Language Studies.* Washington, D.C.: Georgetown Univ. Press, 1970.

Alford, Henry. *A Plea for the Queen's English: Stray Notes on Speaking and Spelling.* Repr. from 2nd London ed. New York, n. d.

Allen, Edward A. "English Grammar, Viewed from All Sides," *Education,* VII (1887), 460–469.

Allen, Harold B., ed. *Readings in Applied English Linguistics.* New York: Appleton-Century-Crofts, 1958; 2nd ed. 1964.

American Council of Learned Societies. *Report of the Commission on the Humanities.* New York, 1964.

Anderson, Wallace L., and Norman C. Stageberg, eds. *Introductory Readings on Language.* New York: Holt, Rinehart, 1962.

Ash, John. *Grammatical Institutes.* 4th ed. London, 1763. Facsimile edition. Leeds: Scolar Press, 1967.

Austin, J. L. *How to Do Things with Words.* 1962; repr. New York: Oxford Univ. Press, 1965.

Ayres, Alfred. *The Verbalist.* New York, 1881.

Baker, Sheridan. "The Error of *Ain't*," *College English,* XXVI (1964), 91–104.

_____. "The Art and Science of Letters: *Webster's Third New International Dictionary*," *Papers of the Michigan Academy of Science, Arts, and Letters,* L (1965), 521–534.

_____. *The Complete Stylist.* New York: Thomas Y. Crowell, 1966.

_____. "The New English," Occasional Papers No. 12. Washington, D.C.: Council for Basic Education, 1967.

Barzun, Jacques. *The House of Intellect.* New York: Harper & Row, 1959.

_____. "What Is a Dictionary?" *The American Scholar,* XXXII (1963), 176–181.

Baugh, Albert C., and Thomas Cable. *A History of the English Language.* 3rd ed. Englewood Cliffs, N.J.: Prentice-Hall, 1978.

Bentley, Harold W. Rev. of *Current English Usage,* by Sterling A. Leonard. *American Speech,* VIII, i (1933), 61–63.

Bishop, Morris. "Good Usage, Bad Usage, and Usage." In *The American Heritage Dictionary of the English Language,* ed. William Morris, pp. xxi-xxiv.

Blom, Jan-Petter, and John J. Gumperz. "Social Meaning in Linguistic Structure: Code-Switching in Norway." In *Directions in Sociolinguistics,* ed. Gumperz and Hymes, pp. 407–434.

179

Bloomfield, Leonard. *An Introduction to the Study of Language.* New York: Holt, 1914.

_____. "Why a Linguistic Society?" *Language,* I (1925), 1–5.

_____. "Literate and Illiterate Speech," *American Speech,* II (1927), 432–438.

_____. *Language.* New York: Holt, 1933.

_____. "Secondary and Tertiary Responses to Language," *Language,* XX (1944), 45–55.

Bloomfield, Morton. "The Problem of Fact and Value in the Teaching of English," *College English,* XV (1953). Repr. in *Perspectives on Language,* ed. Rycenga and Schwartz, pp. 276–281.

Bolton, W. F., ed. *The English Language: Essays by English and American Men of Letters 1490–1839.* Cambridge: Cambridge Univ. Press, 1966.

Brown, Goold. *The Grammar of English Grammars.* New York, 1851.

_____. *The Institutes of English Grammar.* New York, 1853; Copyright 1851; preface dated 1832. First edition published 1823.

Bryan, W. F. "Notes on the Founders of Prescriptive English Grammar," *The Manly Anniversary Studies in Language and Literature.* Chicago: Univ. of Chicago Press, 1923. Pp. 383–393.

Campbell, George. *The Philosophy of Rhetoric.* Ed. Lloyd F. Bitzer. Carbondale: Southern Illinois Univ. Press, 1963.

Carpenter, George R., Franklin T. Baker, and Fred N. Scott. *The Teaching of English in the Elementary and the Secondary School.* New York: Longman's, Green, 1903.

Chapman, Robert L. "A Working Lexicographer Appraises *Webster's Third New International Dictionary,*" *American Speech,* XLII (1967), 202–210.

Chomsky, Noam. *Aspects of the Theory of Syntax.* Cambridge, Mass.: M.I.T. Press, 1965.

_____. *Language and Mind.* Enl. ed. New York: Harcourt, 1972.

Christensen, Francis. "A Case for *Webster's Third,*" *The USC Alumni Review,* November, 1962, pp. 11–13. Repr. in *The Role of the Dictionary,* ed. Philip B. Gove, pp. 22–25.

Ciardi, John. "Manner of Speaking," *Saturday Review,* November 4, 1961, p. 30.

Cook, Walter A., S.J. *Introduction to Tagmemic Analysis,* New York: Holt, Rinehart, 1969.

Corbett, Edward P. J. *Classical Rhetoric for the Modern Student.* New York: Oxford Univ. Press, 1965.

Creswell, Thomas J. *Usage in Dictionaries and Dictionaries of Usage.* Publications of the American Dialect Society: Nos. 63–64. University, Ala., 1975.

d'Anglejan, Alison, and G. Richard Tucker. "Sociolinguistic Correlates of Speech Style in Quebec." In *Language Attitudes,* ed. Shuy and Fasold, pp. 1–27.

DeCamp, David. "Introduction: The Study of Pidgin and Creole Languages." In *Pidginization and Creolization of Languages,* ed. Dell Hymes, pp. 13–39.

Dingwall, William Orr, ed. *A Survey of Linguistic Science.* College Park, Md.: Linguistics Program, Univ. of Maryland, 1971.

Dykema, Karl W. "The Grammar of Spoken English: Its Relation to What Is

Called English Grammar." In *Readings in Applied English Linguistics,* ed. Harold B. Allen, 1958, pp. 95–101.

_____. "Cultural Lag and Reviewers of *Webster III," AAUP Bulletin,* XLIX (1963), 364–369.

Edgerton, Franklin. "Notes on Early American Work in Linguistics," *Proceedings of the American Philosophical Society,* LXXXVII (1943), 25–34.

Ervin-Tripp, Susan. "On Sociolinguistic Rules: Alternation and Co-occurrence." In *Directions in Sociolinguistics,* ed. Gumperz and Hymes, pp. 213–250.

Estrin, Herman A., and Donald V. Mehus, eds. *The American Language in the 1970s.* San Francisco: Boyd & Fraser, 1974.

Evans, Bergen. "Grammar for Today," *The Atlantic,* March, 1960, pp. 79–82.

_____. "But What's a Dictionary For?" *The Atlantic,* May, 1962, pp. 57–62.

_____. "Noah Webster Had the Same Troubles," *The New York Times Magazine,* May 13, 1962, pp. 11, 77, 79–80.

_____. "Let's Stop Maligning the Dictionary," *Chicago Tribune Magazine,* August 25, 1963, pp. 42–43. Repr. in *The Role of the Dictionary,* ed. Philip B. Gove, pp. 40–42.

_____ and Cornelia Evans. *A Dictionary of Contemporary American Usage.* New York: Random House, 1957.

Fillmore, Charles J., and D. Terence Langendoen, eds. *Studies in Linguistic Semantics.* New York: Holt, Rinehart, 1971.

Fishman, Joshua A., ed. *Readings in the Sociology of Language.* The Hague: Mouton, 1968.

_____. "Domains and the Relationships between Micro- and Macrosociolinguistics." In *Directions in Sociolinguistics,* ed. Gumperz and Hymes, pp. 435–453.

_____. "The Sociology of Language." In *Language and Social Context,* ed. Pier Paolo Giglioli, pp. 45–58.

Follett, Wilson. "Grammar Is Obsolete," *The Atlantic,* February, 1960, pp. 73–76.

_____. "Sabotage in Springfield: *Webster's Third Edition," The Atlantic,* January, 1962, pp. 73–77.

_____. *Modern American Usage.* Ed. and completed by Jacques Barzun with the collaboration of Carlos Baker, Frederick Dupee, Dudley Fitts, James D. Hart, Phyllis McGinley, Lionel Trilling. 1966; repr. New York: Grosset & Dunlap, 1970.

Foucault, Michel. *The Archaeology of Knowledge.* Trans. A. M. Sheridan Smith. New York: Pantheon, 1972.

Francis, W. Nelson. "Language and Linguistics in the English Program," *College English,* XXVI (1964), 13–16.

Friend, Joseph H. *The Development of American Lexicography 1798–1864.* The Hague: Mouton, 1967.

Fries, Charles C. "The Periphrastic Future with *Shall* and *Will* in Modern English," *PMLA,* XL (1925), 963–1024.

_____. "What Is Good English?" *English Journal,* XIV (1925), 685–697.

_____. *The Teaching of the English Language.* New York: Thomas Nelson, 1927.

_____. *The Structure of English.* New York: Harcourt, 1952.

_____. *American English Grammar: The Grammatical Structure of Present-Day American English with Especial Reference to Social Difference or Class Dialects.* National Council of Teachers of English: English Monograph No. 10. New York: Appleton-Century-Crofts, 1940.

Fromkin, Victoria, and Robert Rodman. *An Introduction to Language.* 2nd ed. New York: Holt, Rinehart, 1978.

Giglioli, Pier Paolo, ed. *Language and Social Context.* Harmondsworth: Penguin, 1972.

Goodrich, Samuel G. "Schools As They Were Sixty Years Ago: Recollections of Peter Parley," *American Journal of Education* [New Series, No. 5], XXX (March 1863), 123-144.

Gove, Philip B., ed. *Webster's Third New International Dictionary.* Springfield, Mass.: G. & C. Merriam, 1961.

_____. "Linguistic Advances and Lexicography," *Word Study,* XXXVII (October 1961), 3-8.

_____, ed. *The Role of the Dictionary.* Indianapolis: Bobbs-Merrill, 1967.

Gray, Louis H. *Foundations of Language.* New York: Macmillan, 1939.

Greene, Donald. *Samuel Johnson.* New York: Twayne, 1970.

Griffin, Nathaniel E. Rev. of *Modern English,* by George Philip Krapp. *Modern Language Notes,* XXVI (1911), 212-219.

Gumperz, John J., and Dell Hymes, eds. *Directions in Sociolinguistics: The Ethnography of Communication.* New York: Holt, Rinehart, 1972.

Gunderson, Robert G., ed. "Webster's Third New International Dictionary: A Symposium," *Quarterly Journal of Speech,* XLVIII (1962), 431-440; includes reviews by Harold B. Allen, Margaret Bryant, Robert A. Hall, Jr., Raven I. McDavid, Jr., John B. Newman, Allen Walker Read, and Robert Sonkin.

Guralnik, David B., and Joseph H. Friend, eds. *Webster's New World Dictionary of the American Language.* College ed. Cleveland: World, 1953.

Hall, Fitzedward. *Recent Exemplifications of False Philology.* New York, 1872.

Hall, J. Lesslie. *English Usage: Studies in the History and Uses of English Words and Phrases.* Chicago: Scott, Foresman, 1917.

Hall, Robert A., Jr. *Leave Your Language Alone!* Ithaca, N.Y.: Linguistica, 1950.

_____. *Linguistics and Your Language.* Garden City, N.Y.: Anchor, 1960. (2nd. rev. ed. of *Leave Your Language Alone!)*

_____. *Introductory Linguistics.* Philadelphia: Chilton, 1964.

Halliday, M. A. K. "The Users and Uses of Language." In *Readings in the Sociology of Language,* ed. Joshua A. Fishman, pp. 139-169.

Hartung, Charles V. "Doctrines of English Usage," *English Journal,* XVL (1956), 517-528.

_____. "The Persistence of Tradition in Grammar," *Quarterly Journal of Speech,* XLVIII (1962), 174-186.

Hatfield, W. Wilbur. "Editorial," *English Journal,* XVI (1927), 238-239.

Hergenhan, Mildred E. "The Doctrine of Correctness in English Usage in the Nineteenth Century." Unpub. diss. Univ. of Wisconsin, 1938.

Higham, John. *Strangers in the Land: Patterns of American Nativism 1860–1925.* New York: Atheneum, 1963.

Hockett, Charles F., ed. *A Leonard Bloomfield Anthology.* Bloomington: Indiana Univ. Press, 1970.

Hosic, James Fleming. "Editorial: The Significance of the Organization of the National Council," *English Journal,* I (1912), 46–48.

_____. "Editorial: The Policy of the 'English Journal'," *English Journal,* I (1912), 375–376.

Hudson, Hoyt H. Rev. of *Current English Usage,* by Sterling A. Leonard. *Quarterly Journal of Speech,* XIX (1933), 585–586.

Hughes, John P. *The Science of Language.* New York: Random House, 1962.

Hymes, Dell, ed. *Pidginization and Creolization of Languages.* Cambridge: Cambridge Univ. Press, 1971.

_____. *Foundations in Sociolinguistics.* Philadelphia: Univ. of Pennsylvania Press, 1974.

Jacobs, Roderick A., and Peter S. Rosenbaum. *English Transformational Grammar.* Waltham, Mass.: Blaisdell, 1968.

Jagemann, H. C. G. von. "Philology and Purism," *PMLA,* XV (1900), 74–96.

Jespersen, Otto. *Mankind, Nation and Individual.* 1925; repr. Bloomington: Indiana Univ. Press, 1964.

Johnson, Samuel. *The Plan of a Dictionary of the English Language; Addressed to the Right Honourable Philip Dormer, Earl of Chesterfield.* London, 1747; Facsimile edition. Menston: Scolar Press, 1970.

_____. *A Dictionary of the English Language: In Which the Words Are Deduced from Their Originals, and Illustrated in Their Different Significations by Examples from the Best Writers, to Which Are Prefixed, a History of the Language, and an English Grammar.* 2 vols. London, 1755.

Jones, Richard Foster. *The Triumph of the English Language.* Stanford: Stanford Univ. Press, 1953.

Keenan, Elinor Ochs, and Tina L. Bennett, eds. *Discourse Across Time and Space.* Southern California Occasional Papers in Linguistics, No. 5. Los Angeles: Department of Linguistics, Univ. of Southern California, 1977.

Kenyon, John S. "Cultural Levels and Functional Varieties of English," *College English,* X (1948), 31–36.

Kilburn, Patrick E. "The Gentlemen's Guide to Linguistic Etiquette," Union College *Symposium,* IX (1970), 2–6.

Kirkham, Samuel. *English Grammar, in Familiar Lectures.* New York, [1829].

Krapp, George Philip. *The Authority of Law in Language.* University Studies, Univ. of Cincinnati, Series II, Vol. IV, No. 3, 1908.

_____. Rev. of *The Standard of Usage in English,* by T. R. Lounsbury. *Educational Review,* XXXVI (1908), 195–200.

_____. *Modern English: Its Growth and Present Use.* New York: Scribner's, 1909.

_____. "The Improvement of American Speech," *English Journal,* VII (1918). 87–97.

_____. *The English Language in America.* 2 vols. 1925; repr. New York: Frederick Ungar, 1960.

_____. *A Comprehensive Guide to Good English.* Chicago: Rand McNally, 1927.

_____. *The Knowledge of English.* New York: Holt, 1927.

_____. Rev. of *Current English Usage,* by Sterling A. Leonard. *American Speech,* VIII, i (1933), 46–47.

Kurath, Hans. *Handbook of the Linguistic Geography of New England.* Providence, R.I.: Brown Univ., 1939.

_____. *A Word Geography of the Eastern United States.* Ann Arbor: Univ. of Michigan Press, 1949.

Labov, William. "The Effect of Social Mobility on Linguistic Behavior," *Sociological Inquiry,* XXXVI (1966), 186–203. Repr. in *A Various Language,* ed. Williamson and Burke, pp. 640–659.

_____. *The Social Stratification of English in New York City.* Washington, D.C.: Center for Applied Linguistics, 1966.

_____. "The Logic of Nonstandard English." In *Report of the Twentieth Annual Round Table Meeting on Linguistics and Language Studies,* ed. James E. Alatis, pp. 1–43.

_____. *The Study of Nonstandard English.* Champaign, Ill.: National Council of Teachers of English, 1970.

_____. *Sociolinguistic Patterns.* Philadelphia: Univ. of Pennsylvania Press, 1972.

Laird, Charlton. *Language in America.* 1970; repr. Englewood Cliffs, N.J.: Prentice-Hall, 1972.

Lamb, Sydney M. *Outline of Stratificational Grammar.* Washington, D.C.: Georgetown Univ. Press, 1966.

Lambert, Wallace E. "A Social Psychology of Bilingualism," *The Journal of Social Issues,* XXIII, i (1967), 91–109.

_____, Moshe Anisfeld, and Grace Yeni-Komshian. "Evaluational Reactions of Jewish and Arab Adolescents to Dialect and Language Variation," *Journal of Personality and Social Psychology,* II (1965), 84–90.

Langacker, Ronald W. *Language and Its Structure.* 2nd ed. New York: Harcourt, 1973.

Langendoen, D. Terence. *Essentials of English Grammar.* New York: Holt, Rinehart, 1970.

Latham, Robert Gordon. *The English Language.* London, 1841.

Learned, Leila Sprague. "A Defense of Purism in Speech," *The Atlantic,* CXI (1913), 682–685.

Leonard, Sterling A. *English Composition as a Social Problem.* Boston: Houghton Mifflin, 1917.

_____. "'Old Purist Junk'," *English Journal,* VII (1918), 295–302.

_____. *The Doctrine of Correctness in English Usage, 1700–1800.* 1929; repr. New York: Russell & Russell, 1962.

_____. *Current English Usage*. National Council of Teachers of English: English Monograph No. 1. Chicago: Inland, 1932.

_____ and H. Y. Moffett. "Current Definitions of Levels in English Usage," *English Journal*, XVI (1927), 345-359.

Leonard, William Ellery. Rev. of *Current English Usage*, by Sterling A. Leonard. *American Speech*, VIII, iii (1933), 57-58.

Lloyd, Donald J. "Snobs, Slobs and the English Language," *The American Scholar*, XX (1951), 279-288.

_____. "Our National Mania for Correctness," *The American Scholar*, XXI (1952), 283-289.

_____ and Harry R. Warfel. *American English in Its Cultural Setting*. New York: Knopf, 1956.

Lockwood, David G. *Introduction to Stratificational Linguistics*. New York: Harcourt, 1972.

Lounsbury, Thomas R. *History of the English Language*. New York, 1879.

_____. *The Standard of Usage in English*. New York: Harper, 1908.

Lowth, Robert. *A Short Introduction to English Grammar*. London, 1762. Facsimile edition. Menston: Scolar Press, 1967.

Lyman, Rollo LaVerne. *English Grammar in American Schools before 1850*. Department of the Interior, Bureau of Education Bulletin No. 12. Washington, D.C., 1922.

Lyons, John. *Noam Chomsky*. New York: Viking, 1970.

Macdonald, Dwight. "The String Untuned," *The New Yorker*, March 10, 1962. Repr. in *Dictionaries and THAT Dictionary*, ed. Sledd and Ebbitt, pp. 166-188.

_____. "Three Questions for Structural Linguists, or Webster 3 Revisited." In *Dictionaries and THAT Dictionary*, ed. Sledd and Ebbitt, pp. 256-264.

Manning, Robert. "The Editor's Page," *The Atlantic*, May, 1971, p. 4.

Marckwardt, Albert H. *Linguistics and the Teaching of English*. Bloomington: Indiana Univ. Press, 1966.

_____, ed. *Language and Language Learning*. Champaign, Ill.: National Council of Teachers of English, 1968.

_____ and Fred G. Walcott. *Facts About Current English Usage*. National Council of Teachers of English: English Monograph No. 7. New York: Appleton-Century-Crofts, 1938.

Marsh, George Perkins. *Lectures on the English Language*. New York, 1860.

Mathews, William. *Words; Their Use and Abuse*. Chicago, 1876.

Matthews, Brander. *Parts of Speech: Essays on English*. New York: Scribner's, 1901.

_____. *Essays on English*. New York: Scribner's, 1921.

_____. "The English Language and the American Academy," *Academy Papers: Addresses on Language Problems by Members of the American Academy of Arts and Letters*. New York: Scribner's, 1925. pp. 63-93.

McDavid, Raven I., Jr., ed., and Betty Gawthrop, C. Michael Lightner, Doris C. Meyers, and Geraldine Russell. *An Examination of the Attitudes of the NCTE toward Language*. NCTE Research Report No. 4. Champaign, Ill.:

National Council of Teachers of English, 1965.

_____. "Usage, Dialects, and Functional Varieties." In *The Random House Dictionary of the English Language,* ed. Jess Stein, pp. xix–xxi.

McKnight, George H. *English Words and Their Background.* New York: Appleton, 1923.

_____. *Modern English in the Making.* New York: Appleton, 1928.

_____. Rev. of *American English Grammar,* by Charles C. Fries. *Journal of English and Germanic Philology,* XL (1941), 452–455.

Mencken, Henry L. *The American Language.* 4th ed. rev. and abr. by Raven I. McDavid, Jr. New York: Knopf, 1963.

Merrill, Francis E. *Society and Culture.* 3rd ed. Englewood Cliffs, N.J.: Prentice-Hall, 1965.

Mittins, W. H., et al. *Attitudes to English Usage.* London: Oxford Univ. Press, 1970.

Moon, George Washington. *The Bad English of Lindley Murray and Other Writers on the English Language: A Series of Criticisms.* 3rd ed. London, 1869.

_____. *The Dean's English: A Criticism on the Dean of Canterbury's Essays on the Queen's English.* 4th ed. New York, [1865].

Morris, William, ed. *The American Heritage Dictionary of the English Language.* Boston: American Heritage and Houghton Mifflin, 1969.

_____. "The Making of a Dictionary—1969," *College Composition and Communication,* XIX (1969). Repr. in *The American Language in the 1970s,* ed. Estrin and Mehus, pp. 52–61.

Müller, F. Max. *Lectures on the Science of Language.* Oxford, 1861.

Murray, Lindley. *English Grammar, Adapted to the Different Classes of Learners.* York, 1795. Facsimile edition. Menston: Scolar Press, 1968.

"The National Council, 1911–1936," *English Journal,* XXV (1936), 805–836.

Newman, Edwin. *Strictly Speaking: Will America Be the Death of English?* Indianapolis: Bobbs-Merrill, 1974.

_____. *A Civil Tongue.* Indianapolis: Bobbs-Merrill, 1976.

Oliver, Kenneth. *A Sound Curriculum in English Grammar: Guidelines for Teachers and Parents.* Washington, D.C.: Council for Basic Education, 1975.

Oliver, Robert T. Rev. of *Facts About Current English Usage,* by Marckwardt and Walcott. *Quarterly Journal of Speech,* XXV (1939), 497.

Partee, Barbara Hall. "On the Requirement that Transformations Preserve Meaning." In *Studies in Linguistic Semantics,* ed. Fillmore and Langendoen, pp. 1–21.

_____. "Linguistic Metatheory." In *A Survey of Linguistic Science,* ed. William Orr Dingwall, pp. 650–680.

Pedersen, Holger. *The Discovery of Language: Linguistic Science in the Nineteenth Century.* Trans. John Webster Spargo. 1931; repr. Bloomington: Indiana Univ. Press, 1962.

Pei, Mario. "The Dictionary as a Battlefront: English Teachers' Dilemma," *Saturday Review,* July 21, 1962, pp. 44–46, 55–56.

_____. "A Loss for Words," *Saturday Review,* November 14, 1964, pp. 82–84.

Plato with an English Translation: Cratylus, Parmenides, Greater Hippias, Lesser Hippias. Ed. H. N. Fowler. Loeb Classical Library. Cambridge, Mass.: Harvard Univ. Press, 1926.

Pooley, Robert C. *Grammar and Usage in Textbooks on English.* Univ. of Wisconsin Bureau of Educational Research Bulletin No. 14. Madison, Wis., 1933.

Postal, Paul M. Epilogue. In *English Transformational Grammar,* by Jacobs and Rosenbaum.

Priestley, Joseph. *The Rudiments of English Grammar.* London, 1761. Facsimile edition. Menston: Scolar Press, 1969.

_____. *A Course of Lectures on the Theory of Language, and Universal Grammar.* Warrington, 1762.

_____. *The Rudiments of English Grammar.* London, 1771.

Pulgram, Ernst. "Don't Leave Your Language Alone," *Quarterly Journal of Speech,* XXXVIII (1952), 423–430.

Pyles, Thomas. *Words and Ways of American English.* New York: Random House, 1952.

Quintilian. *Institutio Oratoria.* Trans. H. E. Butler. Loeb Classical Library. Cambridge, Mass.: Harvard Univ. Press, 1920.

Ramsey, Samuel. *The English Language and English Grammar: An Historical Study of the Sources, Development, and Analogies of the Language and of the Principles Governing Its Usage.* New York, 1892.

Rand, Asa. "Lecture on Teaching Grammar and Composition," *American Annals of Education and Instruction,* III (1833), pp. 159–174.

Read, Allen Walker. "American Projects for an Academy to Regulate Speech," *PMLA,* LI (1936), 1141–1179.

_____. "The Motivation of Lindley Murray's Grammatical Work," *Journal of English and Germanic Philology,* XXXVIII (1939), 525–539.

_____. "*That* Dictionary or *The* Dictionary?" *Consumer Reports,* XXVIII (1963), 488–492.

_____. "The Spread of German Linguistic Learning in New England during the Lifetime of Noah Webster," *American Speech,* XLI, iii (1966), 163–181.

Read, William A. Rev. of *Modern English,* by George Philip Krapp. *Englische Studien,* XLIII (1910–1911), 426–432.

Reed, Carroll E. *Dialects of American English.* Rev. ed. Amherst, Mass.: Univ. of Massachusetts Press, 1977.

Rev. of *American English Grammar,* by Charles C. Fries. *The Nation,* January 4, 1941, p. 26

Richards, I. A. *Interpretation in Teaching.* New York: Harcourt, 1938.

_____. *Speculative Instruments.* Chicago: Univ. of Chicago Press, 1955.

Roberts, Paul. "The Relation of Linguistics to the Teaching of English," *College English,* XXII (1960), 1–9. Repr. in *Readings in Applied English Linguistics,* 2nd ed., ed. Harold B. Allen, pp. 395–405.

Russell, I. Willis. "Prescription and Description in English Usage," *American Speech,* XIV, iv (1939), 291-296.

_____. Rev. of *American English Grammar,* by Charles C. Fries. *American Speech,* XVI (1941), 128-130.

Rycenga, John A., and Joseph Schwartz, eds. *Perspectives on Language: An Anthology.* New York: Ronald, 1963.

Salomon, Louis B. *"Whose* Good English?" *AAUP Bulletin,* XXXVIII (1952), 442-449.

Sapir, Edward. *Language: An Introduction to the Study of Speech.* New York: Harcourt, 1921.

Scott, Fred Newton. *The Standard of American Speech and Other Papers.* Boston: Allyn and Bacon, 1926.

Searle, John R. *Speech Acts.* Cambridge: Cambridge Univ. Press, 1969.

Seligman, C. R., G. R. Tucker, and W. E. Lambert, "The Effects of Speech Style and Other Attributes on Teachers' Attitudes toward Pupils," *Language in Society,* I (1972), 131-142.

Sheldon, E. S. "Practical Philology," *PMLA,* XVII (1902), 91-104.

Sherwood, John C. "Dr. Kinsey and Professor Fries," *College English,* XXI (1960), 275-280.

Shuy, Roger W., and Ralph W. Fasold, eds. *Language Attitudes: Current Trends and Prospects.* Washington, D.C.: Georgetown Univ. Press, 1973.

Simmons, Paxton. "Coddling in English," *English Journal,* V (1916), 659-664.

Sledd, James. "The Lexicographer's Uneasy Chair," *College English,* XXIII (1962), 682-687.

_____. "'Standard' Is a Trademark," *Consumer Reports,* XXVIII (1963), 551-552.

_____ and Wilma R. Ebbitt, eds. *Dictionaries and THAT Dictionary.* Chicago: Scott, Foresman, 1962.

_____ and Gwin J. Kolb. *Dr. Johnson's Dictionary: Essays in the Biography of a Book.* Chicago: Univ. of Chicago Press, 1955.

Smith, C. Alphonso. "The Work of the Modern Language Association of America," *PMLA,* XIV (1899), 240-256.

Stein, Jess, ed. *The Random House Dictionary of the English Language—The Unabridged Edition.* New York: Random House, 1966.

Sturtevant, Edgar H. *Linguistic Change: An Introduction to the Historical Study of Language.* Chicago: Univ. of Chicago Press, 1917.

Swift, Jonathan. *A Proposal for Correcting, Improving and Ascertaining the English Tongue.* London, 1712. Facsimile edition. Menston: Scolar Press, 1969.

Tibbetts, A. M., "Two Cheers for the Authoritarian," *College English,* XXV (1964), 370-373.

_____. "The Real Issues in the Great Language Controversy," *English Journal,* LV (1966), 28-38.

Tobin, Richard L. "Like Your Cigarette Should," *Saturday Review,* May 14, 1966, pp. 59-60.

Trudgill, Peter. *Sociolinguistics: An Introduction.* Harmondsworth: Penguin, 1974.

Tucker, Susie I., ed. *English Examined.* Cambridge: Cambridge Univ. Press, 1961.

Warfel, Harry R. *Who Killed Grammar?* Gainesville: Univ. of Florida Press, 1952.

_____, ed. *Letters of Noah Webster.* New York: Library, 1953.

Webster, Noah. *A Grammatical Institute of the English Language.* Part I: Hartford, 1783. Part II: Hartford, 1784. Facsimile edition. Menston: Scolar Press, 1968.

_____. *Dissertations on the English Language.* Boston, 1789. Facsimile edition. Menston: Scolar Press, 1967.

_____. *A Compendious Dictionary of the English Language.* Hartford, 1806. Facsimile edition, New York: Crown, 1970.

_____. *An American Dictionary of the English Language.* 1828. Facsimile edition. New York: Johnson Reprint, 1970.

Weinreich, Uriel. "*Webster's Third*: A Critique of Its Semantics," *International Journal of American Linguistics,* XXX (1964), 405–409.

White, Richard Grant. *Words and Their Uses Past and Present: A Study of the English Language.* Boston, 1870.

Whitehall, Harold. *Structural Essentials of English.* New York: Harcourt, 1956.

Whitney, William Dwight. *Language and the Study of Language: Twelve Lectures on the Principles of Linguistic Science.* New York, 1867.

_____. *Oriental and Linguistic Studies: Second Series.* New York, 1874.

_____. *The Life and Growth of Language: An Outline of Linguistic Science.* New York, 1875.

_____. *Essentials of English Grammar.* Boston, 1877.

Williamson, Juanita V., and Virginia M. Burke, eds. *A Various Language: Perspectives on American Dialects.* New York: Holt, Rinehart, 1971.

Wills, Garry. "Madness in Their Method," *National Review,* February 13, 1962, pp. 98–99.

Young, Richard E., Alton L. Becker, and Kenneth L. Pike. *Rhetoric: Discovery and Change.* New York: Harcourt, 1970.

SUGGESTED READINGS

Bryant, Margaret M., ed. *Current American Usage.* New York: Funk & Wagnalls, 1962.

Copperud, Roy H. *American Usage: The Consensus.* New York: Van Nostrand Reinhold, 1970.

Fowler, Henry W. *A Dictionary of Modern English Usage.* 1926; 2nd ed. rev. by Sir Ernest Gowers. Oxford: Oxford Univ. Press, 1965.

Joos, Martin. *The Five Clocks.* 1961; repr. New York: Harcourt, 1967.

Lamberts, J. J. *A Short Introduction to English Usage.* New York: McGraw-Hill, 1972.

Pooley, Robert C. *The Teaching of English Usage.* Urbana, Ill.: National Council of Teachers of English, 1974.

Shores, David L., ed. *Contemporary English: Change and Variation.* Philadelphia: Lippincott, 1972.

Students' Right to Their Own Language. Special Issue of *College Composition and Communication,* XXV (Fall 1974).

Wells, Ronald A. *Dictionaries and the Authoritarian Tradition: A Study in English Usage and Lexicography.* The Hague: Mouton, 1973.

Williams, Frederick, et al. *Explorations of the Linguistic Attitudes of Teachers.* Rowley, Mass.: Newbury House, 1976.

The following works, cited in full in the preceding section, are also suggested for reading: Creswell 1975; Evans and Evans 1957; Labov 1970; Laird 1970; Mencken 1963; Mittins et al. 1970; Trudgill 1974; Williamson and Burke 1971.

Index

NOTE: A brief index to selected usages is supplied following this general index.

Selected Usages